KEEPING THE FAITH

KEEPING
the FAITH

Stories of Love, Courage,
Healing, and Hope from
Black America

Tavis Smiley

Doubleday

NEW YORK   LONDON   TORONTO

SYDNEY   AUCKLAND

PUBLISHED BY DOUBLEDAY
A division of Random House, Inc.
1540 Broadway, New York, New York 10036

DOUBLEDAY and the portrayal of an anchor with a
dolphin are trademarks of Doubleday, a division of
Random House, Inc.

Cataloging-in-Publication Data is on file with the
Library of Congress.

ISBN 0-385-50514-0

PRINTED IN THE UNITED STATES OF AMERICA

First Edition: November 2002

10 9 8 7 6 5

Book design by Jennifer Ann Daddio

The greatest love of all . . . God's love.

CONTENTS

INSPIRATION

FAITH

EDUCATION

Family, Friendship, and Heritage

ACKNOWLEDGMENTS

Keeping the Faith makes book number six for me. I'm proud of that. I am more proud of the fact that the folk who were with me for the early titles are still with me today. Their abiding friendship, wise counsel, and unwavering support have made my life—personally and professionally—rich and rewarding.

Thank you, Denise Pines, Harold W. Patrick, Errol Collier, Ken Browning, and Wendi Chavis. To the only editor I have ever known and hope to know, Roger Scholl, and his able assistant Sarah Rainone, my admiration and appreciation.

To Karen Young, thanks for being on time, on task, and on target. Couldn't have done it without you.

To my personal assistants, Dana Clark and Raymond Ross, and the staffs of The Smiley Group, Inc., the Tavis Smiley Foundation, and *The Tavis Smiley Show from NPR*, I value your sacrifice and support.

Finally, to the two groups of people I cherish most—my family and friends—thank you for keeping the faith in me and in my dreams.

INTRODUCTION

One of my favorite gospel hymns is an old Negro spiritual titled "Love Lifted Me." The verses tell the story of someone—battered and bruised by life—who was "sinking to rise no more." But the joyful chorus triumphantly cries that "when nothing else could help, love lifted me!" I thought I knew a little something about love—and I did. Precious little. Until, that is, I found myself enduring the most excruciating personal and professional pain I could imagine. In one calendar year, I lost a love relationship with a woman about whom I cared deeply, and then I lost, quite publicly, the centerpiece of my air advocacy, my television talk show that allowed me to enlighten, encourage, and empower viewers nightly. I don't know what's worse, private or public pain. I do know that they both hurt and that if you live long enough, you will experience both.

Taken together, these ordeals taught me a few things. One, that bad things do happen to good people. Two, that love is the infrastructure of everything and anything worthwhile. And three, that in the end, through love we can turn pain into power. The power to heal ourselves. The power to help others. The power to hope for better days. The power of possibility.

It is my hope that the stories of love, courage, healing, and hope from Black America that you're about to read in this book will inspire you to keep the faith no matter what you're going through. Sorrow looks back, worry looks around, but faith looks up.

Keeping the Faith is about character, conduct, and courage. Courage is the greatest virtue, says my friend Maya Angelou, because without it, you can't practice the other virtues. I urge you to summon the courage, conviction, and commitment to meet life's challenges with uncommon vigor and zest. For it will see you through. And no matter what comes your way, you keep the faith!

Tavis Smiley
Los Angeles, CA
24 June 2002

 BLACK LOVE

WHAT BLACK LOVE IS . . .

Tavis Smiley

The concept of Black love is how this book came to be. Yes, so many of the stories are about overcoming and succeeding against the odds. But the real and true theme underlying the book is Black love.

I came up with the idea of putting together this book after I was fired from Black Entertainment Television (BET). Prior to being fired, I thought I knew something about Black love. But after I lost my job, the outpouring of Black love shown to me, from California to the Carolinas, was phenomenal. It was Black love that lifted me during the darkest moment of my professional career. It was Black love that lifted me out of my despair. I discovered that, outside of God's love, nothing is more powerful.

One of the greatest challenges we face as Black people is whether or not we can take the notion of Black love and use it *proactively*, as opposed to reactively. Black love is a powerful force. The Black community has a way of coming together and rescuing each other and lifting each other up when someone has been attacked, undermined, or otherwise disenfranchised. But the challenge for us as African Americans is to act proactively with regard to the important issues in our community. If we could harness this notion of Black love and demonstrate it on the *front end* of our life experiences, as opposed to the back end of our struggles, we would become an awesome force to be reckoned with.

Using Black love, we could eradicate Black-on-Black crime, Black nihilism, and Black powerlessness, all of which exist in our communities because of a lack of *self-love*. We could even strengthen Black male-female relationships.

For me, what was so uplifting and rewarding about my discovery of the genuine meaning of Black love was the relationship between one's "value" and love. Value, I learned, is not what you think of yourself, but rather what *other* people think of you. The outpouring of Black love that was shown to me across this country after I was fired from BET made a clear statement about my value to African Americans—who I was, what I was about, and the way that Black America perceived me. I learned that my real value wasn't what BET thought of me or even what I thought of myself. It had more to do with what other Black folks thought of me. I didn't realize the powerful force of Black love that I became the beneficiary of. I was completely overwhelmed.

Of course, I knew that people watched my show, that they would buy my books, and that they would come to hear me if I was speaking somewhere. So I was aware that I had some followers. But when I got fired, it became clear to me that Black people saw me as someone they cared about, someone who tried to represent their best interests, someone who was genuinely concerned about the plight of Black America. Their immediate response was "We're not going to stand for this." That's what I love about being Black: when our backs are to the wall, we come together as a people. When one of us is targeted unfairly or unduly, we go to bat for one another.

Consider the reelection of Marion Barry as mayor of Washington, D.C. Here was a man who had been caught on videotape smoking crack and trying to bed a woman who was not his wife, attempting to run for another term as mayor of a major U.S. city. And he won! Many said the reason he won was that Black folks were crazy—how dare they vote Marion Barry back into office. The more sophisticated, however, realized that Black folk in the D.C. area saw the government create an elaborate sting operation to nail Marion Barry—and use their taxpayer dollars to pay for it. And they suspected he was nailed *because* he is Black. So their vote became their voice and they reelected Marion Barry.

Black love is Black citizens reelecting Marion Barry as mayor of Washington, D.C., when he didn't necessarily deserve their votes. Black love is Black people cheering and rejoicing the day that O.J. Simpson was found not guilty, even though O.J. hadn't done much of anything for Black people. Black love, in its essence, is the awesome capacity and the uncanny ability to love someone in spite of themselves—in spite of their shortcomings, in spite of their mistakes, in spite of their lapses in judgment, in spite of their deserting their community and not giving back to it once they leave. Black love is forgiving.

When I say that Black people have a tremendous capacity for loving others in spite of, I'm not just talking about their ability to love their own, but also the ability to love *others* in spite of. One can make the case, given the historical relationship between Blacks and whites in America, that Black people love white people in spite of all the things that have been done to us. Think about how Black folks had to love America, in spite of the fact we were considered three-fifths of a person, when we fought alongside whites in the Civil War to help America resolve the issue of slavery, even though many of the soldiers were enslaved themselves. We fought in both world wars as well as the Vietnam War; sometimes we came home missing leg and limb, only to be treated like second-class citizens. Yet we learned to love this country in spite of this. To this day, we are still, through amendment, through protests, through boycotts, and through the ballot, trying to make America live up to her truest ideals. We love this country, we love our people, in spite of and not because of. That's what Black love is.

Although so many Black folks in America detest the programming offered by BET, they have shown their love and support for founder Bob Johnson because he was the only one out there attempting to bring certain issues about Black people to the forefront through the use of mainstream media. So they loved him in spite of and not because of.

When your back is to the wall, there is nothing like the power of Black love to pull you through. And that's why I believe that beyond God's love, Black love is the most powerful force in the universe.

The fact that we can love under such dire circumstances—in spite of and not because of—is, I believe, what makes us special. For all the torture, pain, and disenfranchisement that we have had to endure—when we are racially profiled, when we can't get a home loan, when we are the victims of insurance redlining and predatory lending, when we are the last hired and first fired, when circumstances are created to make it more difficult for us to get into college in order to receive a quality education— Black people find a way to love this place called America. That's what Black love is. Other races might have said, "To hell with all this confusion and pain and heartache." We kept right on loving, trying to make America a better nation.

This book represents the very best of what Black love has to offer. To love in spite of and not because of.

LOVE LIFTED ME

Dr. Cornel West

The fundamental theme of Black life and history is freedom, a freedom that is rooted in a deep courage to love. The power of Black love not only sustains our struggle for freedom; it is the prerequisite of our sanity and dignity. If you examine Black literature, you will find that our greatest text is Toni Morrison's *Beloved*. Her book reminds us in many ways of Berry Gordy's autobiography, *To Be Loved*. In many of the Black texts we find a kind of Black ontology that puts a high premium on love, in part because we have been such a hated, haunted, and hunted people.

This same theme is represented in Black music, particularly when we look at the talented and gifted artist John Coltrane. In one of his greatest Black musical texts, "A Love Supreme," he wrestles with pain and anguish as well as joy and ecstasy. Even though love is very much about ecstasy, Frankie Beverly of the popular recording group Maze also reminds us that Black love includes the dimensions of joy and pain, "sunshine and rain." This Black love has been forged in the face of American barbarism (slavery) and American terrorism (Jim Crow, lynching)—over against violence and death.

I experienced the power of Black love in a fundamental way when I confronted three recent crises in my life. This past year I experienced a physical crisis when the doctor told me that my body was nearly incurably infected with cancer. Because of the magnificent and successful surgery performed by Dr. Peter Scardino, all of the cancer has been removed. Looking back, there is no doubt in my mind that what lifted me and what sustained me was the power of Black love. The power of Black love was demonstrated to me in a very deep way by my family, including my mother, my two sisters, my brother, and my close friends (including loyal, non-Black people). My mother and my friend Leslie waited on me hand and foot every day for seven weeks. It was the overwhelming demonstration of Black love, including the prayers of supporters around the world, that constituted the pillar upon which I stood. It became my rock and my foundation as I struggled against the deadly disease that threatened my body. It is hard to put in words the kind of love I felt. It went far beyond any kind of glib formulation of mere family, friendship, and companionship. It was, in fact, a love that was supernatural and translunar and, I contend, unexplainable through mere words. To take it a step further, I believe that all forms of love are unmistakable and indefinable at the same time and this love is clearly what I experienced and what lifted me. Within the history of the Black church, as well as in the history of Black mosques and Black synagogues, there is, at the center of their teaching, the fundamental need to dignify Black people by making us view ourselves as worthy of love. This love can be God's love, the love of significant others, the love of children, or the love of our friends.

The second crisis I experienced was a professional crisis—my struggle with President Larry Summers of Harvard University. Summers attacked my integrity and insulted my character. Because I felt so deeply disrespected and dishonored, it created a sense of rage within me. In many ways, the notion of rage has always been an integral part of Black existence. However, if rage is not channeled in such a way that it is influenced and shaped and molded by love, it can become self-destructive. I was able to deal with the rage I experienced in a way that allowed me to retain my sense of self-respect and integrity, as opposed to allowing the experience of being disrespected and dishonored to cause me to self-destruct. Here again, it was the power of Black love that lifted me and enabled me to maintain my self-respect and to keep things in perspective. Without the love shown to me by my mother, my two sisters, my brother, and my friends, I would not have pulled through.

The third crisis I experienced was a family crisis; I underwent a very painful divorce. This situation was again a crucial occasion in which the sustaining power of Black love was manifested in a mighty and powerful way. I had invested a tremendous amount of time and material resources in my relationship and partnership only to find myself one day having fallen flat on my face. Two things became very clear to me. The first was that I saw myself as I am—a cracked vessel. But the second and more significant thing revealed to me was that I could bounce back. In spite of my faults, foibles, shortcomings, and defects, I was still deeply loved by others. And so, Black love became the impetus that allowed me to bounce back, rather than remain down and out. In all three of the afore-mentioned crises, the power of Black love was the fundamental factor that allowed me to preserve my sanity and dignity.

I believe there is a real challenge for Black people in general and for Black leaders in particular today. We are currently experiencing a crisis in Black leadership in America, in part because we simply do not have enough Black leaders who have a profound love for Black people. We need the kind of Black love that allows us to criticize as well as embrace, to empower as well as to correct, to listen as well as to speak, and in the end, to ennoble as well as be ennobled by the people. I also believe this to be true for many among our Black professional class. Many have become so isolated and so insulated and so intoxicated with the material toys of the world that they have lost sight of the love that made them who they are and that brought them to where they are. I also believe that we are losing the ability to pass that profound love on to our young people.

The major crisis of our younger generation, in addition to the decrepit educational system, inadequate health care, unavailable child-care, and lack of jobs that provide a living wage, is that many young peo-ple have not been loved deeply enough. The major responsibility lies with the older generation. We must bequeath and transmit a genuine love to the younger generation in order to ensure that they will not feel rootless, isolated, unloved, untouched, and simply unattended to.

In the end, I believe that the power of Black love is one of the most precious themes and most significant issues in the history of Black people, past, present, and future. It is Black love, like Black history, that unites these three dimensions of time.

WEDNESDAYS AND SUNDAYS

Elwood L. Robinson

I am the only child of the union of Isaiah and Hannah Robinson. My father spent all his life working for meager wages in rural North Carolina. His highest annual salary was $8,500. We grew up in a small, dilapidated house with no bathroom or running water. It was not until I was a senior in high school that we got a telephone. (The first person I called was the woman who has now been my wife for twenty years.) I never felt ashamed of our living conditions; I always had the feeling of being loved, and the sense that my parents were doing the best they could. I never knew I was poor. The fact is, I was not poor; I was very rich in love. The riches that I accumulated during my childhood are the foundation for my adult perspective on life.

Today I am a professor of psychology at North Carolina Central University in Durham, North Carolina. I was the first person in my family to graduate from college and the first person from my community to receive a Ph.D. My beautiful wife, Denise, and I have two children, Chanita, seventeen, and Devin, eight. My life has been so full of love and kindness that sometimes I get overwhelmed with emotion just thinking about it. I have been blessed to have two parents who loved me unconditionally and would do anything for me. They denied themselves many things and sacrificed so that I would have opportunities that they didn't— and in many ways, were not allowed to have.

My mother had a severe and incapacitating stroke in 1993. Early one Sunday morning, two years later, I received a call that my father was lying motionless in the den of my parents' home; the rescue workers there were trying to revive him. By the time I arrived, the emergency folks were transporting him to the ambulance.

I waited by my father's side as he struggled to regain consciousness. The stroke had caused bleeding in the lower brain structures, and in a short period he would be dead. The hospital staff had briefed me on his condition and told me that the chances of his survival were slim. The attending physician informed me that my father would be dead in a short while and asked me if I wanted to have him resuscitated if he expired. That night was the longest night of my life. His breathing was labored. With every breath he took, I was certain that it was his last.

As the afternoon turned to evening, all I could do was watch him and pray. I rubbed his face and looked in his eyes. I knew he recognized me, but he could not speak. This was the man who taught me the "love of the game." He was a Celtic fan because of Bill Russell, the Jones boys, Sam, and KC. He was a Dodger fan because of Jackie Robinson and Sandy Koufax. And so I became a Celtic and Dodger fan too. He did not appreciate football, but when I became a Cowboy fan, he became one as well. When I was a child, he would come into my room each morning and tell me the baseball scores. I remember his 6 A.M. voice: "You know, the Dodgers beat the Giants last night." And that's all he would say before going to work. But those words gave me comfort, and I immediately felt safe and secure. Somehow, those words told me that everything was right with the world. He taught me about manhood, hard work, and faith by the simple eloquence of his example.

The evening shift at the hospital came on duty at 6:00 P.M. The attending physician came by to see my father at around 7:00 P.M. As he was reviewing my father's chart, I noticed that he was wearing a class ring from North Carolina Central University. Since I had been a professor at NCCU since 1984, I thought it a possibility that I knew him. It turned out that he had been a Minority Access to Research Careers (MARC) scholar while attending NCCU. I was the current director of the MARC program. I had never imagined that a student trained in our program would one day be taking care of my dying father.

He asked me what I had been told about my father's prognosis. I told him that the attending physician said that he would be dead soon. This wonderful Black physician would not be dissuaded by the diagnosis of his counterpart. He simply looked at the chart and said, "Let me try something." I don't know what he told the staff, but there was an immediate flurry of activity around my father. I later learned that this doctor, who would not give up on my father when everybody else had, had ordered that he be given some experimental medication designed to stop the bleeding in his brain. The blessings are overflowing.

My father survived, but he had a very long road to recovery. He spent a month in a rehabilitation center, and I was now faced with an unthinkable situation. Who would take care of my father? I could not take him home because my aunt was already there taking care of my mother, who required twenty-four-hour assistance. While I knew my aunt would never turn down the challenge of taking care of both her sister and her brother-in-law, it would be too much for one person. And I knew that I didn't have the room or the facilities at my house for him to live with us. My only option was the unthinkable: a nursing home.

I had a referral from a trusted social worker who urged me to consider putting my father in Mary Gran Nursing Center. It was where all the local doctors put their parents. Just the thought of having to put my father in a nursing center was horrifying, almost beyond understanding. Black folks didn't put their parents in nursing homes. That was something that white people did. I drove slowly to the center to meet with the administrators to discuss my father's becoming a resident. After I parked in the lot, I put my head on the steering wheel, unable to get out of the car. I prayed and cried out for God to give me the strength to move, and the courage to do what I knew in my heart was best for my father. I felt so guilty about signing the forms that would admit him to this nursing home.

In retrospect, this was one of the best decisions that I would make regarding my father's health care. My father received care that exceeded my expectations tenfold. He became the darling of the nursing center. For the last six years, the nursing staff and other support staff have taken care of my father with the greatest love, support, and professionalism. I often asked myself, "Why have I been so blessed?"

Psalm 30 says, "Weeping endures during the night, but in the morning joy cometh." Since he arrived at the nursing center, my father has developed insulin-dependent diabetes, survived prostate cancer, and experienced the death of six roommates. In spite of this, he approaches each day with a positive attitude. He has taught me more about love and life during his disability than I could have imagined. His attitude about his illness has been inspiring. He still believes that he will walk again unassisted. He still believes that he will work again. And he still believes that he is improving each day and will have a complete recovery. Words cannot express or capture his spirit and resiliency.

The nursing home is approximately ninety miles from my home in Durham, North Carolina. For the past six years, I have visited him every Sunday. He likes Sundays. I take him to see my mother, who has been bedridden for the past eight years. If you did not know him before the disability, it would be difficult to detect how the stroke has changed him. Order and consistency are important to him now. He calls me every Wednesday at approximately 7:30 P.M. We talk for a few minutes about sports or politics, but he always wants to know how I am doing. And he always encourages me, and asks me to be careful.

Today, my father and I are closer than ever before. His motivation and determination are inspiring. He lives life to its fullest in spite of his disability. He often talks of his life now by using the words of Apostle Paul, who wrote, "I have learned, in whatever state I am, therefore to be content." I get up early on Sunday morning in anticipation of my weekly pilgrimage to Mary Gran Nursing Center. It is not a job, a chore, or an inconvenience; it is very simply an act of love. When I was a baby and could not walk, my parents carried me; when I could not eat, they fed me; when I could not put on my clothes, they put them on for me. The very least I can do for them during this time is to return their love.

The Women of Minende

Erica Johnson

At age twenty-five I had it all together. I had bought a house with my mother at age twenty-one, and I had a good corporate job that I had been at for six years. The job was able to pay for my college education and my car, and help pay my mortgage as well. Then the unthinkable happened. My boyfriend of five and a half years ended our relationship. I felt like my life had fallen apart. Gone was all my confidence and self-esteem. I was a complete mess.

A friend suggested I visit her to get my mind off my troubles. While at her home, I picked up a book from her dresser: *Value in the Valley*, by Iyanla Vanzant. The book changed my life! I cried after every page. I immediately put myself on the Inner Visions mailing list, and received an invitation to attend a workshop. I jumped at the opportunity! That is where I met the nine women in my sister circle; they attended the workshop as well.

After the completion of the workshop, our coordinator suggested that we start a support group and keep in contact with each other, which we agreed to do. As with any group, we had some growing pains; however, over the last five years we have evolved into a committed family. In the year 2000 we decided to formalize our group by giving it some structure and a name, and thus Minende was born. *Minende* is an Aboriginal word that means "yolk." We support each other as our lives unfold just as an egg yolk nourishes during the transformation from egg to hatchling. Our group of sisters range in age from thirty to fifty and come from a variety of social and economic backgrounds.

Being in the presence of these women has taught me self-acceptance. Now when I look in the mirror I see a divine daughter, no matter what my hair looks like or how my day is going. I still have insecurities, but now I know to trust the process of life.

The concept of a sister circle has changed my life for the better. I now know what it is to be accepted and loved unconditionally. The women of Minende opened their hearts to me at a time when it was critical for my growth and development, as well as my survival. They allowed me to learn the lessons that only living life could teach me, and they did it without being judgmental. I've learned what it means to trust my instincts and not doubt my abilities. Their support has given me the courage to experience all the joys in life.

I am proud to say I am a member of a sister circle. I truly love and respect the women of Minende. They have shown me that strong, proud Black women don't talk about what they can do or are capable of doing—they just do it!

My Baby Brother

Roslyn Perry

On January 23, 1970, my baby brother, George, was born. He had cocoa skin, full lips, beautiful brown eyes, and a head full of gorgeous silky Black hair.

George looked perfect on the outside, but he was born with a defective heart. My parents were crushed. But they were determined that they would get through this crisis.

The doctors informed my parents that George would need open-heart surgery to try to correct the defect in his heart. At this point, George was only weeks old. But it had to be done in order to prolong his life. So my parents agreed, and the battle began.

Through the course of his life, George would have several open-heart surgeries. To make things worse, when he turned two years old, George became ill with an extremely high fever. My parents took him to the emergency room at the local hospital only to be told by the attending resident physician that he had a minor illness. He was sent home. George's fever spiked so high that he had a stroke, which left him paralyzed on his right side and developmentally disabled.

My parents, however, never wavered and never crumbled. The love that they had for George always outweighed any obstacle; as a family, we were determined that we would get through this.

Throughout his life, and through all of his adversities, George was the most positive, kind, and loving individual imaginable. Even when he was in the hospital having yet another surgery, he was always happy and laughing. When he was undergoing physical, occupational, and speech therapy to learn how to walk and talk, he was always positive. George went to special schools for the mentally challenged and was later mainstreamed into regular schools. Even though at times children could be cruel and hurtful toward him, my baby brother remained positive, happy, and loving.

My family made sure that whatever we did, George did as well. We took summer vacations together; when we all went to camp, George went too! George even went to his prom, which was a major accomplishment. He taught everyone who came in contact with him to make the most out of life.

The doctors told my parents at the outset that George would not live past the age of five. My parents did not believe that, and their love and care, along with George's zest for life and his will to live, proved them all wrong. George lived to be twenty-eight before he passed away in 1999. When he died, he died at home in his room, with his two favorite people with him. My mom was holding him, and my dad was sitting at the foot of his bed watching TV with him, something they loved to do together.

George taught us so many things before he left this earth. I thank God every day for the time I had with him. I believe that people are put into our lives for different reasons and purposes. George was put into my family's life so that we could come to know a special kind of love and closeness, and to this day we do. I know I am a better person for having had him as a brother. A lot of families would have given up from day one, but not mine. Today we are so much stronger because of the love that my baby brother brought us.

My Pillow of Strength

Rayetta Johnson

The Valentine's Day dance, the homecoming dance, the winter formal, and all the other dances at my junior high school always ended up the same for me. I was a chubby and neurotic girl, with a preteen body that appeared as though it would develop into a big, bloated human pimple!

With my body in its already "fluffy" state, I would swallow every crumb and sip every high-calorie drink I could get my hands on prior to the dance. Consequently, whatever custom-made outfit that my mom had sewn, during the few free swatches of her busy time, would appear to magnify my chunkiness even more. My face would turn into an acne-filled mess, or so it seemed to me. To my mom, however, I was always a beautiful princess.

All of the dances would end the same. My dad would come to pick up the princess at the end of the dance. He would always ask me how everything had gone, and I would always say "fine." I'd babble on and on about some unimportant details to avoid bursting into tears. As soon as we'd arrive home, I'd trudge to my room. Within a few minutes, a gentle knock could be heard, and in would walk my mom.

Without anything having been said, the tears would silently begin to stream down my chubby cheeks. At that point, my mother would take me in her arms and the saga would rush forth from my lips in between my sobs. The story I related was always the same. I'd recall all the girls who had been asked to dance and the boys who'd asked them, but I was always left out of the recollection.

During the dance, I would talk and laugh with my friends, each of whom, throughout the evening, had been asked to dance by someone, whether it was the captain of one of the sports teams or the chess champion. The point was that someone had asked them! In between their invitations, dances, and refusals, we would huddle to swap experiences. Well, at least they could swap experiences; all I could do was listen! This back-and-forth carousel would last the duration of the dance. To my dismay, I was never able to take a turn in participating. Sadly enough, not even the president of the insect club had asked me to dance.

Whenever I returned home and shared my experiences with my mother, she was always my pillow of strength. Her warm arms, soft lap, and soothing but strong words chased my pubescent problems away. She would tell me how special and beautiful I was, and she'd make sure I knew how much she, my dad, and my sister loved me. Then she'd immediately launch into praise of my talents and highlights of my accomplishments. Finally, she would tell me that someday I would have to run from all the boys because they'd all be chasing me for a dance!

Others tried to convince me of the positive attributes I possessed, but they were unsuccessful. There was something special about the way in which my mother approached these things, however. I don't know if it was the sparkle in her eye as she would talk to me or the dimple in her cheek as she smiled at me. Perhaps it was the stroke of her hand as she brushed back my hair; or maybe it was a combination of all of these things.

Whatever it was, I believed her when she said it. And there in the warm, soft lamplight in the quiet of our home, my "pillow of strength" would soak up my tears, kiss away my hurts, and infuse my soul with esteem, strength, and hope!

THE POWER OF BLACK LOVE

Tina Marshall-Bradley

I fell in love with the man that I am going to be with for the rest of my life when I was fifteen years old. Since that time we have married, reared two beautiful children, and been blessed to have loved and been loved by literally hundreds of people. There is nothing particularly special about us, except that by the grace of a power higher than any of us, we understood at an early age that happiness, strength, and prosperity all lie in the power of Black love, and together we consciously resolved to manifest that love in the decisions we made in our lives. As we grew and developed as young professionals, we made deliberate choices to live in African American communities, use the services of African American professionals, patronize Black businesses, work for Black organizations, and immerse ourselves in Black culture.

While in the middle of living the American dream (our first home, good jobs, two children, two cars, an active social life, and credit card debt), we decided to sell everything, pack up the children and our few remaining belongings, and enroll in graduate school in the Midwest. With no family and very few African Americans in the area, we clung feverishly to anything and anyone affiliated with Africa. We created programs so that our children could interact with African and African American children. We organized community forums at the Black Culture Center on campus so that we could be steeped in our culture while our formal studies were steeped in another culture. We went out of our way to create a sense of community for ourselves and our children as well as the young African Americans and Africans who came to this small midwestern town from cities such as Chicago, Detroit, and Minneapolis, and countries such as Nigeria, Sudan, and Mauritania, only to find themselves in a sea of white. Last weekend I saw one of the students who used to attend those forums at a mall in Virginia. We recalled those days as if they were yesterday. There is not a week that goes by that we don't make some kind of contact from someone we met during that dynamic three-year period.

Through our advanced studies at this predominantly white institution, we met a number of African Americans who had gotten their start at historically Black colleges or universities (HBCUs). We wanted to contribute our skills to these institutions. After defending our dissertations within a week of each other, my husband and I took positions at an HBCU on the East Coast, where our careers took off. Through these positions we were both afforded opportunities to work with movers and shakers in education, government, and social organizations and have been doing so ever since. Our careers have been meaningful and fulfilling, and we are constantly challenged to manifest the greatness that has gone before us and continues to surround us.

After completing our formal studies, we were also determined that our children would live in a community and attend schools with African Americans. We purposely identified a Black realtor and told him we wanted to live in a Black neighborhood. He took us to a dilapidated house in the 'hood and asked us if that was "Black enough" for us. We chose not to use his services and identified another Black realtor who found us a home in a wonderful community where our children attended the small Black community school and made friends that they still communicate with to this day. When we moved out of the house, our realtor managed our property for six years. We were able to move out of the state to advance our careers without worrying about our investment. The only trouble that occurred was when most of the plumbing in the house had to be replaced. Thankfully, my husband's former college roommate owns a plumbing company in Atlanta. The brother left his home on the weekend and picked my husband up in South Carolina, and they drove to Virginia to replace all of the pipes in the house for the cost of supplies. After eleven years, we sold the house last month. We stayed with our dear friends and former neighbors while we closed on the house. We will be attending the wedding of our realtor's son in Charlotte, North Carolina, the first of May. People come into your life for a reason, a season, or a lifetime. The brothers and sisters that we associate with are a part of our lives forever.

Our lives have been richly blessed; my husband, my children, and I have had opportunities to teach or study in different countries, where we have interacted with many people of African descent. Together we have studied or lectured in Bermuda, Egypt, Ghana, and Colombia. In fact, I will be lecturing with two of my dear colleagues in Nigeria this year. Currently, my husband and I both work for HBCUs in South Carolina. We are purchasing a house that one of the colleges is refurbishing as a part of a neighborhood revitalization program. We are committed to lending our energy to a community that has so much rich history but which in the recent past has had its resources depleted as African Americans move to suburban areas. Our son is attending a university on a full athletic scholarship, and he is majoring in urban planning and international development. Through our involvement in the Black community he has "uncles" who are judges, CEOs of companies, professional athletes, university presidents, electricians, and every other type of hardworking, upstanding brother one can imagine.

Our sixteen-year-old daughter is an exchange student in Brazil, an opportunity she won while attending the all-Black high school in the city where we live. People warned us not to send her to the school because it had a reputation for being dangerous. But there are fantastic things happening in urban schools, even though there is a lot of work to be done here (and in all other schools where the majority of students served are African American).

We are convinced that, as strong African Americans, we have a responsibility to stand up for those whose voices have not been traditionally heard. Our daughter e-mailed us last week and asked us if she should honor a request by a professional organization in Brazil to speak about American racism. We told her that it is her responsibility to provide information to those who request it, and reminded her to recall what she has learned through the literature she has been exposed to and lectures she has attended since she was a toddler.

Our children have been taught that "for unto whomsoever much is given, of him shall be much required" (Luke 12:48). The sacrifices of Mary McLeod Bethune, Harriet Tubman, Marcus Garvey, and Paul Robeson were constant topics of discussion in our house and always will be a part of our children's formal studies, even if they are not required by the schools.

Our conscious decision to love ourselves and those who look like us is necessary because of the constant barrage of negative energy and information that is leveled at individuals of African descent, particularly in America. This decision has given us rewards beyond our imaginations. We are not wealthy in the traditional sense of the word. However, our friends, who are like family members, are so numerous that we have a hard time keeping up with them. Our children relish the knowledge that they have "aunts" and "uncles" literally all over the world who have their backs, support them with prayers and well wishes, and take pride in having had a hand in rearing them. Because of the love that we have for our collective selves and our community, we continue to patronize Black businesses and professionals, live in the Black community, and steep ourselves in the magnificent cultures of the African diaspora. The stories of how consciously loving our brothers and sisters has brought us fulfillment and spirited wealth are too numerous to mention. Suffice it to say that we are convinced that the power of Black love has brought us the kind of prosperity that the Creator wishes for all mankind.

TRIBUTE TO MY HUSBAND

Donna M. Johnson-Thomas

Black love, Black hope, and Black healing—my story involves all three. It's a story that ends prematurely, some would say sadly; yet it gave me hope for the future and eventually healed me. As I watched the love of my life slowly slip away, his body ravaged by pancreatic cancer, I felt a part of me was dying with him, the part that was the best because of knowing and loving him.

Our story began in 1979, after a lot of cajoling on the part of my friend Grace to meet a friend of her and her husband, Ray. I had just gone through a divorce, and frankly, the last thing I was interested in was the prospect of a new relationship. Fortunately for me, fate stepped in. Grace was as tenacious as a bulldog, and I finally acquiesced to her suggestion of a small dinner party to meet this "nice guy." I went to their house not expecting anything; in fact, I had made up my mind not to like him. To my surprise and complete amazement, he was all Grace had said: poised, amusing, a good conversationalist, and not hard on the eyes. Maybe it was the ambience of my friend's home or the amount of wine that I had been drinking (to which I was not accustomed), but I was relaxed and very glad I came.

After the party he escorted me to my car, inquiring if I was all right to drive home. I was saying to myself, "N——, please, I didn't drink *that* much," but to my surprise he was sincerely concerned, and moreover a true gentleman. I was again impressed. But first impressions can be deceiving (been there and done that). We exchanged phone numbers; he said that he was going home for the holidays to Montgomery, Alabama, where his mother, brother, and sister-in-law reside, but he would call me when he got back.

Thanksgiving came and went; no call. You know what I was thinking: "Mr. Right was only Mr. Right Now." Then one bright and sunny Saturday, as I was driving along, I noticed a familiar face. The Renaissance Lions Club members were out selling candy canes for their annual Christmas

Cane Drive. For a moment I had forgotten his name—was it Herman? Harold? Oh yes, Hubert. I rolled down the window with my dollar in hand, and as he approached the car I wondered if he remembered me (it had been more than a month since we first met). At first he didn't; then with that wide, infectious grin he said, "I've been meaning to call you." I laughed, asked if he still had the number, paid him for the candy cane, and said I was looking forward to hearing from him. I have to admit I would have been very disappointed if he hadn't called, but he did. Slowly, cautiously, we both let our walls down. We found out that even though there was a wide gap in our ages, seventeen years, we had a lot in common. Momma was right—the way to a man's heart is still through his stomach. I baited my hook for that fish with collard greens, candied yams, homemade rolls, and all sorts of other delicacies.

After eight years of being together, the idea of marriage never crossed my mind. It wasn't until the day that I accompanied Hubert to the emergency room that I was slapped with reality. He was taken into the examining room, and I was left to give his personal information to the triage nurse. She got to the question about next of kin and asked what my relationship to him was. I said I was his girlfriend. To my amazement, she gathered up her clipboard and walked away, without so much as a thank-you. It was then that I realized girlfriends and significant others meant zilch, nada, nothing, less than nothing. This was the turning point of our relationship.

Every woman, if she really knows her man, knows when to bring up the Question! Especially to a Lion (Hubert was born August 7). To make a long story short, after he accused me of giving him an ultimatum, a female friend asked him if he loved me. He answered affirmatively. She said, "Then you've answered your own question." Shortly afterward he proposed. We were married on a Thursday evening in November 1987.

In June 1990 I lost my love to cancer, just five months short of our third wedding anniversary. At his bedside were Ray, Grace, and myself, just as we had begun that glorious journey eleven years earlier. I thank God for every moment spent with him. Our vows stated that we would love each other in good times and in bad, in sickness as in health. There were never any bad times. Even through his sickness Hubert showed me how to die in dignity, just as he had lived.

THE PERFECT WIFE

Dale S. Johnson

One day, I found myself unemployed. I had always considered it something that happened to other people. After all, I had done things the right way in my life. I had not taken drugs; I had graduated from a "name" college; I had played the corporate role as well as any young Black midlevel executive was allowed to play it. Nonetheless, I found myself unemployed, thanks to corporate politics and economic conditions. How would I be able to tell my wife?

We had been married for fourteen years. As in any marriage with its ups and downs, we had experienced a couple of bad years, but for the most part we had a strong marriage. Yet I wondered how she would deal with a newly unemployed primary breadwinner.

Less than six months prior, we had finalized the adoption of our little girl, Khristyn. We had moved into our new house (a house that both sets of parents bragged about) less than three years before. Although we had been relatively successful in eliminating most of our credit card bills, there was still the house note and two car notes, utilities to be paid, and groceries to be bought. I was scared!

When I told Judy, she just wrapped her arms around me and said those four magic words: "We'll be all right!" At that moment, my worries fell away. As she released me from our embrace, she smiled and repeated those same words over and over again.

It would have been easy for Judy to go on the attack. Two weeks earlier, I had begged her to resign from her job to stay home with Khristyn. I was making over twice as much as she was and was convinced that we could survive on my income alone. After all, my parents had done it, and they raised four kids!

Judy, being her own person, refused. She said that she had a college degree just as I did; that she wanted her own identity, and her own money. She didn't care how much money I made. She wanted to work, and she was going to work! Now her income was the only income that we had, yet she never mentioned any earlier conversation.

I'd always believed it was the man's responsibility to provide for his family. I couldn't help thinking, "What will my parents and Judy's parents and our friends think?" I feared that we would have to sell the house and leave the state to relocate to an area where I could find another position in my profession. Finally, the voice of reason popped into my head; in reality, survival is the name of the game!

My wife continued to work as I began looking for a job. Over time, I was overcome with feelings of depression. One day, Judy brought home flowers for me. Judy handed me the flowers and gave me a big, toe-curling kiss! The card attached to the flowers read, "I love you, and don't ever forget that!"

I've come to realize every man needs someone to whom he can expose his vulnerabilities without worrying about losing face in that person's eyes. Judy taught me that. She taught me what real love was all about.

LESSONS FROM A THREE-YEAR-OLD

Nikitta A. Foston

Watching the rear lights of the Saab fade into the sunlit afternoon, I waved good-bye to my six-month-old daughter, who was strapped securely in her infant seat. Even though she was out of sight, I could feel her presence as though her small body were still cradled in my arms. Wiping the tears from my eyes, I tried to remind myself of my daughter's relationship with her father, and—more importantly—the effect on her life without it.

For months, my daughter's father and I had struggled to reach an agreement on how to provide her with the benefit and privileges of both parents, given our separation. Yet, despite our efforts and good intentions, we continued to disagree. As the mother, I automatically assumed that my daughter should be with me primarily. Certainly, I welcomed the involvement of her father, but I did not believe in separating a child from her mother at such a young age for any extended period of time.

My ex's argument was that he was entitled to the same rights, the same access, and the same privileges that I enjoyed, and that his role should not be defined by my limited perceptions of fatherhood. Refusing to accept society's notion of single fathers as passive at best, he advocated splitting our daughter's time equally until she was of school age, when a primary location (not a primary parent) would be necessary.

While I respected his position, I did not understand the origins of his inexhaustible devotion to sharing so equally in the life of our child. Without question, he loved her and was committed to her well-being. But there was something more. Something, I believed, that stemmed from his childhood without his father. It was an absence that he seldom spoke of but which was evident in his every word and deed since learning he was to become a father.

I too had missed my father's presence following my parents' divorce when I was a child. Yet my father's absence did not ignite in me an allegiance to the importance of fatherhood. Instead, his absence only seemed to strengthen my belief in the power and importance of motherhood. Watching my own mother raise my younger brother and me without my father's assistance reinforced the notion that mothers are dominant—not by choice, but by necessity.

For the sake of my daughter, however, I tried to set aside my perceptions of parenting in order to make decisions that were best for her, even if they were difficult for me. With that in mind, I agreed to a one-week stay with her dad when she was six months old. I packed bottles of breast milk, clothes, and diapers, and tried to prepare myself mentally for her departure.

I contacted her pediatrician to inquire about any health issues that I should be concerned with and was comforted and relieved with her response. "So long as your child receives the same care and love in the alternate environment," her doctor assured me, "she will be fine." But before I could feel completely at ease, I called my pastor for spiritual support and was encouraged with a thought that continues to sustain me: "God is a father, and He seeks a loving relationship with His children; your daughter's father wants nothing less."

Three years later, my daughter adores and respects her dad. Well aware of those who love her, she has grown into an inquisitive and energetic child with an intellect well beyond her three-and-a-half years. Her initial one-week stay with her dad began a regimen of one-week stays each month that we adhered to until she reached a year and a half. At that point, given her exceptional development and adaptability to both environments, and in the interest of fairness, we divided our daughter's time equally: two weeks with Mommy, two weeks with Daddy.

In accordance with our arrangement, her father drives to pick her up from my home, and I drive to pick her up from his, or we meet at a midpoint and exchange our "little love." Sometimes when it's nearly time for her to leave, she'll place her hands on her imaginary hips, stare from behind her big brown eyes with a frown, and exclaim, "Mommy, can you *please* tell Saturday to hurry up—my daddy is coming on Saturday!"

Some say I'm lucky to have a break from being Mommy each month, to have time for myself. But I know that I'm blessed to have a beautiful little girl who is in turn blessed to have the love and presence of both Mommy and Daddy.

What I Never Knew I Always Needed

Ebuni McFall-Roberts, M.A., L.P.C.

During the two years that I was completing my master's degree in counseling, my idea of the "right man" had undergone a profound transformation. I had decided that I would let God lead my husband to me, instead of me looking for him. I revised my list of "needs" in a mate, shortening it to the following: (1) he had to be a man of God, (2) he had to be a man of integrity, and (3) he had to know that no woman deserved to be beaten, cheated on, or called derogatory names, ever. I had been celibate for many months and was committed to graduating and looking for a job. Dating was not high on my priority list. I realized that I deserved more than I had been receiving. I believe that when you truly "let go and let God," God will deliver far beyond what you could ever imagine or hope for. I had asked God to send me a good man for many years, and what I found didn't meet my then-longer list of "needs." Once I shortened the list to what was truly important, though, God sent him to me.

Meandering down the hall at the psychiatric hospital where I was completing my internship for my degree, I met my future husband. He was sitting in his office, the office of the director of adolescent services, as I was passing by, looking for his boss, who was also my clinical supervisor. I thought he looked interesting, although "not my type." I circled back around, though, and said hello. His hello was so engaging that we ended up talking for over two hours. But I was still certain that this was just a chance conversation with a fellow employee. While talking with him and to him was the easiest thing I had ever done, that still did not change the fact that he was not my type.

Later, it occurred to me that if God was in charge, my type was whomever He wanted for me. We spoke once more, and he asked me out on a date that afternoon. I later learned that he'd wanted to ask me out that first day, but he was in the process of ending a relationship and wanted to "clean house" first, which I deeply respect him for. From our very first date, he impressed me. It was not the car he drove, nor his clothes; it was his attentiveness to me. We went to a restaurant on the south side of Charlotte that had trivia and bingo contests during dinner. When the waitress presented us with the option to play bingo, he declined, saying, "I just want to focus on you." That evening we talked and laughed for hours. I enjoyed his company. He actually saw me through the attractive exterior. He looked beyond my credentials and got to the heart of me. We went out and shot pool the next night. He knew I was not interested in a sexual relationship until marriage, and he respected that. He didn't even try to kiss me. I think I finally kissed him on our fifth date, just to get it over with. However, it was on our third date that he began talking about marriage; he told me, "If you're not the one, you're pretty close to the one."

We became engaged on New Year's. We faced our first major test the week before our wedding. The hospital where we had met was closing, and he would be unemployed. This did not interfere with our wedding; we simply trusted God that an answer would come. We honeymooned in Florida and took suits for interviews in case calls came in. He already had an interview scheduled in Atlanta, and then I received a request for an interview there as well. We left our honeymoon early so that I could interview. I was given the job, with only two weeks to pack our apartment in Charlotte and move to Atlanta. This time cemented us in many ways, however. We actually had a twenty-one-day honeymoon where neither of us worked, for he received a very generous severance package from the hospital.

Before marriage, I was wedded to ideas about being married that have not all come to fruition. I didn't know that it was possible to trust that someone will truly be there for me and love me so completely and unconditionally. My husband has become my rock of Gibraltar, and we have weathered many storms. His consistency and his dedication to our marriage, to God, and to our personal growth have made the journey special. He has taught me so much about stick-to-it-iveness, and about the importance of not giving up.

We had a baby at the end of last year; the next chapter in our lives is beginning. It is so incredible to see him with our son, to be married to a man who wants to get up with the baby at night. He never just baby-sits his child, he parents.

Just as children don't come with instructions, neither does marriage. Sometimes I think back about the first time we met and how just a year earlier I probably wouldn't have been interested in him. I was still figuring out what I needed from another person. I realize now that God sent him in His time. It is the simple things that keep our love growing, like his waking before me and turning my curling iron on, or his rubbing my shoulders while I feed the baby. My husband is everything I never knew I always needed.

Love is what keeps us trying every day, and prayer has brought us through what we could not come through on our own. While it has not always been easy, it has always been worth it.

These Three Words

Cherryl Floyd-Miller

I had been one of four women selected to appear on the *Oprah Winfrey Show* for the *Heart of a Woman* book club episode. It was my fifteen minutes of fame. My friend Enessia had taped the show and was hosting a viewing party at her home. I sat with friends and work colleagues, watching the show intently, when I heard the words I'd said: "I've never heard my mother say 'I love you.'"

A quickened heartbeat drummed in my ears and throat. My mother was hosting a viewing party for the show at her home too. *My God, what did she think of this?*

The sentence that followed what I had said had been edited out. The complete statement—"I've never heard my mother say 'I love you,' but I know that she does"—had been hacked to suit the clueless tastes of some ratings chaser. I started to write the producers of *Oprah* a letter. But the truth stopped me, and the truth was that I had never heard my mother say "I love you." Even if the full statement had been broadcast, the first part of it was still true.

I was accustomed to being the odd one in my family, frequently misunderstood and likely to bear the brunt of dissent from all the folks who disagreed with my decisions. I am a writer, and that makes me weird to begin with. This new drama, however, lowered me a step down from black sheep squarely into the role of traitor. What I'd said was selfish. I was ungrateful. I had no right. And it was as far from the truth as a lie could get. That's what the family said about me. Those who didn't say it thought it.

For the next year I braved rooms at family gatherings that fell silent when I entered them. I trudged through the slush of double talk and hidden meanings in carefully laid sentences. I waited to be slugged by judgments from the eyes of people with my blood in their veins. I felt alone and small. I began to speak to them only of what was necessary—

Hello; Happy birthday; Yes, the kids can come to the cookout; Yes, we're doing okay. The very thing I'd spoken out against—silence—started to root itself in me.

It wasn't that I was a stranger to silence. Growing up in the South among spirits of women who I was convinced could grab misery by its ugly face and sell it back to the devil, I was spoon-fed silence daily. It was how we got by, speaking *around* the things that ran deep in us like rivers. I was never to let anyone who was against me see me cry. This gave them a victory they didn't deserve. Some things, like pain or betrayal or agony, were not to be spoken about aloud. Having breath in your body was a blessing; complaining was a blasphemy against the Father and His Son. And what I had done, going on national television and talking about what my mother didn't do for me, was definitely blasphemous. I had sinned against God and my mother.

As it always happens when you believe, I was tested. I had resolved that this friction between me and my mother would forever characterize the way we connected. I had accepted that we would never be friends, but I would find a space inside my own dignity to honor my mother as the vessel that gave me life. She was twice my age and less likely to change. I believed I had to be more charitable than the rift between us so far had allowed.

Then a call came from my aunt in the middle of the night. My mother was scheduled for surgery early the next morning, and she'd been asking for me. Over the past year of not speaking, she'd changed her phone number and didn't have mine. The doctors were not sure what would happen once the procedure began, but the family planned to be there to support her during the surgery.

The next day, I entered the waiting room, shocking everyone already there. But I didn't arrive in time to see my mother before the surgery began. I sat in the sterile hush of the hospital trying to remember how we'd grown so far apart.

As a girl, I had watched my mother work as a head cashier in a grocery store to make ends meet for herself and us three children. My father repeatedly missed paying the $35 a week he owed for child support for the three of us. I'd seen the look of despair in my mother's eyes during our weeks of navy bean and grilled cheese dinners. I knew in her quiet dismay what she wanted . . . *hoped* for us: better lives. Hard luck filled our house; hard money eluded us all the time.

I wanted what my mother wanted. The oldest of three children, I bore much of the responsibility for keeping our house clean and in order when my mother worked. I matured quickly, cooking elaborate dishes, changing my baby brother's diapers, answering calls from bill collectors, all before I was twelve. When I got married at twenty-three, I had only one request of God and my then-husband: I did not want to live my mother's life.

She wasn't a wretched woman by any stretch of the imagination. In fact, she had a quick wit and a youth about her that made her the most trusted mom among all my friends. And I trusted her. Before my teen years, my mother and I carried on like sisters. When she wasn't working herself into a tired frenzy, she was vibrant and fully engaged with our childhood joys.

I do not know anyone as strong as my mother. She has survived a horrific divorce, an inner-ear infection that mysteriously caused blackouts and stole her balance, bleeding ulcers, a stroke, and for nearly fifteen years a brain tumor. She ignored the gloomy prognoses of doctors who gave her a virtual death date on each successive visit. Only she could look death squarely in the eyes and laugh at it.

So, what right did I have to complain? My mother had made the most incredible sacrifices. Without them, my life could have taken so many more fatal turns. I had gratefully embraced my mother's willingness to forfeit herself for her children. It's what mothers do.

But while I had learned the language of need, of uttering what is essential for your survival, I missed hearing my mother say she loved me. I have forever craved the sound of it in my ear. As music legend Carlos Santana says, sound alters the molecular structure of the listener. In my case, the sound of those words, I believed, would have configured every cell in my body into an anatomy that was whole and not fragmented with doubt. These three words, to me, are the most eloquent of any in human language, because they have the capacity to change our marrow and not merely our flesh.

My mother survived the surgery. Over the next two years, we spent a lot of time getting to *know* each other. Part of our difficulty was that neither of us truly knew who the other was outside the scope of our pain. I got to see my mother war against the ravishes of disease . . . and win. She got to see me mother my children and give birth to my art.

Last summer, I got a call from her when I was in the middle of a difficult time. I gave her an update on what was going on in my life and she listened. Just before I was ready to replace the phone in its cradle, the words I'd long been waiting for came crackling through the receiver: "I love you," she said. Somewhere deep in my bones, the marrow shifted at the sound of it, and we both were significantly altered.

A Support Group Based on Black Love

Gay Wheeler-Smith

Black love is phenomenal on every level. It has been the social fabric of our existence and survival for hundreds of years. It is unconditional, quiet, patient, sweet, and genuine. Black love is a pot of collard greens with smoked neck bones and corn bread on a cold winter night. Black love comes from our parents, siblings, cousins, and many, many, many great friends. I mean real good sistah-inspirin', sistah-supportin', sistah-cryin', sistah-laughin', sistah-understandin', and sistah-feelin' friends! Sisterhood is something—it's one of a kind.

I left my husband when my daughter was eighteen months old. I packed my clothes, my baby's clothes, some furniture, and left the Big Apple, headed for Atlanta, Georgia.

I started working immediately as a community health nurse. I traveled approximately eighty to a hundred miles a day into unknown territory and was generally greeted by southerners whose belief system was very different from mine. I began to feel a bit frightened—alone, unworthy, inadequate, and depressed due to my failed marriage and my new status as a single mom.

Believe me, this was not my original plan. My mother came to Atlanta with me and was as supportive as a mom could be. I am forever grateful to her. Later I met some sistahs in Georgia who helped pull me out of my slump. Joy, Gay-lynn, Sherry, and Maritza gave me strength, energy, courage, laughter, love, and much-needed healing. They did it not by gossiping, judging, demeaning, or humiliating me. With open, loving hearts, they allowed me to experience the grieving process, cry, be angry, and ventilate my pain and anguish. I was allowed silent moments; while few words were spoken, their actions were crucial.

Joy demonstrated for me how to be a single mom. She had driven alone from New York to Atlanta with a two-month-old, bought a house, painted it herself, and mowed the lawn. Joy did this single-mommyhood thing with energy, grace, style, charm, and much wisdom. She taught me how not to be afraid of parenting alone, and how to travel and engage in activities with my daughter solo.

Slowly, Joy broke through my anger and hopelessness. She made single parenting look so easy. I was fortunate because she and I worked together. As health care professionals, we often worked in the same geographical location. I can remember many hot, sunny days we would see each other unexpectedly and begin to talk. Joy inspired me and taught me how to empower myself.

Joy would often say you cannot control other people, but you can control how you respond to a situation and what you will and will not engage in. She also said you could dictate how a person will treat you. Ultimately, you learn the ability to empower yourself and teach your daughter to do the same. Moreover, she taught me that what you put into the universe is what you receive in return. I began living life more lovingly and openly. Joy gave me the courage I needed to return to New York, take the bull by the horns, and win!

It has now been eight years, and I love being a single mom! Great children come from single-parent households! My daughter and I engage in empowering activities all of the time. Joh'vonni, now ten years old, purchases stock on the Internet and runs a small chocolate lollipop business.

She is a mean backstroke swimmer, participates in Girl Scouts, plays the flute, writes poetry, rides a ten-speed bike, and is a B+/A student in school. And I am now the president of an investment club and conduct financial seminars and workshops for parents and children. My daughter and I were featured on the cover of *Black Enterprise* and are currently writing a book together. I say, hats off to single moms and dads. Now I wear the brand proudly!

Although Joy is married now, she understood my turmoil then and took the time to show me Black love. More now than ever, I pay tribute to her because she recently underwent brain surgery to remove a tumor that was pressing on her spine. I want everyone who reads this story to send light, energy, love, and prayers to this beautiful sister.

I pray for Joy every day. My dear friend helped me be who I am today. In this small way. I want to give back to her what she has given to me: acceptance of self and Black love. A candle burns every day for you to continue to heal and gain strength. Continue to grow, my sistah!

INSPIRATION

BROTHER HOGAN

Tavis Smiley

When I was thirteen and growing up in Indiana, there was a man named Douglas Hogan Jr. who lived in the same town as I worshiped, Kokomo, Indiana. Douglas Hogan was the superintendent of the Sunday School at our church, New Bethel Tabernacle. Because I was very active in Sunday School, I got to know Brother Hogan rather well.

As it turns out, Brother Hogan was also a member of the city council in Kokomo. Prior to meeting Brother Hogan, I had not been interested in learning how the political process worked. But when I started spending time with Brother Hogan, I began to understand the impact he had in empowering Black folks in his district. It became clear to me that Brother Hogan was making an important contribution to the community, making a difference in the lives of the folks who were his constituents.

I started spending time at Douglas Hogan's house and worked with him at his office while I was still in junior high school. I opened his mail and tried to help him respond to citizens' complaints, concerns, and requests on his behalf. The majority of the requests focused on the usual—getting potholes fixed and trees trimmed, locating government assistance checks that had not arrived, and helping kids find summer jobs. Not only was I able to see how good it made Brother Hogan feel by working in the community, but in working with him, I began to feel good myself about the impact I was having in helping to respond to the concerns and needs of the community.

Working with Douglas Hogan taught me how the political process really worked. It was my first understanding of the greater good involved in public service, and my first opportunity to witness someone determined to make a difference in the community, fighting for the things the people believed in. The more time I spent with the councilman, the more I became intrigued by the political process and the more convinced I became that public service was a worthy cause. I came to believe that service to the community is the price we pay for the space we occupy—the rent we owe for our place on earth, if you will. Most of all, I enjoyed the feeling I received by helping Brother Hogan help other people.

I learned a lot over the years I worked with Doug Hogan. I learned that Black people want the same things as whites from their leaders in the community. People want leaders to have the courage, the conviction, and the commitment to do what is right. I learned that being of service to others is tremendously rewarding. I learned that when it comes to sharing and caring and mentoring and community, each of us has to find a way to give back.

Mentoring has become one of those politically correct words; who is opposed to mentoring? The reality is, however, that there aren't enough of us who spend quality time with a young person on even a semiregular basis. There is no greater challenge facing our community than the challenge to mentor our young people to achieve to the best of their ability, and to give back to their community. And there is no greater reward.

I learned about mentoring because I was fortunate to have had Brother Hogan mentor me. I gained a passion for helping the community because I worked with a man who cared deeply about the community. Some of the best experiences of my young life were those times when I got to hang out with Douglas Hogan. I wish that every kid had the opportunity to spend time with a leader in the community who is really making a contribution. It was the leadership and mentorship of Douglas Hogan that was the impetus for the mentoring work I engage in through the Tavis Smiley Foundation. Thank you, Brother Hogan—and thanks to all the unrecognized brothers and sisters in towns across our nation who are helping to shape our communities in a positive way, and to guide and mentor our future generations.

Unselfish Love

Tavis Smiley

I have often been asked what I value most about my mother and my father and what traits and characteristics I gained from each of them. My mother Joyce happens to be a Pentecostal evangelist; from her I inherited my abiding faith. From my father, Emory, I inherited my work ethic and my discipline. He is, undoubtedly, the hardest-working man I've ever known. But what inspired me most about them was their example of selflessness that I saw daily.

In the early seventies, my mother and father had three sons, and my mother was pregnant with her fourth child. (She went on to give birth to a total of six sons.) While she was pregnant with her fourth child, she learned that her sister had been murdered in Mississippi. She left behind five kids—three daughters and two sons; the two youngest children weren't in kindergarten yet. Social services prepared to make arrangements for the children to be taken care of, and since there were five children, the agency couldn't find a family that wanted to take in all five. Their solution was to split the kids up by sending them to different foster homes.

My grandmother, Big Mama, had been born and raised in Mississippi and still lived there at the time of my aunt's death. Even though my grandmother's health was failing, she could not bear to see her grandchildren split up, and decided to take four of the five children herself. The father of the last child came to retrieve his daughter and raised her.

Several years later, Big Mama's health began to deteriorate further. She was no longer able to raise four grandchildren. Social services once again prepared to step in and split the children up.

It was at this juncture that my mother and father decided that, rather than have these children split up and be sent to foster homes, they would become the legal guardians of my deceased aunt's kids. So they set out on an eighteen-hour drive from Indiana to Mississippi to retrieve the four children.

My mother and father raised all of us as if we were brothers and sisters from birth. None of us received any more than the other; we were all given equal amounts. This was true for love as well. My parents loved us all the same; they disciplined us all the same; they shared with us all the same; and they sacrificed for us all the same. And never did I hear my parents complain, not even once, about the extra responsibility they had taken on, despite the fact that my parents' income hadn't increased and the space in the trailer we lived in hadn't gotten any bigger. My father had a full-time job as an Air Force officer, and at one time he was working six part-time jobs just to make ends meet. And these weren't even his kids; they were his nephews and nieces by marriage.

A few years ago, I was preparing an acceptance speech for an award I was about to receive. My parents were scheduled to be in the audience that night as I accepted the award. While preparing remarks for the occasion, for the first time in my life it struck me what my parents had actually done. I did the math and discovered that when my parents became the guardians for my aunt's kids, they were only twenty-seven and twenty-eight years old! They were still kids in many respects. I am thirty-seven years old now, and I still don't have a wife or any kids (as my mother so often reminds me!). To think back on what my parents had accomplished completely overwhelmed me. They never complained, nor let us complain. They raised us together as one family.

Years later my grandmother's health deteriorated further and my parents took her into our home as well. In the end, we had thirteen people living in one small trailer in a trailer park. And, in spite of it all, I never heard my mother or my father voice a note of regret.

So when people ask me, "Who inspired you as a child?" it's an easy question to answer, because nothing inspires me as much as the sacrifices my parents made around the issue of family. It brings home to me what the notion of sacrifice is really all about.

RUN ON ANYHOW

R. Lee Gamble

Even in a hospital bed, my mother found a way to appear regal. There she sat, back straight, head held high as she listened to the words her doctor spoke. The prognosis was not good. The tests had confirmed that she had non-Hodgkin's lymphoma. At sixty-eight my mother was facing her mortality.

I sat back in the chair stunned. There had to be a mistake. I asked the doctor if they were sure, but he told me they had ruled out everything else. He turned to my mother and told her that he was going to set up a schedule for her to begin chemotherapy treatments right away. My mother, without even the slightest change in her demeanor, thanked the doctor and told him she trusted him to continue taking care of her.

My sister, Carol, and I looked at each other; we felt the air in the room getting heavier. Carol said she was going to go get a soda, and left my mother and me in the room.

I had no idea that this brief moment alone with my mother would, for the rest of my life, define who she was for me. Out of all of the times we had shared, nothing was as poignant as the moment she and I together faced the fact that she was dying.

"Okay, puddin'," she said in her serious voice, which let me know she expected me to be as straight with her as she was about to be with me. "What is this non-Hodgkin's thing?"

I was determined in that moment to show my mother that she had raised me well. I was going to be strong and tell her exactly what I knew about the disease.

"It is a form of cancer that attacks the lymph nodes," I replied. "There is a lot of research being done, and a lot of medicines are available to treat it." I paused at this point, wondering if I should go on or just leave it like that. It was the look in my mother's eyes that decided for me. She wanted the truth, and she wanted it from me. "It's not curable, but I am going to make sure that you receive the best treatment that is available," I said.

My mother smiled at me, and it was as if all the thickness in the air had just evaporated. She kept smiling as she straightened the covers and fiddled with the remote to adjust her bed. I sat on the edge of my seat and waited for her to break down. I wanted to scream for her. She was too young to go through any of this. This was my mother! I'd expected her to live to be a hundred, and now I was realizing that she might not make it through the year.

I wanted her to fall apart. I wanted her to be angry. I wanted her to give me an excuse to feel all these things. My eyes started to sting as I tried my best to fight back the tears. I struggled to find the right words to say to her.

Turns out my mother said it all. "Don't you start worrying about me. You and I both still have too much living to do. Besides, you know what I have always told you—no doctor or anybody else can decide what will happen in your life. Only two people can determine that—you and God. This is between God and me now. You know, it's like the song we sing in church all the time—sometimes you just got to run on anyhow." She never mentioned the word *cancer* again.

Run on anyhow is exactly what she did. My mother walked out of that hospital and went on with the business of living. Five years later she was still maintaining her life as if that day in the doctor's office never happened. Although she was undergoing chemotherapy and didn't always have the energy she used to have, she still tried to live her life as she always did.

She continued to baby-sit a little girl she had been taking care of since the child was an infant. She still cleaned her home and cooked her meals. I saw her or spoke to her every day, and every day she would let me know she was running on.

In the summers she traveled—one year to St. Louis, another year to New York. She even attended her high school reunion in her hometown of Augusta, Georgia.

Amazed, I watched her and I learned. She taught me that living or dying is all a state of mind, and my mother's mind was set on living for as long as she had breath.

On the day that I gave birth to my third child, her eleventh grand-child, she had a chemotherapy treatment scheduled. I spoke with her on the phone to let her know that her granddaughter and I were fine. She told me to rest and that she would see me later. I thought she meant when I got out of the hospital. Chemotherapy usually left her weak and tired, so I knew she would need to go home and get her rest.

Later that evening, as I began to try to force down what the hospital called dinner, I heard the voice I had recognized since the day I came into the world. There she stood. She looked thin, and her once plump face had started to sag. But the beauty that was my mother still radiated around her. "Where is my baby?" she said as she walked in with my sister and nephew in tow.

"What are you doing here?" I asked, stunned. "You should be home resting." I looked at my sister, bewildered.

My sister looked at me, shook her head, and said, "She insisted."

"Of course I insisted," Mother said in her huffy tone. "Nothing was going to keep me from seeing my grandbaby."

As we walked down the hall toward the nursery I had no idea that we were heading into the last stretch of our time together. My mother's health began to rapidly deteriorate after that day.

The chemotherapy was being given in stronger doses, and her hair began to come out. Not one to let anything just happen to her, she took control of the situation and cut the rest of her hair off. She called me and told me to come over and see her hair. My husband and I, along with the kids, piled in the car and headed over. I was preparing myself to cheer her up about losing her hair, and instead she flipped the script on me.

When I walked into the house she was sitting in her favorite chair at the kitchen table. How sick my mother was becoming was made clear to me when I walked up those stairs into the kitchen and saw her with peach fuzz across her scalp. It took everything in me not to run and hold her and beg her not to leave me.

Instead I composed myself and told her that she looked like a newborn baby. My daughters ran up to her, asking could they rub her scalp. They giggled as they looked at their grandmother, which made her laugh. "You don't recognize your grandmother without her red hair, do you?" she asked, laughing.

"How do you feel about losing your hair?" I asked her. Anybody who knew my mother knew how important her hair was to her. She'd always kept her hair looking good. I had already told my husband that we were probably going to have to spend the afternoon cheering her up about it.

Instead, she said very matter-of-factly as she hugged the girls, "I would rather be here with all of you with no hair than be lying in a coffin with a head full of hair. Losing my hair is a very small price to pay for this."

At that moment I thanked God for my mother and for the experience he was giving me. Although it was difficult to watch her illness finally get the best of her, I was comforted by knowing that she treasured every day God gave her to share with us.

When I knew that the end was drawing near, it was the strength that she had shown throughout her illness that gave me the courage to pray with a clear conscience the hardest prayer of my life—for the Heavenly Father to take her home so she could rest.

On the day that my mother passed I left the hospital and came home to my husband and children, who were waiting to comfort me. My oldest daughter was four at the time, and through tears she asked me, "Mommy, what are we going to do without Grandma?"

Picking her up, I held her in my arms and I rocked her. I told her that we were going to do exactly what Grandma would expect us to do. We were gonna run on anyhow.

THE LIFE AND SPIRIT OF NATHANIEL BRISCOE

Donnella L. Rucker

My father, Nathaniel Briscoe, was a community man in Washington, D.C. When there was nothing for the boys in our neighborhood to do, he started the Pioneers boys' club in our area in 1961. Our house was literally open to the neighborhood. He set up football, basketball, baseball, boxing, cheerleading, and track teams. He raised money through donations for uniforms and equipment. My father and the neighborhood boys would go door to door asking for donations. The boys that he worked with were labeled "the worst of the worst." These young men had no fathers in their homes and were headed for jail or the grave. My father was the only father that a lot of these guys ever had.

After a few years, the District of Columbia Metropolitan Police Department started to sponsor the programs. Through my father, his friends, and the Metropolitan Police Department, they were able to help these young men complete high school. He was even able to get some of them into prestigious high schools and colleges in the D.C. area. He worked within our community until 1989, when he retired.

My father also raised five children. Two of my sisters became involved in drugs. My parents never stopped supporting and encouraging them. After many prayers and much support, my oldest sister received the job that she has always wanted, teaching in the D.C. public school system. She started her job one month before he died.

In March 1998, for my father's seventieth birthday, we decided to give him a surprise birthday party. We invited all of the guys he helped and nurtured over the years. Some even brought their wives and children to meet him. These loving Black men, most now in their late thirties, forties, and fifties, came from as far away as New York, Philadelphia, and Chicago to celebrate his life.

They told my father what he meant to them and what a positive effect he had had in their lives. Some claimed they owed him their very lives. They were now businessmen, teachers, ministers, police officers. Even those who hadn't done as well for themselves came.

Less than a year later, these men returned for my father's funeral, grieving and loving alongside my family. One of my father's "mentees" who is now an ordained minister led the prayer program at the wake; everyone wanted to be an honorary pallbearer. My father left this earthly life on August 5, 1999, but I continue to speak of him in the present tense—because his spirit and life are all around me.

WE HAVE WHAT IT TAKES

Marsha Kelley-Sutton

Working for a program that strives to assist minority students interested in the medical field, I know that God shows us all the time through various experiences that people of color are born quality caregivers. One hot June day in the summer of 1997, I reached home to find that a message had been left for me to return to campus as soon as possible. One of the program participants had been hit by a car while crossing the street at a major intersection. The students had been on campus for only four days, yet when I entered the emergency room approximately fifteen minutes later, it was standing room only. The students had already formed a close bond, something rarely seen on an inner-city campus.

We were informed by the ER physician that the student's arm, which she had used to shield her head during the accident, had been torn open from her wrist to her elbow during the impact, and emergency surgery would be necessary. The student was released from the hospital two days later and the surgeon informed the director of the program that her recovery time would be six weeks. It was truly a blessing that the injury was not as serious as it could have been, but the bad news was that the program was only six weeks in length.

When the student was told, tears began to stream down her face. You see, the main perk of the summer program she attended was a guaranteed interview at our university medical school for the top fifteen of the program's 125 students. This was the prize that attracted the majority of students to our program. This program, which could possibly open the doors of medical school to her, was closing before her eyes. She made a plea to stay in the summer program; the director respected her wish, and she was allowed to continue.

After she was released from the hospital, I went to her dormitory to take her extra pillows to prop up her arm. I arrived to find her eating a breakfast that had been prepared for her by a student next door. Her bandages had to be changed daily, and when I phoned to see if she needed assistance, I discovered another fellow student had already carried her to student health, where her bandages had been changed. Other students washed and cared for her hair, carried her books, painted her nails, helped her prepare for class, and shared their class notes. Everyone pulled together to make sure this injured student had what she needed to complete the program, as well as compete for her dream.

At the closing ceremony, the last event of the program, the fifteen students chosen to receive a guaranteed interview to our medical school were announced. Students waited as the names were called one by one. By the time the fourteenth name was called, everyone was perched at the edge of their chairs. The program director became silent, as did the room of students. Who would the final recipient be?

Instead of calling a name, the program director began to retell the story of the car accident. With the help of her fellow classmates, the injured student's dream had come true. As she rose to go onstage and receive her certificate, the crowd rose to their feet to applaud her. Tears were streaming down her face. She requested an opportunity to speak, and after thanking God, she shared how generous her classmates had been and recounted all of the help she had received from them. Before the evening was over we were all applauding each other.

The memory of the summer of 1997 will be embedded in my mind forever. In a time when we are struggling to increase the number of physicians of color, I had a group of 125 students of color who displayed the compassion, care, and concern so necessary and so needed in the medical field. In my heart, I knew that each one of them had what it takes to grow and develop into our great physicians of the future.

BIOGRAPHY OF A SCAR

Karen Williams

"Keep frowning, and your face is gonna freeze like that," my father would say to me when I was younger to coax my periodic sadness into a smile. Not that he wanted me to be falsely happy, but to learn that sometimes it's more advantageous to grin than scowl. The brilliant smile I gave him in response could easily pass for that of other Black girls my age, save for the prominent keloids that framed it, protruding around and underneath my jawline. The cause of these growths was an atypical case of chicken pox I contracted a year earlier. These scars, which formed on my face, torso, arms, and legs, left me hypersensitive, and led to a beleaguered childhood and adolescence.

Only a second-grader when I was stricken in 1970, I became the butt of jokes and pranks, and was labeled "Chicken Pox Girl" and "Cootie Face." I begged my teacher, Mrs. Frederick, to let me stay indoors at recess—"They keep teasing me"—and she and my parents agreed. As a result, I read SRS reading booklets until their ink colored my hands, joined the Service Squad, and because of my mother's generosity and fashion sense, became consistently the best-dressed girl in my class. I morphed into a model student, deciding that if I have to be ugly, I'm going to be smarter.

My mother, then a pediatric nurse, ferried me to a local dermatologist at the suggestion of a coworker. His office was located in Dearborn, notorious for its segregationist mayor, Orville Hubbard. The city wasn't one many Blacks frequented unless to work on the line at Ford Motors or as a housekeeper in a white household, as my grandmother did. It was also my first medical visit beyond an annual checkup from my pediatrician. However, I discovered that the doctor's staff weren't comfortable seeing me, either.

After my mother unwrapped the soft cloth around my neck and led me into the examining room, a curious staffer dressed in white took my trembling jaw in her hand. I vaguely recall her white face as she peered closely at my jaw; someone announced (I don't remember who) that the office had never seen a case of chicken pox scarring like mine, and (I remember this assertion quite vividly) there was nothing they could do. When my mother insisted on a referral, someone suggested she take me "downtown" to Detroit's Henry Ford Hospital, an urban facility known for its dermatology procedures and work with ethnic (read "Black") cultures.

At Ford Hospital, Dr. Clarence Livingood, a physician who doubled as the team physician for the Detroit Tigers, became my dermatologist. After his initial consultation with my parents, I began years of intensive steroid treatments. I entered the examination room, lay on the table, and waited for the syringes, two-and-a-half-inch needles filled with a stinging liquid anesthetic, Xylocaine. Dr. Livingood explained that the liquid would help flatten and reduce the redness of the scars. A chemical in the liquid, when it entered my scar tissue, would break down the levels of what he called collagen. "That's what makes a keloid a keloid," he'd say. "It's skin, or what we call tissue, filled with too much collagen. And the fact that there's too much collagen in your skin makes your scars hard, puffy, and plump. If you had a certain chemical in your skin, your scars would be flatter, like those of other children," he said.

The routine became indelible in my memory. Prior to each round of injections, a nurse would roll a small shallow pan on wheels, something like a cookie sheet, up to the table. Atop a sterile cloth in the pan lay an assortment of needles in shiny packages, two kinds of forceps (blunt and needle-nosed), packets of unfilled syringes, Xylocaine bottles, as well as snowy squares of gauze. Tucked in the pan's corner were miniature tubes of Kenalog cream, extra cloths, and packets of dry ice. Usually she'd tell me to lie on my right side if the doctor was going to tend to the right side of my face, on the left if that was the side to be treated. Later, when the treatments took another turn, I undressed, donned a cotton gown, and lay on my stomach, ready to receive injections into the scars on my back.

When Dr. Livingood arrived he'd always greet me with "Now what I'm going to do is numb you up first." He'd take a packet of dry ice, open it, and wrap it with a sterile cloth before giving it to me to hold it against my chin. "Now hold it tight," he'd continue, "and try not to wiggle it. I know it's cold, but this will help it hurt less." The first few times, he walked me through the procedure. "When you're nice and numb, we'll"—

it was amazing how he'd say "we" instead of "I," to make me feel more empowered and part of the process—"gather a bit of skin between my fingers. Don't worry, I won't hurt you. You'll feel a little prick, then some pressure. That's the Xylocaine flowing into your skin," he said. "It's going to sting a little. Afterward we'll lightly massage the spot we injected to make sure the medicine goes into your tissues really good. Then we'll put a little of this cream on there," he said, holding up the tiny Kenalog tube. "This will stop the itching. We'll also give you some to take home. Afterward we'll put on a bandage, and zap! You'll be finished." Remembering his remarks and demeanor makes me realize how I learned to cherish what I eventually recognized was an exceptional doctor-patient relationship. Good physicians, like Dr. Livingood, talk to their patients, explain the procedures, and do their best to make you comfortable—to make you feel more human and more protected.

By the time I graduated from the sixth grade, I had been seeing Dr. Livingood for four years, twice a month. It didn't occur to me a time would arrive for my visits to cease, but I learned they would during the visit nearest my twelfth birthday. "Karen's getting older," Dr. Livingood said, "and progressing well, and I'm thinking this should be the last visit we schedule for her. I think we should give her the opportunity to decide whether she wants to continue treatments." He said he and his colleagues felt that since I was entering puberty, the surface of my skin would soon grow faster than it ever had during the growth process, causing my remaining scars to stretch and fade with time. "But," he cautioned, "they'll never disappear completely. By the time you turn eighteen, you'll pretty much have the face you'll have for the rest of your life." I recall quietly saying, "I hope so." The teasing I had been receiving from my classmates hadn't decreased.

One day, in a scene that mirrored a key passage of Shirley Jackson's "The Lottery," two schoolmates followed me home through the woods near our home and pelted me with pebbles. My mother shared what happened with my father. He waited for me at the corner the next afternoon. His voice was curt and rough as he told the boys, "If you ever mess with my daughter again . . ."

When does a person's beauty, ugliness, or disfigurement fail to count? I wondered if those boys' cruelty was predisposed by something outside my body. Are children *that* eager to harm or to potentially maim?

Though I wanted to continue treatments (my parents had exceptional health insurance plans), part of me screamed to live normally—free of needle pricks and teasing, feeling "special" or freakish. I chose to make that visit my last and to learn as best I could how to live and be in my own skin. But when I left the office for the final time, I was in tears. Dr. Livingood gave me a final hug of encouragement. "You're a pretty little girl, Karen," he said. "Remember that, okay? Anything you want to do and be, you can do. Don't let another's words, another's insensitivity, stop you."

Years later, my skin clear of the keloids (though I now have the most stubborn adult acne, which often leaves its own brand of dark spots to be dealt with), I decided to return to see Dr. Livingood to thank him for the time and care he offered over the years, helping to transform the quality of my skin—and of my life. But just as I was getting ready to make that visit, I read in a local paper of his death. I spent the afternoon weeping before my mother for a man who would never know how much he had taught me about ugliness and beauty, self-esteem and confidence.

DADDY'S HANDS

Donna M. Woodard

When I was seven or eight years of age, I remember sitting on the side of my parents' bed while my father sat on a chair at the foot of the bed. During these times, my father would impart the kind of knowledge and wisdom to me that only the school of hard knocks and lack of opportunities could teach.

During one of our conversations, my father told me that he never wanted my hands to look like his. I guess I must have looked at him with a bewildered expression on my face, for in my mind, Daddy's hands looked fine.

The look I gave him must have said it all, because right then he began to explain to me what he meant. As my father began to speak, I will never forget the words that came from his mouth.

"Donna," he said, "do you see these calluses and frostbite marks on my hands? One of the reasons I go to work every morning and come home tired every evening is because I don't want your hands to ever have to look like mine. Daddy did not have the opportunity to go to school back when I was a kid because there just weren't many schools for Black children. All we knew was that we had to work. Daddy wants you to get an education because knowledge is power. And as long as you have an education, your hands will never have to look like mine."

One of the proudest and happiest days of my life came when my father attended my college graduation and said to me, "You've done a good job, Donna! Now don't stop here—you just keep on going and get yourself some more education!"

Today, as the youngest of eight children, I am still following Daddy's advice. Currently, I am earning my master's degree from Florida State University in communication disorders and speech pathology. And all because of the inspiration of my daddy, who wanted to make sure my hands don't ever look like his.

BAD BOY ON BOARD

Booker T. Washington

As I sat awaiting the announcement by the chairman of the board of the name of the new CEO, I couldn't help but reflect on how I'd arrived at this place in my life. Only a few short years earlier, if I had run across the chairman in the street, he would have been in serious trouble.

I started out a military brat who got into general mischief. You know, breaking and entering, petty theft, vandalism—the kind of things associated with juvenile delinquents. Somehow my comrades and I eased into our roles as hoods, and the hood in us quickly spiraled downward into something closer to pure gangster.

The term "Uncle Charlie," for me, represented all the white people that had done evil deeds to Black people: like turning fire hoses on Black folk to break up a civil rights rally; setting vicious dogs on a Black man simply for requesting his dignity; leading Rosa Parks away for suggesting that a Black person had the right to sit down on a bus anywhere they pleased; murdering Dr. Martin Luther King Jr. in cold blood; the memory of white schoolkids spitting at me from their bus windows as I walked five miles to a wooden shack of a school while they rode a half mile to a beautiful brick edifice. Most of all, I remembered the look on my father's face after being chastised by his "Uncle Charlie" colonel.

My family arrived at my father's posting in Frankfurt, West Germany, from Fort Hood, Texas, in September 1968. I was in the ninth grade and attended Frankfurt Junior High School. I was somewhat of a geek. I simply loved mathematics and science. It was there that I met my comrades Eric, Ron Ron, Zack, and Jeff. They had formed a gang, but were just thugs really.

One day they hemmed me up for my lunch money, and I put a whupping on each one of them. After that, Eric, Zack, Ron Ron, Jeff, and I became fast friends. Zack said, "Now there's a bad boy on board," when I joined the gang.

On my way to school I had to pass my father's compound. I would usually see my father standing in formation with his unit while the colonel inspected the squad. We had a special signal that he would send me to say have a good day, even when he was standing at attention. One cold November morning, however, formation was already over and as I approached the fence I could see that the colonel was in my father's face.

No one got in my father's face. He was one of those ol' school guys who would cut you before you knew what happened. To see "Uncle Charlie" leaning in on my ol' man shocked me. I could see the hurt in my father's eyes as he caught a glimpse of me. It was as if he knew, at that moment, that his stature in my eyes had been diminished, and by someone who epitomized the deep-fried southern good ol' boy.

At that moment I decided "Uncle Charlie" needed to be taught a lesson. When I told my comrades what had happened, we agreed it was time to dispense some Black justice.

Two weeks after the incident, we arrived at the colonel's house about one o'clock in the morning. I went to the back of the house and busted in, while my comrades held vigil out front. We knew the colonel was a party animal and usually hung out with the rest of the white officers at the officers' club until two or three in the morning.

I opened the front door for my comrades, and we proceeded to reduce the place to rubble. But we were so engrossed in the destruction of the colonel's home, we didn't notice a key turning in the lock.

Just as I was about to smash a lamp onto the floor, the door opened and in walked the colonel. I quickly spun around and shattered the lamp on the colonel's shoulder. That was all it took for my comrades to jump in. He never knew what hit him. Zack hit the colonel so hard I could hear his jaw snap. Jeff body-slammed him, and he hit the floor with such force that the bone in his right leg popped through the skin. We were like a pack of wild dogs, kicking, stomping, spitting, and crushing bones from head to toe. I left the house feeling that my comrades and I had recovered a piece of dignity for all the times that "Uncle Charlie" had disrespected Black people.

I couldn't wait to hear the news about the colonel spread across the compound, but nothing was said. I started to think that he had died and they were secretly searching for the killers. I became nervous and very anxious. One day I was having a general conversation with my father and eased into the topic of military life, to see if he would divulge any information about the colonel. I was in awe of my father's ability to handle the stress of racism while maintaining the decorum of military life. He explained the military rules and regulations and how soldiers needed to follow these rules in order to survive in times of war. He talked about the racial strife, as it existed for him both outside the military and inside the military.

Finally, I couldn't contain my curiosity about the colonel any longer, so I asked him about the day I'd seen the colonel in his face. He explained that the colonel was showing him some of the techniques he could use for his preparation for drill instruction school. My father had been talking about being a drill sergeant for months, and the colonel had commanded a camp for new recruits earlier in his career.

Then my father said that someone had broken into the colonel's house and crushed most of the bones in his body. They'd had to ship him back to the United States because he was in critical condition; they thought he should be closer to family in case he didn't recover.

I sat there for what seemed like hours, trying to shut down the hurt that I was feeling for nearly costing a man his life. I had been so wrapped up in my own hatred of "Uncle Charlie" that I had likened the colonel to a redneck, just for being white. According to my father, the colonel had marched with Dr. King and was a member of the NAACP. I had never heard of such a thing—a white man associated with a Black organization. My comrades and I had nearly beaten to death a man who was trying to right the wrongs and injustices of this crazy world. My father wasn't being chastised at all that day; he was being mentored.

That day, I had so much respect for my father, and felt so much guilt about my actions, that I decided to change my life. I couldn't let my anger at the racism around me hip-check my life. Fortunately, we moved back to the United States shortly afterward, when my father received his drill sergeant assignment.

In Europe, I had accumulated more credits than were necessary to graduate from high school in the United States. I used the additional half year of school to raise my GPA from 2.7 to 3.6. That gave me options.

I applied to and was accepted at Purdue. Given my love of math and science, I decided to become an engineer.

I was accustomed to being around white people, but this campus was white on another level. I was one of two Blacks in my freshman class to actually matriculate in the engineering program, and I completed it in three years.

I discovered that racism remained rampant in the United States. Black people were still marching in the streets and begging "Uncle Charlie" and his cousin "Uncle Sam" for jobs, housing, equal access, and equal rights. Disproving all the racist beliefs about Blacks being less intelligent than whites became my quest.

When you decide to go head to head with "Uncle Charlie," you soon find out that if you are too good, "Uncle Charlie" will change the rules on you quickly. He likes to declare that you should get an education, work hard, and pull yourself up by your bootstraps. What he fails to tell you is that he determines (1) how much education you will need to get the same job and (2) how to lace those bootstraps (you know Black people can be creative with them bootstraps, too). Black people know they need to be three times as good to get the same job. Our mistake is in thinking that the playing field is level.

Toward the end of my senior year, I was one of two people at the top of the class with a 4.0 average. The other was a white guy named Rick. He was quick-witted and very smart. He and I weren't friends, but we were respectful of one another. Rick was weak in the area of calculus programming, and I knew that there was no way he could get any better than a B out of our final class, which would leave me as sole valedictorian.

I went to see my professor before the end of the semester, and as I approached his office I overheard the professor speaking to someone about Rick. Turns out he was talking to Rick's father about his son's grade, and it wasn't going to be an A. Rick's father started talking about his contributions to the university and how his son needed this grade not only to graduate as valedictorian but to give a kick-start to his professional career. My professor bent, folded, and collapsed as fast as the market for a two-dollar bill. Rick became valedictorian.

Upon graduation, I went to work for a major computer company. At the time that I joined, they were among the first in the industry to establish an internal campus for continuing education. Their purpose was to mold engineers and computer scientists into managers and project engineers. Upon completion, each one of us would graduate with an MBA. Although it was 1976, I was the only Black in the Program.

To get through the Program, you had to complete a project that the company could put into practice. To do this the project had to be original and plausible. I took the concept of the banking system and turned it into a product system where everything you bought could be processed through one system processor, using one card—the software, of course, being supplied by our company. Not only did I get my MBA, but I also once again graduated at the top of my class. The company adopted my project and made billions.

During the next ten years, I was promoted to many midlevel management positions. I finally came under the thumb of a chief information officer (CIO) named Bob. This guy constantly addressed me as "the genius," in a way that made it clear he thought of it as a joke.

I came up with an idea about selling our services to individual businesses via the Web. The CIO didn't see any benefit to this. Today, the Web is commonplace, but in 1990, when I made the presentation, it was virtually unheard of for businesses to sell commercially over this medium. Over the next five years the company, through my Web management, became the leader in Web site creation services and products. And I took Bob's place as CIO.

As CIO, I was responsible for planning future ventures and acquisitions for the company. I interfaced with the new vice president of marketing, a gregarious guy who made friends easily and ostensibly was next in line for the CEO job. The marketing VP saw me as a threat, and time and again instigated marketing changes without notifying me. This caused programming changes and other overtime costs for my departments, affecting my budget.

Nonetheless, when it came time for the chairman to announce the new CEO, the person he chose was me. I had been selected to run a multi-million-dollar company.

At any number of points in my life, I could have broken down, given in, and succumbed to racism. What kept me going were the dreams, blood, and sweat of Black folk who had come before me. No matter what obstacles "Uncle Charlie" erected, I knew that I could not let Black people down. Zack had it right about me long ago when he said, "Now there's a bad boy on board."

REPAYMENT

Ronald R. Lawson

I'm forty-nine years old. I graduated with a B.A. from Holy Cross College in 1975, an M.S. from Carnegie-Mellon University in 1978, and received a postgraduate certificate in accounting from the Kellogg Graduate School of Management at Northwestern University in 1979.

I spent fourteen years working in the financial services arena on Wall Street. Then, in 1991, I lost my job. Given my educational background and my professional experiences, I thought it would take me only a few weeks to find a job. I was wrong. Weeks turned into months. At the same time, I tore my knee up skiing and had no medical insurance. So I spent a significant part of the lowest period in my life on crutches. I lost my apartment in Brooklyn because I couldn't pay the rent and found myself basically homeless. There were many nights I ate cereal because that's all I could afford.

A friend of a friend of mine, whom I barely knew, offered to put me up. Having no recourse, I agreed. I put all my possessions in storage (which I lost when they auctioned them off because I couldn't pay the storage fees), except for my mattress and three wardrobe boxes of clothes. I'll never forget the night I moved in, because I spent it sleeping on the floor with a sheet over me, tucked under the mattress so the roaches on the floor wouldn't crawl on me.

Fortunately I was, and still am, blessed with a remarkable group of friends. One of them, Westina Matthews, Senior VP at Merrill Lynch, invited me to church with her one day. It was there that I met the minister, Dr. Paul Smith, who is still my minister, mentor, and friend. I would visit Paul on a regular basis and pray and counsel with him. He continually told me to keep my head up and stay strong because "hard times don't last always!"

When I would leave Paul, he would often give me an envelope with maybe fifteen or sixteen dollars and one or two subway tokens. He told me it was from a fund the church had for people who needed help. Well, I've been a member of the church board for the last five years and I now know there is no such fund. Paul was giving me whatever he could from his own pocket!

Another friend, Ken Glover, was asked by then Mayor David Dinkins if he would serve as his treasurer for his 1992 reelection campaign. Ken asked me if I would work with him to set up the appropriate campaign financial systems. I agreed, and after several months Ken and Bill Lynch, the campaign manager, asked if I would stay on as finance director.

So, in a matter of months I went from having no job, no money, and no home, to being finance director of the largest and most important political campaign in the country in 1993. I managed an $11 million campaign budget and had a staff of twenty-five, and was called to strategy sessions and receptions at Gracie Mansion, the mayor's residence.

Because of my campaign involvement, I met my wife, a woman I had met twenty years before but had not seen or heard from until we were reacquainted during the campaign. We got married six months after the campaign ended and now have a beautiful five-year-old daughter.

When I reflect upon that period in my life, I remember saying to all my friends, and those who supported me during those difficult times, "I can never repay you all for all that you did for me." To a person, they told me, "We don't expect you to, we expect you to do it for somebody else."

And so I do.

FAITH

THE SUBSTANCE OF THINGS HOPED FOR

Tavis Smiley

The book of Hebrews declares that "Faith is the substance of things hoped for, the evidence of things not seen." There are three things in life that I think sustain us. I call them the three F's: faith, family, and friends.

I don't know how people survive, let alone thrive, without having an abiding faith in something bigger and beyond them. Faith is what makes this universe work.

I believe the ultimate compliment is to have someone put faith in your ability to deliver. People do not necessarily put their confidence in you or believe in you because the evidence is there for them to do so. Rather, they are doing it in light of the biblical definition of faith: the substance of things *hoped for* and the evidence of things *not seen.* In other words, people often have put faith in us simply because they believe in us, not because they have evidence to support their belief. It's easy to bet on Tiger Woods and on Michael Jordan in their respective sports if you've seen them play before, because the evidence abounds that they are the best at what they do. Faith is not really a factor here. Let me tell you about faith.

I ran for a seat on the Los Angeles City Council in 1991. I was a twenty-six-year-old kid who had never run for public office before. My opponent was the incumbent, and early on I realized that I was going to be vastly outspent. But I just campaigned harder, and the closer it got to election day, the more it appeared that I had a reasonable chance of forcing a runoff with the incumbent, although there was never any evidence to suggest I could beat her. I was running a "faith" campaign.

As we neared the end of the campaign, with literally just weeks to go, I ran out of money. My funds were so depleted that my campaign manager and my staff had not been paid in weeks. I didn't have the money to print any more brochures or lawn signs. I was completely dry.

My mother apparently had talked to someone on my campaign staff and found out that I had run out of money. She had enough faith in me (and was crazy enough) to go down to her bank and mortgage *her house* to get me the additional money that I needed to finish my campaign.

Fortunately, I overheard someone on my staff share this news with another campaign staff person. When I caught up with my mother, she was actually on her way to the bank to get the money. I had to stop her from going through with it. But I cannot tell you how moved to tears I was that my mother thought enough of me and had enough faith in me to mortgage her house on my behalf. My mother has always believed in me, and the myriad ways she has demonstrated this have helped me to develop into the person I am today.

Having just one person truly believe in you is one of life's greatest and most precious gifts.

If more of our young people had someone who really believed in them, who demonstrated unwavering faith and trust in them, I think they would be capable of achieving great things. More often than not, our young people deliver what is simply ordinary because we adults don't expect the extraordinary. Nor do we give them the proper tools to perform at a high level. In this respect, there is much that we adults can do to help advance our young people on their journey through life.

Sometimes you have to believe with all your heart in someone else, and conversely have someone believe in you in exactly the same way. We owe this to each other, as African Americans, and we owe it especially to our young people.

Detour of Faith

Cynthia Gary

The summer following my college graduation was one of those moments in time when it seems as though everything in the universe is in perfect alignment. I had decided to stray from my original plans and take a year off before going on to graduate school. Thus began the detour that I would never forget.

I returned to my hometown to find a summer job. Before long, I was hired as a part-time instructor for a six-week summer youth program. I had decided to work with middle and high school students; there was no way I was going to work with the smaller children. All that noise and running around—I didn't want any part of it! I arrived for my first day, but there were only a few teenagers signed up, so I volunteered to go to a different location. When I arrived at my new location, the program manager led me into a large classroom. She discovered no one was in charge of that class, so she cheerfully said to me, "Great, this can be your class." As I slowly looked around, I struggled to maintain my composure. Twenty-five pairs of kindergarten eyes locked onto mine. My detour had just hit a speed bump.

I knew next to nothing about teaching children. I had just graduated with a degree in biology, so while rats and frogs were no problem, five-year-old humans made me queasy. However, I knew that children are like sponges and that the amount of knowledge they can soak up is astonishing. Contained in that classroom was a miniature version of the world. Every personality was completely distinct from the next; a few of the faces, however, stand out in my mind. There was a girl I called "chocolate baby doll" because she had one of the prettiest complexions and faces I had ever seen. There were boys who, I was told, had difficulty learning. There was a girl who smiled at everything and was upset by nothing. Then there was the little bossy girl who could run faster than any of the boys. For a parent or a teacher, none of this is a revelation, but for me it was a new perspective. In a few short weeks I had gone from petri dishes to pandemonium.

Because I knew very little about teaching children, I taught them what I thought they should know—reading, writing, and 'rithmetic. Ignorance *is* sometimes bliss. I did not realize that my lessons were too advanced for five-year-olds, and they did not know what their lessons should be. So there we were, twenty-six peas in a pod, about to embark on a six-week journey.

As each day went by, I became more and more determined to teach them as much as I could. Although there were the typical rules the children had to obey, I had only one edict—*no excuses*. There would be absolutely no excuses why they could not do their best. Ignorance, stubbornness, and my mother's expectations were the architects of my proclamation. I spent my own money to buy supplies for them: addition and subtraction flash cards, activity books for the first and second grades, construction paper to draw the outline of the African continent. Too much for a five-year-old? Maybe, but what did I know? The funny thing is, they were catching on to everything I threw at them. These little chocolate-faced children were learning more than they should have—more than many would have expected of them.

I sometimes tease my mother that she never told me that I was a little Black southern girl and that there were just some things I should not know—such as math and science. I kid my mother that because of her negligence in explaining about the limited expectations of a little Black girl, I actually believed I was smart and that I could do absolutely anything. I simply did not know that odds were against me. I just read and learned everything I could because I truly believed I was just as good as any student in my class or in the world. I often teased my mom about that. But I was being negligent in just the same manner that summer. For those six weeks the twenty-six of us believed we could read and learn, and so we did.

It was not until close to the end of the program that I knew I was neither hated nor feared. I had been not the conqueror of this little world, but rather simply a guide, and the children had been my companions on the trip. The parent of one of my most challenging students said to me,

"So you're Miss Gary. My son talks about you all the time—Miss Gary this and Miss Gary that." I could not believe the boy who had gone from having the most excuses to no excuses would even give me a second thought! I discovered that children are full of wonderful surprises.

I have seen only a couple of those children since that summer, and I am no longer a teacher today. So what was the purpose of that detour in my life? We must learn to trust the process of life, regardless of the turns, twists, bumps, delays, construction zones, or detours. Yes, the summer following my college graduation was a detour—but, because of my faith, I did not speed through the construction zone. I enjoyed the scenery and the rainbow of twenty-six different shades of chocolate. They were my sign that my trip was right on schedule.

THE KIND ASIAN MAN

John Pettiford

I remember the sweet smell of warm sugar doughnuts against the agonizing self-consciousness of a nine-year-old boy in a family once again on the move. It was 1989, the fourth time we were forced to leave a homeless shelter in southern California. Too weary to keep fighting the system, my mother had become strangely complacent. Eight months pregnant, she went through the motions of daily tasks only because there was no one else to do them. This strange reality was becoming commonplace to her. But I could tell many times, as I caught her daydreaming, that she was actually calculating a means of escape, a desperate route to lead us back somehow to the life we'd once known.

It was 5 A.M. The Asian man's eyes behind the counter met mine as he put two doughnuts into a bag. They were still warm, fresh from the oil. My stomach grumbled. The dollar bill in my outstretched fingers suddenly looked overly crumpled and worn, like an old friend.

I could feel the man's eyes on my back as I shuffled back to a bus bench by the road. I gave one to my mother, for the baby, and the other to my little brother, half asleep against the duffel bag containing everything we had left in the world. I could not stop my fingers from reaching into the bag to catch the warm crumbs at the bottom and bring them to my lips.

A few minutes later the Asian man from behind the counter appeared, holding a bulging bag emitting the same fresh, delicious sugar aroma. I watched my mother's exhausted eyes fill with tears as he held it out to her. She sat rock still, hesitating, head held high with dignity even as my pleading eyes were trying desperately to catch hers.

The man stood his ground. "You don't take, I throw away."

In broken English, he offered to let us sit in his ragged yellow Volkswagen to wait for the buses to begin their morning run. Warm and full, our little family gratefully slept until the fierce California sun and the rumble of the morning traffic awakened us. Waving a rushed good-bye to the man, my mother ushered us quickly back to the bus stop. To my brother and me, we were merely on to the next adventure. To my mother, this generous stranger seemed to give her the strength she needed to face another day, her faith in humanity refueled by his immeasurable act of kindness.

Today, at age twenty-one, this memory stands out among all others from that nomadic visit in California. My mother went back to her native New Jersey after my sister was born, and took the steps to rebuild our lives. A few years later, at fourteen, I found within myself a deep love for music, handed down from my grandfather, Oscar Pettiford, the great jazz bassist. An honor student at the oldest historically Black college in the country, I look forward to preparing myself to help other children of single parents as they struggle to find their own place in the world.

HAVING THE COURAGE TO DREAM

Vonda Paige

In 1981, I was a junior at Stonewall Jackson Senior High School in Manassas, Virginia, a small suburban town about thirty minutes outside of Washington, D.C. One day while I was walking through the library, one of the business teachers stopped me. I didn't know her name, but I knew from other friends that she taught stenography and bookkeeping.

"You're Vonda Paige. I haven't seen you in the business classes. You should take stenography," she said from behind a pair of cat eyeglasses.

"Why?" I responded. "I don't need it. The only business class I'm taking is typing, because I'm going to be a reporter and I will need to learn to type before I get to college."

"Well, you should consider some business classes and take them just in case," she continued.

While the teacher in the library did not come right out and say it, the look on her face and the tone of her voice conveyed her underlying message: *Black girls do not go to college, they become clerks or secretaries.* By the time I got to my typing class later that day I had a really bad attitude; I didn't want to be there learning to set margins and tabs.

I didn't think less of anyone who chose clerical or secretarial fields. I really had no opinion about it. I just knew that I was a writer, and I was annoyed that someone who didn't even know me would try to step on my dream.

At Stonewall Jackson I was one of a handful of Black students pursuing an academic track. I was part of that group of students that I know exists in schools around the country and which I like to call "the only Blacks." I was the only Black writer for the *Jackson Journal*, the only Black in the National Honor Society and the Model United Nations and It's Academic clubs. I was the only Black in advanced orchestra playing the violin. My brother, Reggie, played cello for a while, but he bailed on me, preferring the drums in the marching band. Fans cheered for the band at football games, but few kids showed up for orchestra concerts.

If you're smart and Black in a predominantly white school, you're subject to grief from other Black kids who think you're trying to be white. If you stand out too much, you get grief from some white kids who are surprised you're *that* smart. My saving grace was my mother, who believed in me.

I was still fuming when I came home from school that day. "You don't have to take stenography if you don't want to," she said. "In fact, you can drop typing if you want. I always hated it too. You need more important classes to get into college." Relieved and encouraged, I set about working on my goal.

By the middle of the year, I had landed my first job as a school correspondent for my hometown newspaper, the *Potomac News*. The first year I covered only my school, but because the other student correspondents from the four neighboring high schools usually failed to meet the deadlines, I was given their columns to write as well.

"You're really blessed," my mother exclaimed, beaming at me. "Few people get a job right away in the field they want, and you haven't even started college yet!"

By my senior year I was appointed editor of my school's newspaper, the *Jackson Journal*. Some of my well-meaning relatives figured I could get into college, but they wondered out loud how in the world my mother would pay for it.

"We're not worried about that," she told them. "It's going to work out." And she was right—it did!

At the graduation ceremony in 1982, I received several scholarships, as well as the prestigious Charles Colgan Citizenship Award for a report I had written about a Black woman who founded a school for Blacks in Manassas. (My name was called repeatedly during the ceremony, and a classmate told me afterward that an audience member remarked, "Who was that n—— winning everything?" My classmate told him I was his sister, which shut him right up!)

Four years later I earned a bachelor's degree in communications from Virginia Tech. When I entered college some of my classmates told me I was wasting my time at the student newspaper because I would never get a chance to write there. When I graduated, I was the paper's first Black news editor.

After internships at the *Roanoke Times and World News* and the *Richmond-Times Dispatch*, I landed my first full-time professional job as a general assignment reporter and columnist at the *Progress-Index* in Petersburg, Virginia. From there I worked at the *News-Leader* in Springfield, Missouri, where I won writing awards for features and news reporting. In 1989, the Associated Press offered me a job in its Philadelphia bureau. Today, I am a freelance writer and public relations consultant.

Biographers often recount that Harriet Tubman rarely told her passengers the route to freedom. If they wanted to leave the plantation, they had to meet her at a certain time and do exactly as she instructed. Since she was often chased by bounty hunters, she needed to be careful about those she trusted.

But I also think she knew that not all slaves had the faith to see that they could be free. If they were fearful, they would not follow her instructions; they could lose their lives, and risk hers as well. She knew the purpose God had for her life, and she followed it.

While in the tenth grade I wrote a list of goals for myself. They included writing for newspapers. I didn't know when it would happen, but faith told me it would. That's why my spirit flared when that business teacher suggested I change course.

In Romans 12:6, Paul urges believers to walk in the talents and gifts God has given us. God's design for our lives is perfect. He has it all figured out. If you're a leader, you should govern well. If you're a teacher, you should teach well. If you are a giver, you should give generously. But never, ever tell a writer she should take stenography!

FROM WELFARE TO FAREWELL

Ken Brown

I am a thirty-five-year-old African American owner of two McDonald's restaurants, and people often ask how I got so lucky. My response to them is always the same: "It has nothing to do with luck. It's all about faith!"

Growing up, we did not always have enough food, but "Mudear," as we affectionately called my mother, always had enough faith for everyone. There were times when we did not have a house to call our own, but my parents always provided us with hope for a better tomorrow. Our dollars were in very short supply, but our dreams were always in abundance.

I was born to teenage parents who by the age of twenty had five children under the age of eight. They stressed to us while growing up, however, that we not let ourselves get into the same situation, and they constantly emphasized that we should make education our top priority. I tried to remain focused on my education, especially during my high school years. We were evicted from three different houses during this period, but I refused to let this deter me.

Growing up, we were able to subsist on welfare benefits. My father used to say, however, that even though welfare was our means of subsistence, we never possessed a welfare mentality. At some point, we recognized that welfare was simply a bridge to help us get through the tough times we had to endure. At no point in our lives did we become dependent on welfare as a way of life. My parents always encouraged us to keep a good attitude about our situation and not to become discouraged about life and the hand it had dealt us. Both my mother and father would constantly remind us that God had something bigger and better planned for us and that the Lord would not give us more than we could handle. "If you can conceive it," they said, "then you can achieve it!"

They were correct. All five of their children graduated from high school and went on to college. Three of the five children went on to earn master's degrees, and I became the proud owner of two McDonald's restaurants. Because of the faith and determination my parents instilled in us, they were able to change our thoughts, and ultimately change our worlds.

NOT HIRING

Dawne J. Harris

Having a preacher for a dad afforded me an above-average belief in miracles—at least for others. I had yet to see my own faith accomplish anything extraordinary. That is, until the summer of 1986.

I was in my first year of college and sweating it out in a low-paying job at a convenience store. I despised the getup I wore to work every day, and the hours weren't the best either. I was certain to miss all the summer fun with my nighttime and holiday work schedule. But because I wanted to purchase a car, I kept on working.

One day, my sister Beth and I heard that Chrysler was hiring. They were looking to hire about 105 employees and pay them $14 an hour! We made plans the very next day to go to the local employment agency and put in our applications.

On the way to the employment agency, we purposely took a longer route and drove by the job site. We were perplexed when we saw a big black-and-white sign on the lawn that read Not Hiring. Our hearts momentarily sank. Suddenly, Beth said, "You know what? We're going to have faith and go on down to the employment agency to put in our applications anyway!"

When we arrived at the agency, there were long lines of people there who had also heard that Chrysler was hiring. When I saw the long lines, I said to my sister, "What's the use going through with this? We couldn't possibly have a chance." There were at least 150 people waiting in that line already.

Beth, who was a few feet in front of me, said, "Hey, sis, remember we said we were going to keep the faith?" We stood in that line for over an hour before we finally reached the front. The tired clerk hadn't so much as looked at us when we saw her point to a bank of file cabinets with five drawers full of applications. Sounding like a robot that needed a tune-up, she informed us that there were yet other file cabinets full of applications from other job hunters who were after the same jobs we wanted. She looked at us and asked, "Still want to apply?"

Beth gave me a signal with her eyes that suggested we keep the faith. Breathing deeply, we filled out the little cards and watched as the clerk filed them away in the sea of others.

A few weeks passed, and I was discouraged, thinking that Chrysler would never call. Then the unexpected happened—Chrysler called my sister to come in for an interview! I was happy for Beth but disappointed for myself. I imagined my sister buying new clothes and a new car from her wages, while I still took the bus and slaved away at low-paying jobs.

On the morning of Beth's interview, I was still asleep when my father burst into my room and boomed, "Get up, get dressed, and go down there with your sister and ask those folks for a job!" I thought he was crazy! I figured those old-time tactics where you walk straight up to someone and ask for a job might have worked forty years ago, but things were more organized and sophisticated now. I imagined marching down there with Beth and being publicly humiliated. I tried to convince my dad to leave me alone, but my father would not listen. He said to me, "How about exercising a little bit of faith?"—my sister's words again.

So I got up, got dressed, and got in the car with Beth. I worried myself sick, however, all the way there.

As I went into the personnel office with Beth, my knees were knocking and my mouth was dry. I gave the gentleman at the window my name, and I sat down and waited, with sweaty palms and cold feet, as Beth was called in for her interview. A short while later she emerged from the glassed-in area with a big smile and a new job!

As I waited, I heard my name called. I got up and approached the stern-looking gentleman who stood behind the window. He looked at me over his glasses and said loudly, "We don't have your name listed for an appointment." My heart sank, and I became embarrassed and frightened as the man stared at me in anticipation of a response. Just as I was about to reply, the gentleman's face softened and he continued, "But maybe we made a mistake. Come on in and take a seat." I regained my composure and stepped into the glassed-in area. Still in shock, I almost bumped into the door a few minutes later as I exited the office that day, work ID in hand and a new job at Chrysler!

A few days later, I drove past the location where I would be working. The black-and-white sign reading Not Hiring was still there. I laughed to myself and said, "Oh, yes, you *are* hiring; it just takes a little faith!"

WITH THE GRACE OF GOD, I SURVIVED

Denise Bride-Frazier

In 1993, I was working for Guy Carpenter in the World Trade Center, on the fifty-third floor. On February 26, a bomb went off in the basement of the World Trade Center complex. It took me an hour and a half to get out of the building. Shortly after we were allowed to return to our office in May 1993, my entire department was laid off. My family from all over the United States called and advised me never to work in the World Trade Center again.

In 1999, after being laid off from another job six months earlier, I was hired by Morgan Stanley Dean Witter. I was working in the World Trade Center again, in the same building, Two World Trade Center, on the sixty-seventh floor.

Two years later, on September 11, 2001, when One World Trade Center was hit by a jet plane, our building, 2 WTC, shook. A coworker told us to look out of the window (our window faced the Hudson River). We saw debris and fireballs falling from the sky. I told my colleague, "Let's get out of here." As we started down the steps, I don't remember all that I said, but later my coworkers told me I was telling people not to panic and that we would be all right. I do know I was praying as I went down the stairs. Then our building was hit by the second jet. "Dear Lord, please get those who can hear my prayers to you out safely," I prayed. But I never once thought that I would not get out alive. I had faith the Lord would carry me through.

Although I was hurt, I was blessed to be able to be reunited with my family and my two-year-old daughter. Many of my former coworkers from Guy Carpenter were lost. With the grace of God, I survived. I guess my work here on earth is not yet done. I offer my prayers to all the families that lost loved ones and friends.

WHAT IF GOD SAID NO?

LaShanna R. Price

It was December 10, 2001, my last day working with the kids at Cornerstone Schools of Alabama. I had been helping the seventh-grade class polish up their performance of James Weldon Johnson's *The Creation* for their Christmas program. I was doing a favor for a friend I attend church with, since acting and directing are my field of expertise. I'm always excited at an opportunity to do theater in my own backyard. Besides, who was I to turn God down? I knew He was calling on me to use my talents to help those kids, so I gladly accepted the request to help.

For two weeks, I spent an hour a day working with some of the most amazing and funniest kids in the world. The "troublesome" kids in the class had been pulled from the program by the administration, but I quickly reinstated them and made them work. I discovered that they were some of the more talented students in the class. They just needed an outlet and someone to give them encouragement.

All the children were inquisitive and wanted more responsibility than I could give them. I soon found myself looking forward to those daily sessions as much as they did! And on that last rainy day, they proved even further how grateful they were for my help by giving me a beautiful watch and earring set with a homemade card.

I laughed at the meaning implied by their gift: that time is valuable. It was a message I tried to impart to them every day, particularly when they tried to goof off or argue with one another instead of focusing on their performance.

The day of their performance I was scheduled to be in New York for an audition. At the dress rehearsal, however, we had a great run-through. The rehearsal was so good that one boy boldly told me not to cancel my audition in New York because of them, and to just forget about them and do what I needed to do.

"I am going to do just that!" I told them proudly. And after our last rehearsal, I took up my gift, bid them good-bye, and told them I would see them Thursday after the performance. Little did I know.

Returning to work, I was driving on an interchange ramp. The roads were wet and slippery. I was barely driving forty-five miles per hour, but I slowed my car down even more on the overpass.

As I tapped the brake, my SUV suddenly swerved to the left, then slid to the right and banged a car in the right lane. I fought to regain control of my vehicle.

My car swerved to the left again, then to the right, and banged the car next to me once more before spinning in a semicircle. My eyes took in the cement guardrail looming before me, with the racing traffic on the highway below. All I could do was shut my eyes and scream, "Oh, my God! Jesus!"

The SUV slammed into the guardrail; the impact was so hard that all three airbags released. I jerked forward against the restraint of my safety belt and gasped, too shocked to cry.

The stench from the airbag powder burned my nose. I scrambled out of the car, shaking uncontrollably as the drizzle from the rain spotted my glasses. My left shoe was caught underneath the pedal of the clutch. When I looked down, I saw I was standing on the overpass with one shoe on, oil, water, and dirt seeping into my white socks.

I was so grateful to be alive! And I came out of the accident with only a scratch on my right knee. At that moment, I knew that God had heard me when I called out to Him as my car hit that guardrail.

My supervisor was kind enough to pick me up after my car was towed away. He smiled sadly at me and said for some unknown reason, "Look at it this way; no good deed goes unrecognized."

When I replayed the accident over and over in my mind, I realized that yes, I had sacrificed my time to help the kids with their theatrical performance. To do so required getting over to the school. But what if I had said no when I was asked to help? I could have been traveling on any highway, on any ramp, at any given time when my car malfunctioned. Had I turned down the offer to help these kids and had an accident, would God have been there to answer my call and take care of me?

I'm a firm believer that God grants us gifts to fulfill our purpose here on earth, which is to minister to other people's weakened spirits, no matter what capacity you find them in. When we choose not to use our talents, we run the risk of losing them.

Every now and again, I catch a faint scent that reminds me how the airbags protected me that December day. A chill comes over me and I am back in my SUV on a rainy day slamming into a guardrail. Only this time, I see a band of God's angels protecting me on all sides, keeping the car from flying over the rail, or flipping over, or exploding. I am reminded that time really is valuable, and life is so precious. I can't let any opportunity to use my talents for God slip by, and run the risk of Him telling me no at just the point when I need Him most!

WHEN FAITH IS TESTED

Judge Trudy M. White

Never in my wildest imagination had I expected that my faith would be sorely tested. I had always done what my parents had taught me: Do unto others as you would have them do unto you. I was very active in the ministries of my church, and involved in many community organizations where we helped needy people. I am an attorney, and most of the cases I handled outside of my government job I did for free or at a nominal cost. I took care of sick family members. I was supportive to friends and family.

And then a course of events happened that changed me for the better. I was an attorney for a state agency. Just before Thanksgiving 1996 I was called into the office by the agency head and advised that allegations had been made against me and that they were going to terminate me. After this pretermination hearing was over, I was escorted to my department and told to remove all of my personal belongings from my office as the human-resources director stood over me and watched. The human-resources director had been directed to retrieve my permanent badge and place me on forced leave. I was given a period of time to respond to the allegations, and would be advised by telephone when I would be allowed to return to the agency.

After filing a response to the allegations, I received a telephone call advising me when I could return. Upon my return I reported to the human-resources division and was given a temporary badge.

With temporary badge in hand, I went to my office and found that the locks to my door had been changed. I had to wait for an hour until the key could be located. Once inside my office, I found everything had been deleted from my computer. In my gut I knew that my termination notice was imminent.

It was standard practice that notice of disciplinary actions be given on a Friday. This helped to minimize the office gossip, as employees would be home over the weekend. True to form, two weeks later the agency notified me on a Friday that my services were no longer needed. With tears in my eyes, I was escorted out of the building for the last time as an employee. My head was held high. I said to myself, "I will not be railroaded."

Although it's been said that it takes an act of Congress to fire a government employee, I found this not to be true. In my case, it took only the stroke of a pen.

I left the parking lot feeling like my world was coming to an end. I did not quite know what to do. How could the agency terminate me when I'd had nothing less than satisfactory ratings? How could I be terminated when my immediate supervisor had never counseled or admonished me for inadequate performance? How could an attorney who had been appointed by two governors to executive positions in the agency be fired?

I knew the agency would have unlimited resources to fight me should I decide to appeal my firing. My faith would be tested, and they would try to break me financially. None of my former colleagues would talk to me for fear of the same thing happening to them. The agency would see to it that I would not be able to get another government job.

Nonetheless, I knew deep inside that the agency had underestimated my tenacity in facing such challenges. The agency might have stripped me of my job, but I still had my dignity. I decided I could either lie down and let them walk all over me or I could fight them. I decided to fight.

Reality began to set in quickly. How was I going to pay my bills? How was I going to afford health insurance with no job? All my plans and dreams would have to be placed on hold. There were nights when I literally cried myself to sleep.

The Monday following the termination, I applied for unemployment compensation benefits. The eligibility caseworker determined that I was eligible to receive $164 a week in employment benefits after taxes. I was not ashamed about filing for unemployment benefits because I knew that I did nothing wrong. If I rolled over and did not fight back, others who might not be able to fight for themselves would be at risk as well.

I took solace in the fact that I come from a line of great people who had endured hardships that I could not imagine. I am a descendant of the fittest and bravest Africans who survived the Middle Passage. I knew that I too would survive this.

Over the weekend I dissected the allegations against me in preparation for filing a civil service appeal. I prepared a chronology of events and pulled together documents that supported my position. Early on in my career I had been advised by a senior government official to leave home each day as if it were my last day. For the most part I had heeded this advice, and so I had copies of documents that I'm sure the agency did not think that I had. With these documents I would be able to reconstruct the truth and prove my case.

Having represented the agency in personnel matters, I felt that I could handle the agency's appeal of the Department of Labor's decision granting me unemployment benefits myself. On the other hand, I knew that I needed an attorney for the civil service appeal. I had a good idea as to the background information that needed to be pulled together. I got up every morning as if I were going to the agency, and worked on my legal cases.

The agency contested my eligibility to receive unemployment benefits and appealed the decision to the administrative law judge. At the first setting of the hearing scheduled before the administrative law judge, the agency asked for a continuance because a witness had a conflict.

More than six months elapsed after the termination before the administrative hearing was held. By then I had received unemployment benefits for twenty-three weeks, and the agency demanded that I reimburse them for the benefits.

At the hearing, agency representatives stated mistruth after mistruth. Perhaps the witnesses felt that they would meet the same fate as me if they did not slant their testimony in the best light of the agency. I promised myself then that I would never put myself in a position where I would be hesitant to speak the truth for fear of losing my job.

The administrative law judge ruled in my favor, but the agency appealed the decision to the Louisiana Board of Review. The Louisiana Board of Review affirmed the administrative decision. Then the agency asked for a judicial review in the court. More than a year elapsed between the administrative hearing and the judicial review.

I had retained a lawyer from a firm that represented the local union to handle the civil service appeal. This firm represented over 50 percent of the appeals to the Louisiana Civil Service Commission.

The services of my lawyers cost money, and paying them was difficult.

As I waited for final decisions in my cases, I was left in limbo. Just to pay for basic necessities, I was forced to deplete my savings and sell real estate that I owned.

The lengthy litigation took an emotional toll on me as well. I began to run stop signs and red lights. When I realized that the distractions caused by the litigation were injuring my health, I decided having closure was more important.

Almost two years after my termination, I bypassed the attorneys on both sides and, with the agency's concurrence, entered into negotiations with the top African American in the agency. Despite the fact that she was representing the agency, I felt that she had integrity. We were successful in negotiating a settlement whereby I was reinstated to my former position, after which I would resign. I dismissed my civil service appeal, and the agency dismissed its appeal of my unemployment benefits. I accepted less than 100 percent of my back pay and unused leave. But I got the closure I wanted and needed. As I understood it, the New Orleans law firm that represented the agency billed the state in excess of $75,000 to defend my entitlement to approximately $5,000 in unemployment benefits and handle the civil service appeal.

But the termination turned out to change my life in so many positive ways I never would have imagined. Six months after my termination, I was hired as the staff person for an inner-city community development corporation (CDC). I had previously helped Zion City CDC with the preparation of its articles of corporation, 501(c)(3) application, and board training. The board members knew of my reputation and character. Though they were only able to pay me 25 percent of what I was paid by the agency, this liberated me in many ways.

It was important to me to be embraced by the Black community at large, and the Zion City community in particular, during this difficult period in my career. I had worked with community organizations and churches throughout the Baton Rouge area over the years and was well known for my public service. They had not forgotten me.

While employed with the Zion City CDC, we built four houses in the community, where there had been no new construction in over thirty years. Teacher's aides, bus drivers, homemakers, ministers, and other community activists worked together to make these houses a reality.

After I had been working for the Zion City CDC for more than a year and a half, Preston Castille Jr., then president of the Black lawyers' association (the Louis A. Martinet Legal Society), asked me to be the staff person for the Legal Society's pro bono program. With the help of many people, especially James A. Wayne Sr., Executive Director of Capital Area Legal Services, we established a viable pro bono program. The program operated out of the Leo S. Butler Community Center in South Baton Rouge. I became the receptionist, secretary, payroll clerk, and lawyer all rolled into one. About a year into the life of our foundation, we added a mentoring program.

By working at the community center, I was able to take the pulse of the community, and the public had daily access to a free lawyer. People would stop by and ask me questions about legal issues that concerned them. Working to win social security appeals on behalf of the indigent was one of the most rewarding experiences in my life. It was such a great feeling.

Shortly afterward, people in the community approached me to run for a vacant judicial seat. I prayed fervently about this and realized it was what God wanted me to do.

I campaigned for over a year, despite limited financial resources. I needed to run a grassroots campaign and meet as many people as possible. It was a hotly contested election, in that I was running against two Black men. To make it tougher, one of the candidates had an identical twin brother who was a judge.

Day after day I would walk the streets in ninety-five-degree heat, speaking with as many folks as I could. It took two months of campaigning just to explain that I was running not against the sitting judge but against his brother. It was a hard-fought campaign that left me with a campaign debt to this day.

Nevertheless, every door that needed to be opened was opened, even if it was just a crack. I led in the primary and went into the runoff with the judge's twin brother. In the runoff election, I won a decisive victory. I was sworn in on December 6, 1999, as a Baton Rouge City Court judge, Division B.

My journey from having my job taken away from me to my new position as judge stretched out over several years. I had been ridiculed, scorned, and accused of all kinds of mistruths. But in many ways it was my wake-up call, and I had heeded it.

I did not know what God had in store for me that Thanksgiving holiday back in 1996, but I knew I had to remain faithful. Had I not been fired, I know I would have become complacent working in that state job. I believe my termination was the catalyst that moved me closer to my real destiny.

THE MOUTHS OF BABES

Carmen Lashley

We never know where we are headed when we first step out on faith. We never know where God will lead us. My goal was to pour out my heart and soul on paper and become a famous author.

Well, God had another plan. While I was working on my book, my thirteen-year-old daughter, Sierra Myers, wrote a collection of poems. She had been reading since she was three years old, and lately she had been entering poetry contests on the Net and receiving prizes in the mail. She told me it was easy to write a book, and why was it taking me so long to finish mine?

A coworker named Stacy suggested that I take Sierra's poetry collection and the art done by Donovan, my fourteen-year-old son (he had been winning art contests since he was in elementary school), and combine them into a book. "Let the little children lead the way," she said.

I put my book on hold and started my own publishing company, Siedon Publications (named after Sierra and Donovan). My daughter and son's *Under the Do-Rag,* a collection of poems targeting teens and dealing with issues such as drugs, gangs, suicide, peer pressure, love, relationships and suicide, became our first teen title. The book offers tributes to Tupac, Martin Luther King Jr., the civil rights movement, and victims of the Holocaust tragedy. The message of the book is to look beyond the clothing and musical preferences of teenagers and to search under their do-rag for what they possess in their minds and hearts.

Sierra and Donovan's book has been lauded in publications such as *Girls' Life, National Geographic World, Sister's Dialogue,* and *Baltimore Café,* and on the WEAA-FM morning show. They received an award from the Fullwood Foundation in January 2002, and Sierra received the Maryland Girls and Young Women Shaping the Future award from the Maryland State Department of Education and the Maryland Commission for Women. Sierra and Donovan have been speaking to youth organizations and church groups throughout the state of Maryland. And the journey continues.

Sierra has gone on to write a second book, titled *Buds of Promise.* Recently Donovan wrote a gospel rap that was released on a soundtrack entitled *The Mission,* by Minister John Johnson.

Today, Siedon Publications prides itself on promoting the works of teenagers and spreading the word through the mouths of babes. Perhaps we still have not reached our final destination. But boy, does it feel good to be moving in the right direction.

When It Is So

Sheila J. Grant

One Saturday, as I was preparing to go to what theater majors call a tech rehearsal, I received a phone call from a close family friend telling me to come home right away; my father had been rushed to the hospital. I was sixty-one miles away from Chicago at Northern Illinois University. A friend who was visiting drove me home. I had no idea what would be waiting for me when I arrived.

When we arrived at the hospital, my father was still in the emergency room. He had suffered a brain aneurysm. The doctors wanted to send him to another hospital for a CAT scan, but his blood pressure was so low he couldn't be moved. I remember hours and hours of waiting and tears. I also remember a visit from the pastor of our church. Later that night they moved my father into intensive care. The family stayed at the hospital all night in a small waiting room near intensive care. At some point during that time the doctors came and told us that we needed to call the rest of the family. They explained that there was so much blood and swelling in my father's brain, there was nothing they could do—Daddy would inevitably die. I don't remember anyone saying a prayer, but I know we all did.

I stood at the pay phone in the hospital lobby with a bunch of quarters, calling all of my father's relatives in Denver, Colorado, explaining to each of them what the doctors had said. I called his brother first, who said he would come to Chicago right away. Next I telephoned his sister, and she said she would come too. Soon our house would be filled with relatives coming into town, hoping to arrive before my father passed away. Once I finished making my telephone calls, I returned to that little waiting room. Everyone was silent with the exception of my aunt, who talks incessantly when she gets nervous. She appeared to be talking ninety miles a minute.

Throughout the night we took turns checking on my father. The next morning, I spoke with a nurse who informed me that my father's condition had not changed. I convinced her to speak to my mother and encourage her to go home, eat, and take her high blood pressure medication. She did, and my mother reluctantly agreed.

The next day there was no change, with Dad still unconscious and hooked up to every kind of machine imaginable. Some of the machines buzzed, some of them beeped, and some hummed while releasing liquid that eventually went into his veins. There was even one very loud machine that forced the air in and out of his lungs, since he wasn't breathing on his own.

Another day passed, and still no change in my father's condition. The family went home briefly to change clothes. When we returned, the neurologist who was treating my father met us in the doorway of intensive care. His exact words to my mother were "Mrs. Grant, you must know somebody in heaven!" My mother responded by saying, "I do!" At that point, the doctor went on to explain that the blood that had filled up in my father's brain had drained out on its own, and the swelling had gone down as well. The doctor had absolutely no explanation for what had happened; in fact, he commented that he had never seen anything like it before. He explained that in the upcoming days my father would need to undergo spinal taps in order to determine where the blood had gone.

When we went to see my father shortly thereafter, he wasn't able to talk yet but he was responding coherently to questions. When asked by hospital personnel how many children he had, he was able to answer by raising his fingers. After several days had passed, the same doctors explained to us that although my father had survived the aneurysm, he would never be the same. "We will be able to release him eventually, but he will probably be bedridden and require twenty-four-hour nursing care for the rest of his life," the doctor said.

I was so grateful for my father's life being spared that I didn't think much about all the things the doctor had said. Later, my mother and I talked about hiring a nurse, getting a hospital bed, and trying to figure out if there would be enough medical insurance to cover all of this.

I took a leave from school so that I could be home with my mother and visit my father on a daily basis. He ended up spending three months in the hospital, and finally the day came for him to be released. We never had to buy that hospital bed or hire any nurses. My father walked out of that hospital on his own two feet. He wouldn't even let the staff wheel him to the door in a wheelchair, which was hospital policy. The only lasting effect of the aneurysm was the loss of Daddy's immediate recall. He could talk to me easily about things that happened when he was twelve, but sometimes he would forget during a conversation that he had already said something and he would repeat it.

I returned to school later that summer, but I had learned two of the greatest lessons of my life. I learned that God makes doctors and even endows them with the expertise and talent to treat patients, even if that sometimes means speaking words of comfort to heartbroken families. But the more important thing I learned is that nothing is so until He says it is so.

"Your Child Has Leukemia"

Keisha M. Brown

Okay, Jesus, tell me what to do now. Breathe, you say? I don't think I know how to do that at this very moment, seeing as how all time, space, and being have ceased to exist. And even if I, somehow, by some small miracle, was able to remember how, I don't think I would take the chance of moving and missing this doctor say, "Oops, I'm so sorry, I'm looking at the wrong chart. I'm not talking about your child at all—please forgive me."

But I never heard those words. The doctors, having seen this look of terror on the faces of a thousand other parents, thought it best to leave the room to let the family digest the jagged pill that had just been shoved down our throats, cutting and burning the entire way down. Things then began to move in slow motion. The heel on my husband's boot was all I saw exit the door before it closed behind him, to seek what I know was a small, dark corner to cry and pray. And there I sat enveloped in my in-laws' arms, crying and screaming, "He's just a baby!" And the more I screamed and heaved, the faster I slid into the realization that I felt worse with every breath. My insides wanted so much to come out to get air, but could not. My eyes wanted to cry harder, but the tears wouldn't come any faster. And through all the commotion, my head was yearning to understand but failed to conceive.

"I need to be near him . . . I need to touch him . . . he needs his mother's touch." Mommy will make it all better. I broke away and darted to the bed where my child—my firstborn, my love—lay. I picked him up and held him and rocked him, wanting to be a Band-Aid for this big bruise called Leukemia: but to no avail . . . and reality had set back in. It was time to deal with this monster.

The doctors explained that there were cancerous cells in my baby's blood and that there was a series of medications that would need to be started. This medication would, they hoped, kill the cancerous cells. Oh, by the way, they told me, these are not smart medicines, so while they are killing the bad cancerous cells, they will be killing some of his good, strong cells also. This will break his immune system and, unfortunately, leave him open to infection. But, they added, he was young and strong, and they saw a good prognosis. With that, the white jackets lined up and walked out of the room, vowing to return to begin treatment and answer any questions.

With that, I called my mother and explained it the best I knew how. The voice that had been so familiar and comfortable to me all of my life gave me no more comfort than that of a total stranger, as hard as she tried. I then called my father, who had been such a friend and confidant to me throughout my life. I explained the matter as best I could muddle through, and his response was, very matter-of-factly, "Oh, okay. Call me and let me know what happens." His response made me feel as if I had just explained that my child had the common cold. Maybe I hadn't been clear. So I repeated, "Yeah, this *is* what happened, Daddy. They say my child has leukemia." His response again: "Okay, keep me abreast of what goes on." With that, I had to hang up or else the little sanity that I was so desperately trying to hold on to would surely leave.

I sat by my child's bed all night, forced to be alone with my own thoughts. Now, let me think, what could I have done differently? Could I have fed him more nutritiously? Did I take him off breast milk too soon? Did I not pay enough attention to the warning signs? Did I not act quickly enough? Then in chimed the doctors' voices telling me that this disease is not hereditary, it has a quick onset, and the cause of it is unknown. Leukemia is less prevalent in the African American community, and it has a cure rate of approximately 80–85 percent for children with this particular form.

80–85% Cure Rate = Hope

You see, God made me, and He knows that Keisha needs to see some hope to hold on to, and he loves me enough to give that to me. God knew that if I was to put on my armor and fight the good fight, he would have to show me a small ray of hope. Thank you, Jesus!

For the next eight days, I lay in that hospital bed alongside my child, dealing with it the only way I knew how: praying and holding him close to me and not letting go as though I was trying to allow my love to come from my body and sink into his to heal his little body. And my husband coped by doing what works best for him, spending long hours in the hospital library reading all that he could about this disease. And my mother-in-law (the matriarch) continued to have us pull ourselves up by the bootstraps by not letting us forget what a great God we serve.

At the end of eight days of medication, spinal taps, blood draws, needles, and blood testing, the doctor walked into our hospital room and asked, "Who wants to go home?" I felt again the disbelief that had clouded my head with the news of the illness, but this time it was a little different:

LOOK AT GOD!

We were sent home with a frail and sick-looking little boy and a boatload of medication. I remember thinking, "God, there's so much of it, why is there so much of it, and how am I supposed to remember when it is supposed to be given?" Then I thought about how much I loved my child and, so I said to myself, Keisha, you can do this! I proceeded to spread the medication out, grouped it by days, and began to mark up my calendar with a definite schedule.

In the next few years, little did I know that the Lord would allow me to experience many hurts and pains. In this time I would watch my son blow up like a balloon, lose weight, become sick to his stomach, experience mood swings, and lose and grow back his hair twice. In addition, I experienced employment and unemployment, which brought on financial problems and, in turn, marital troubles. I would go to the hospital at the first sign of a fever and sit in the emergency ward until the wee hours of the morning, sometimes staying longer. I say that God allowed me to experience these things because He loved me enough to know that these things would only strengthen me, and that through these experiences I would have no other alternative but to give God and only God the glory. He knew that only these experiences would allow me to appreciate the miraculous recovery that my son is experiencing now.

My son is now five years of age, soon to be six. He began kindergarten last September and, with God's grace and mercy, will be finished with chemotherapy in March of 2002. My son has never had to have radiation or a bone marrow transplant and has remained in remission since eight days after his diagnosis on December 22, 1998. These are my blessings. Some may wonder how having leukemia can bring or be a blessing. I say that when your child or loved one has this disease, you find the blessings. I can remember my husband calling me on his way home from a late night of work once, about one year into our child's illness. He was upset because, for whatever reason, on this particular day many people had inquired about our son's health. He said, "Keish, I told them that he was okay, but also that my wife is so strong and does better with it than me." I then responded by saying, "Stop telling people that, because if it were up to me, I would be a mess and things would have fallen apart a long time ago. You tell them that the Lord is our strength."

AMBAY'S GIFT

Michael W. Catledge

Spring Break 1987 found me a twenty-one-year-old sophomore architect major at Florida A&M University, at a time-share condo at Indian Rocks Beach. Mother had just signed on with one of those time-share outfits that were booming up all over the Suncoast in the mid-1980s. As we lived in nearby Tampa, Mother thought having a time-share would be a good investment for the family—something we could enjoy once a year without having to journey far from home.

Her first "time slot" popped up just in time for my spring break. Unfortunately, Mother couldn't take the time off from work to enjoy the time-share herself. Rather than pass over her time, she decided that James and I could use the condo for the week; she would join us on the weekend. Although not many twenty-year-olds would have welcomed the notion of having their six-year-old baby brother tag along, to me, spending time with Jimmy was a treat.

He was always in a happy spirit, and was very intelligent for his age. He taught himself how to read by thumbing through the *TV Guide* and matching the program listings to the broadcasts as they came on air!

On the third day of our vacation, Jimmy had slept restlessly and woke up crying. When I asked what was wrong, he told me he had had a bad dream. In the dream several people were standing over him, many were crying, and Mother was somewhere nearby with some hysterical woman. Noticing my distress, Jimmy took my hand and said, "But don't worry, Mike. I was all right. Everything was a-okay in the end." With that, Jimmy bounded out of the room and returned to his happy-go-lucky self.

Still a bit unnerved, I mentioned his dream to Mother when she called later that morning. Bothered herself—Jimmy had never had bad dreams before—she decided that after work she would hop over the bay and pay us a visit to make certain Jimmy was okay.

Jimmy and I continued to have fun that day, and didn't even think about his dream again until Mother came bounding through the front door just after sunset and practically interrogated him about the dream. I understood, though. We are a deeply spiritual and earthy family that takes such occurrences seriously. Confident Jimmy was fine, Mother decided that she would take him on a moonlit stroll on the beach while I prepared dinner. Fifteen minutes later, she returned without Jimmy, looking quite puzzled. "Michael, did James come back up here?" she asked, glancing about the condo. "No, he didn't," I replied. "I thought he was with you?" "He was," she said, "but I stopped to speak to someone downstairs and when I turned around he was gone."

Mother and I ran back downstairs to the resort's back patio facing the beach. Mother, thinking Jimmy might have wandered on shore, decided to search there while I tried to figure out where else he might have gone. Then, out of the corner of my eye, I caught sight of some guy who, as he had stuck a pole under the surface, I thought was cleaning the pool. Which was odd, given the time of day. Suddenly, someone shouted, "Oh, my God! There's a child at the bottom of the pool!" My heart dropped.

"No!" I screamed, as I dashed toward the pool area. Mother came running behind me. I reached the edge of the pool and looked down. I could barely make out a small fuzzy form lying motionless on the bottom. I'll never forget the sight. By this time, Mother realized it was her child that the stranger was trying to fish out of the pool. She let out a bloodcurdling scream as she called out Jimmy's name. Several women seemed to come out of nowhere to hold my mother back, refusing to allow her to see Jimmy's body. Mother sat down and started to pray as the ladies tried to comfort her.

Without thinking, I threw off my glasses and jumped into the pool just as the stranger snagged the netted end of the pole around Jimmy's legs and scooped him off the bottom. I swam over and grabbed hold of Jimmy's motionless body. He was limp. It was awful. By then several people had gathered at the edge of the pool. They helped me lift Jimmy out of the water and onto the deck. Instinctively, the stranger who had pulled him off the bottom and I began administering CPR—I've never been so thankful of my high school gym teacher's instruction in it in my entire life. I won't describe the anguish I felt as I tried to pump air into the waterlogged lungs of my six-year-old brother, while the stranger tried to jump-start his heart. As I struggled to keep my mouth over his, those once bright sparkling eyes never moved, never blinked. Mother was unusually calm, surrounded by hysterical ladies. People stood around crying. It was then that I remembered Jimmy's dream. I get chills even now just thinking about it.

After what seemed like hours, but was in actuality only a few minutes, the paramedics arrived and ordered the stranger and me to stand back while they tried to resuscitate Jimmy. One of them shouted, "We've got a pulse!" I ran over to Mother and told her that James was still alive. The look of despair in her eyes finally made me bust out in tears. Until then it had not really registered that this was happening. I was simply going through the motions and operating on adrenaline. Now it hit me—my baby brother might have died. I fell apart.

Later that same night, we received word from Key West that during the hour of Jimmy's resuscitation, my mother's aunt, Ambay, died of emphysema. It was as if she gave her last breath so that Jimmy could live. Certainly Jimmy's revival was a gift to us all.

Note: The author of this piece has since gone to be with my aunt Ambay, my father, and my mother. He died in a car accident on January 17, 2002, eight days after his thirty-sixth birthday. There was not enough time for him to be given CPR, but thank God he was able to do that for his little brother. More important, thank God for his talent that enabled this piece to be written and preserved. May he continue to oversee us as we travel through this earthly journey. Jimmy (or James) is now twenty-one years old and eternally grateful to Michael and Ambay.

 —Juliette Catledge, mother of Michael, Gregory, and James—all of whom I will forever be proud of.

GRIEF AND HEALING

HEALING

Tavis Smiley

When I was in the seventh grade, my sister Phyllis and I were accused of doing something at church that we had not done. To understand the context, my mother and father were both leaders in our church; my mother was a missionary, and my father was on the trustee board and on the deacon board.

We had attended an afternoon service at the church, and some disruptive behavior took place during this program. Somehow the fingers got pointed at my sister and me as the ringleaders, even though we were innocent. In a subsequent church meeting, the minister of our church stood up in front of the entire congregation and accused Phyllis and me of being the culprits. He proceeded to scold us publicly.

I knew that Phyllis and I were in deep trouble when we got home. We tried to convince our parents that we were not responsible for the disturbance—we were simply somewhere in the vicinity when it happened. But my parents, as leaders in the church, were embarrassed at having their children's names called out in front of the entire congregation. Unfortunately, we were unable to convince our parents that we were telling the truth.

My father in particular took our minister's word over ours. When we got home from church following the evening service, my father was absolutely enraged. I had never seen him so upset before in my life. I knew we were going to get a whipping, as usual, with a belt or with switches. But it didn't happen right away. My father, because he worked several part-time jobs to take care of the family, had to leave again to go to one of them. He didn't return home until the wee hours of the morning.

When my father did make it back home Sunday night, he came into my bedroom, turned the light on, got me out of bed, and proceeded to give me the beating of my life. But he didn't use a belt or switch. He used an extension cord. He beat both my sister and me. He beat us so badly that night that the flesh on our bodies was ripped and torn. We were in so much pain that we couldn't lie down on the bed after he finished beating us. We had so many open wounds that the sheets stuck to the bloody cuts.

The next day we tried to take a bath before going to school but could not do it. We were both in a great deal of pain and felt absolutely miserable. When it came time for gym class, neither one of us wanted to get undressed to put on our gym clothes. We were too embarrassed at what the other kids would see on our legs, arms, and backs.

Finally, I was sent to the principal's office. Once there, I was ordered to take my clothes off. The teacher thought I was trying to hide something; indeed, I was. After they discovered the condition my body was in, they called Phyllis into the office and saw the marks on her too. The police and the ambulance were called. Phyllis and I were rushed to the hospital, where we stayed about seven days. Shortly after, social services became involved, and eventually the matter went to court, and both Phyllis and I were taken out of our parents' home and sent to separate foster homes.

After months of living in the foster home and being away from my parents, I eventually went back home and stayed until I finished high school. It wasn't always easy, because my relationship with my father and mother had been severely impacted. Indeed, when I went off to Indiana University five years later, our relationship was still so rocky that my parents refused to fill out and sign my financial aid forms. And when I left for school, they did not accompany me. Phyllis never returned home from the foster family she had been placed with.

To this day, Phyllis and I are trying to heal from this experience. It was a painful experience for us both, as well as an embarrassment to us as a family. When the police and social services became involved, the story was put in the local newspaper. We were from a small town, and everybody started talking about our family, including the people at our church. Phyllis and I both felt a deep sense of shame because we felt we had brought embarrassment to our family, even though we had been beaten for something we hadn't done. My parents felt bad as well. It was just a horrific ordeal.

I often think about what happened, mostly because of my sister. The incident affected us in drastically different ways. I used the incident to motivate me, to empower me to never allow myself to be humiliated in the eyes of my community again. I decided that I would not let the scars on my body determine the destiny of my future. I ended up using the incident as a motivating force to achieve, achieve, and achieve, to the best of my ability.

Phyllis, on the other hand, allowed the incident to beat her down. Emotionally, she was never able to overcome the incident. Nor was she able to forgive my father for his actions. She went on to have a number of kids out of wedlock, and wound up becoming a crack addict. It literally wrecked her life. Her life spun out of control. She continues to live with scars all over her arms and her legs. In the summertime, she can never feel comfortable wearing short pants or a swimming suit because of the marks.

Sometimes we are able to deal effectively with the hurt and pain that others inflict upon us. Sometimes we exacerbate that pain and slow down our healing process because of our inability to forgive those who have hurt us. I believe that we have to forgive in order to live. My sister is not yet able to do this. (But as I write this she is doing well, working and staying clear of drugs.)

Healing is an everyday process. There isn't a day that goes by in my life that I don't think about this incident in some way. Many times, as African Americans, we try to avoid dealing with our pain; as a result, it makes it impossible for us to heal. We can't ignore the hurt or the pain in our lives and expect ourselves to heal automatically. We have to deal if we want to heal.

I meet all kinds of Black folks who have gotten emotionally stuck for years over an issue or incident in their lives. They end up languishing personally, professionally, spiritually, and psychologically because they become afraid to acknowledge it, afraid to deal with it, afraid to confront others, afraid to forgive others, and afraid to let go of it. When we are afraid to address these issues of hurt and pain, we jeopardize our own progress.

My father and mother have profusely apologized to me, and we have worked hard to repair our relationship. In many respects, my healing has already taken place.

I continue to pray for my sister, that she will one day be able to heal and live the kind of productive life that I know she is capable and deserving of living. No matter how severe the pain in our lives, we must strive to do whatever is necessary to turn our pain into power.

A Dream, Not Deferred, but Fulfilled

Marilyn Smith

On September 10, 2001, I had just returned home from working three twelve-hour shifts at Moses Cone Hospital in Greensboro, North Carolina. I was completely exhausted. Even in my exhaustion, however, something in my spirit was troubled. When I lay down to sleep that night, I dreamed that I saw a whole bunch of people in a building and they were burning up. I knew it was a familiar building, but I couldn't make out exactly which building it was. I am a nurse, and in the dream I was a nurse as well. I kept trying to get to the people in this burning building, but somehow I couldn't reach them. Then I began to see the people disintegrating before me. I wondered what I had done to land myself in Hell, because that is where I thought I was in the dream. All of a sudden, the dream shifted and I found myself in the desert, high on top of a cliff as I looked down into a pit. I saw one familiar hand come up and I thought to myself, "Oh my God, I've got to reach this one person." As I reached down to help this person and grabbed their hand, I started to fall. Right before I hit the bottom, I woke up.

When I woke up, I was full of perspiration and I didn't have a blanket or a sheet on me; they were strewn about all over. I got up to open the blinds and it was a beautiful day outside. I started praising God, because I

realized I hadn't gone to hell, that I was still alive and well. I had the feeling, however, that something was going to happen to someone I knew; I
just didn't know whom and I didn't know what was going to take place.
It was September 11.

Something said to me, "Call the firehouse." So I called the firestation
in Brooklyn Heights, New York, where my husband worked. When they
put him on the line, he was his usual jolly self. He wanted to know how I
was doing and how the girls were doing. Our twin daughters had recently
enrolled in Johnson C. Smith College in Charlotte, North Carolina,
and he informed me that he had just put some money in the mail to pay
some of their expenses. I told him that I was tired because I hadn't slept
well the night before. He asked me if I had seen the news and I told him
I hadn't. When I started to tell him about my dream, he said, "That's
weird, because what you dreamed is what's happening right now in New
York. We're being attacked!" I turned on the television just in time
to see the plane fly into the South Tower of the World Trade Center.
I immediately started crying; I felt as though this was the dream I had
experienced the night before. Just then, my husband informed me that he
had to get on the fire truck and head down to the World Trade Center.
The phrase he used was the same one he used whenever he had to answer
a fire call: "We have to rock 'n' roll." In the midst of my tears, I begged
him not to go down there, but I knew he had to. He had wanted to be a
fireman since he was eight years old. Nothing was going to keep him from
doing his job.

Before we hung up, I told my husband I loved him. During our twenty
years of marriage, things had not always been perfect for us and we had
been separated a number of times. "Leon," I said to him. "I want you
to know that I really love you and no matter what we've been through
in life, you have always been my hero and you have always been our
daughters' hero. I'm going to pray for you, and I want you to pray before
you leave." Then we said a prayer together and he told me he would call
me later. When I hung up the phone, I couldn't take my hand off the
receiver. I felt as though someone had just cut me with a knife and the
blood was running out of my body. I just knew that something was going
to happen.

My husband and I had known each other since I was fifteen years old.

When we got together as a couple, we made a promise to each other that we would never do drugs or engage in criminal activity, and we leaned on each other to keep these promises. In addition to working as a fireman in Brooklyn, Leon held three other jobs to raise enough money to send the twins to college. He was active in all kinds of charity organizations, he mentored kids in the neighborhood, and he had gained a reputation as the neighborhood mechanic, working on everybody's car, including those of firemen at other firestations. In August 2000, I moved to Greensboro, North Carolina, from Brooklyn to be closer to my daughters.

My daughters were contacted at the college and notified that their father had responded to the call for duty at the World Trade Center. I became concerned about their well-being and decided to make the one-and-a-half-hour drive from Greensboro to the school to see how they were doing. It was important to me that they know I was okay and that I was holding up. When I arrived at the school and found the girls, we exchanged prayers and hugged and I let them know that I was holding up okay and that I felt everything would be fine. But when I got in the car and started driving home, I just knew I was going to have that phone call that I had always dreaded would come one day as a firefighter's wife.

When I arrived home, my answering machine had eighteen messages. I knew this was not a good sign. I did not want to listen to those messages alone, but since I had recently relocated to Greensboro, I didn't really know anyone there. Finally, I went over to my neighbor's house across the street and explained my situation to the woman who lived there. I asked if she would come home and listen to the messages with me. My neighbor left her kids and came over to the house with me. When we played the messages, there were calls from Leon's mother, my brother and sister, and then the dreaded message from the firehouse. "Hello, Marilyn? This is the firehouse. Give us a call when you get this message."

I started running around in the house like a crazy person. I held on to my neighbor as I made the call back to the firehouse. "Marilyn," they said. "We are sorry to inform you that Leon and all of Brooklyn #118 went into the World Trade Center and they were in the building when the building went down. No one has been recovered yet and we do not know their whereabouts."

I can't tell you what happened immediately after that. All I remember is that I was on the floor, crying and hurting in a way I had never hurt before. After I calmed down a bit, I called the Greensboro Fire Department and spoke to the chief. He and several other firefighters from the station came over to the house to console me. He also sent some of his workers down to Charlotte to pick up my daughters.

For the next five days, I did my best to get to New York with the girls, but we couldn't get a flight out. When we finally did get to New York, I knew that Leon was gone. I couldn't feel his presence anymore, and I knew that he had left us. I went to the firehouse where my husband worked and it was like a nightmare there. Because Brooklyn Heights #118 lost all the men on the truck they sent to the World Trade Center that day, there was weeping and wailing all around. The Brooklyn Heights fire station had taken a big hit.

One night in Greensboro several weeks later, I was sitting in the family room mourning the loss of my husband, and trying to make some sense out of what had taken place in our family's life. I thought about Leon and how much I missed him. I thought about how he would affectionately call me "little mama" or "sweet little mama." It was about 11:30 P.M. and suddenly the sprinklers came on outside. I thought that was strange, especially since they were programmed to come on at 5 in the morning. Then I heard a noise; a book had fallen over on the shelf. I got up to set the book back up and noticed the title of the book was I Love You Mama. Finally, I went downstairs to see what was happening with the sprinklers. When I reached the bottom of the stairs, the most eerie thing happened. A huge spirit or dark form passed right in front of me. It happened so quickly that I thought I was going to run into it. Immediately afterward, I smelled Leon's cologne; it seemed as though Leon had walked right through me. At that moment, I felt that Leon was there in the house with me, and he had come back to let me know that he was still with his family in spirit.

Since that day, the girls and I have tried to console one another. We would kid each other that we knew Leon was up in heaven bargaining with God to work things out for his family still on earth.

In the wake of 9/11, all I kept worrying about was how I would ever be able to afford to get my daughters through college. It turned out that Johnson C. Smith College was contacted by the United Negro College

Fund to find out if there were any students attending the school who had parents that were lost in the 9/11 tragedy. My daughters' names were submitted to UNCF, and they were selected to receive a scholarship. The scholarship was presented to my daughters by the First Lady, Laura Bush, in Washington, D.C.

The City of New York joined with the United Negro College Fund in contributing toward the scholarship my daughters received. We went to New York to attend another awards ceremony in which Mayor Giuliani and the governor of New York presented the girls with awards as well, just to let the rest of the world know that the City of New York was taking care of the children affected by the tragedy. The Red Cross made us recipients of their help, as well. I often thought back to the times when I would get mail from the United Way and the Red Cross, and would send some money back in those envelopes I received, even if it was only five dollars. I never dreamed that the money I was giving would one day come back to help me and my family.

In Greensboro, people started coming from all over the city to bring me food or to ask how they could help. I really appreciated everything that was being done for me and the girls. But, in my silent moments when no one was around, I felt like I was sinking deeper and deeper into despair. My daughters, who were still out of school, said to me, "Mama, we have to get back in school. We can't allow Dad's death to knock us down. We have to do well in school and become productive citizens in the community, and give back by pulling others up along the way. We have to fulfill the dream he had for us." So after a semester out of college, the girls returned. Yolanda stayed at Johnson C. Smith in Charlotte. But Tiffany became too worried about me and chose to attend Bennett College to be closer to me here in Greensboro. Now that some time has passed, the girls have gotten back on track and are doing well in school again. They are carrying out their father's dream for their lives.

When the girls were children, I began my study toward becoming a nurse. Leon encouraged me to pursue this course, and he worked three jobs to make sure there was enough money to take care of the household. I earned my associate's degree in nursing, but Leon kept encouraging me to go all the way and earn my B.S. in nursing. I wasn't able to continue on with my education, however, due to financial and time constraints.

After 9/11, I received a call from the fire department; they were offering scholarships for the girls' education, and they offered me a scholarship to pursue my education as well. In the midst of all the tragedy, it seemed as though I could hear my husband's voice saying to me, "You get back in school, Marilyn. You go all the way and earn the nurse practitioner's and the B.S. in nursing degree."

I accepted the scholarship from the New York Fire Department and I enrolled in the University of North Carolina here in Greensboro. At the end of my first semester, I had earned all A's. A feeling of inspiration arose in me, and made me hungry to achieve my goal.

I still feel like I am living in two states, traveling back and forth from North Carolina to New York. My husband's mother still lives in New York, and Leon was her only child. She had just lost her husband in December of the year before. I try to be a source of support for her whenever she needs something.

In spite of all that has happened, I am filled with feelings of gratitude and thankfulness. Whenever I am not in classes at school or studying for my courses, I do volunteer work in Greensboro. Sometimes it takes a tragedy to make you appreciate life and put things in perspective. I feel blessed because of what all the various organizations and the fire department did for not only me, my daughters, and my mother-in-law in our time of need, but for other dependents of firefighters, as well. In my heart, I feel like it is my time to give back to others, even if it is only an hour or so here and there.

These days I find myself trying to make decisions for my family that I know my husband would have made were he still alive. I have taken a lot of the insurance money I received from his death and placed it in a fund for his current and future grandchildren's educations, because I feel that's what Leon would have wanted. Because Leon always celebrated the twins' birthday by taking them shopping at every store they wanted to go to, this year the girls and I are spending his birthday in New York with his mother, going out to dinner, and buying him a gift from us all. And I'm planning on planting a Japanese red maple tree in my backyard and placing a brass plate with Leon's name on it in honor of him.

Today, I am taking joy in living a simple life. I am trying to teach my children to do the same. Tomorrow is never promised to any of us. Each of us has to live life to the fullest each day we are blessed to stay here on this earth. It's not how long we live measured by the years we stay here, but it's the quality of what we do with the time we're allowed.

When I went down to Ground Zero, the most memorable scene for me was seeing the construction workers and the rescue workers. I had never seen such unity in all of my life: Blacks, Latinos, Chinese, Japanese, and Caucasians, sitting together, breaking bread, working, and hugging each other.

When I went to the closing ceremony at Ground Zero, it didn't give me closure because I didn't feel like Leon was there. I felt like he had gone to a better place. They still have not recovered Leon's body. He is the only one from Brooklyn Heights #118 that they have not recovered. The children and I continue to swab out our mouths and send our samples to New York to help with the DNA identification process; we'll be glad when this part is over.

Although we already had a memorial service for Leon, if his remains are ever found, our family will have a private ceremony for him. It will be the closest we can come to having closure in celebrating the life and death of a very special man.

On a Rainy Night: A Christmas Blessing

Kaye Barrow Ziglar

We knew Christmas was not going to be the same. Our baby, Lauren Grace, had passed away nine months earlier, at only seventeen and a half months of age. It had been a tough year.

Early in the holiday season we both agreed on a simple Christmas. Neither of us had the desire or energy to deal with the commercialism of the season. For once, we were taking care of us instead of complying with the wishes of others. It felt very good not to have the pressure and anxiety of shopping for everyone, deciding whom we were going to visit, or if we were going to have Christmas guests over. We wanted neither. It would be just the three of us; me, our five year-old son, Garrett, and Rod, my husband of seven years.

I asked Rod to bring in the two huge boxes of decorations so that I could begin decorating for Christmas. At the very top of the first box, wrapped in clear plastic, were our Christmas stockings. Lauren Grace's was on top, and I wondered for a while if I should put it up. During grief counseling, I was told, "Don't try to make your holidays like the ones from the past, because things will not be the same." So I asked my son Garrett if he thought we should put Lauren's stocking up. He replied, "Yes, Mommy, let's put it up."

Lauren Grace's stocking was the first one to be hung on the mantel. Then we put up our tree. In years past, we had always had ornaments on the tree that represented our marriage and our children. Two doves represented Rod's and my bond, which began in April 1994. Another ornament with a photograph reminded us of our first Christmas as husband and wife. In another, a dove represented the children that we hoped to produce to make our family complete. A hand-painted Noah's Ark ornament always adorned our tree in memory of our firstborn, Matthew, who was stillborn in 1995 during my fifth month of pregnancy. Ornaments representing our son's first Christmas honored little Garrett, who was born the following year. This year we chose two ornaments for Lauren Grace. The first was a tiny ornament depicting little cherubs of all races and nationalities singing. In addition, we bought a tiny angel made of Lauren's birthstone, sapphire, with golden wings and a diamond face. Now the tree was complete.

Though we did not talk about it, Rod and I both knew that on Christmas Day we wanted to visit the cemetery to include Lauren Grace in our Christmas celebration. I had prepared a wonderful Christmas dinner with all the soul food trimmings, and I wondered if going to the cemetery before dinner would zap our appetites along with our spirits. But Rod said, "We'll be all right. Let's go now."

Very nervously and anxiously, I took off my Christmas apron and grabbed my jacket, and the three of us hopped into the car. We had a poinsettia to bring, but I wanted to keep it beautiful for as long as I could, so we decided not to take it yet. Rod had seen a little holiday bear with some flowers encased in a clear tube while he was out earlier in the season, and suggested that we place that on Lauren Grace's grave.

Lauren's grave was at the extreme rear of the cemetery. It broke my heart to leave each time we visited; it felt like I was leaving my baby back there all alone. "Oh, my Lauren," I thought. "How I wish you were here with us this year, as you were last year."

As we approached her grave, we all called out, "Hi, Lauren Grace, Merry Christmas. We miss you, Lauren!" We stood around the grave in silence for a moment, and then Rod affixed the little Christmas bear around the urn of flowers. As usual, we wiped the headstone off to make it presentable. We stood close together at the foot of the grave. As I stared down at the grave marker, I noticed that the lamb carved there—which had been tiny, about the size of my pinky—was now much larger. I said to Rod, "Do you notice something different about that lamb?" He replied, "Yes, it's bigger."

How could that be? When the marker was first placed, we had been a little upset that the lamb was so small; we'd wanted one that would be more proportionate to the size of the stone and would balance the wording on the stone.

Garrett, in his slightly stuttering little-boy voice, said, "Mommy, mmmmommy, I, I, I know how that lamb got to be so big! Naybe"—he couldn't at the time say *maybe*—"God came on a rainy night and just made the lamb get bigger! God did it, Mommy, on a rainy night." Rod and I just looked at each other and smiled.

"Garrett, I think you're right about God coming and changing that lamb," I said. And with that Rod offered up a beautiful Christmas prayer. Of all the many times that I have visited my daughter's grave, I have never again left in such great spirits and without tears. I felt a sense of hope and healing, assured of God's presence with us on Christmas day. Afterward we went home with more of the true spirit of Christmas in our hearts.

Challenges, Not Obstacles

Norma Gaines-Hanks, Ed.D.

In the fall of 1997, my mother, the Reverend Naomi Gaines Winchester, was diagnosed with breast cancer. She was sixty-seven years old and had recently started a new career, serving as the pastor of three small churches in New Castle County, Delaware.

We were very fortunate in that the surgeon was family-oriented and insisted on meeting with the family before the surgery. He was extremely reassuring. On the day that he performed the biopsy confirming the malignancy, I broke down in tears. As my mother was coming out of the anesthesia, she realized I was crying. When she asked me why I was crying, I lied and said that my contact lenses were bothering me. The doctor, overhearing my response, immediately chastised me for being dishonest and suggested that we needed to be up front with my mother. She accepted his report, said a prayer, and immediately asked what she needed to do next.

Mom underwent aggressive chemotherapy prior to her mastectomy. The chemo weakened her and she lost her hair, but never lost her spirit. She kept the faith and continued to serve the churches, as well as tried to keep up with her busy schedule of serving on various boards and committees. Just a week or so before her scheduled surgery, she participated in her mother's hundredth-birthday celebration, despite her discomfort from the chemotherapy.

On the day of her surgery, my mother had been giving instructions to everyone who had come to the hospital to support her, including expressing concern about my then ten-year-old twin nephews, who lived with her part time.

The surgery took longer than expected, and the recovery was difficult. There were some days when it was hard for Mother to be optimistic, but she never gave up the fight. As soon as she awoke following surgery, she wanted to be sure we were all right. She expressed concern that her grandsons were not being fed properly and that someone at one of her churches might have needed her. It was very hard for her to accept that the tables were turned and that she was the one who needed attention.

Her Delta Sigma Theta sorority and church members assumed responsibility for providing meals for her a few days a week. Her grandsons developed survival-cooking skills and willingly washed dishes, did the laundry, and vacuumed the carpets so that their grandmother could rest properly.

In 2000, Mom participated in the Relay for Life campaign, sponsored by the local chapter of the American Cancer Society. It was the first time it had been held in Wilmington, Delaware (it was usually held in a suburban city), and this time it was targeted at the Black and Hispanic communities. With the support of her sorority sisters, Mom became the highest individual fund-raiser, and Delta Sigma Theta became the highest group fund-raiser in both 2000 and 2001.

Today, despite lymphedema and diabetes—both outcomes of her chemotherapy—Mom works a few days per week for a local United Methodist church, visiting members in nursing homes, hospitals, or at home. She also substitutes for the senior pastor when he is absent. This is all in addition to providing support and care to her sister (who at age 81 underwent a leg amputation), her 104-year-old mother, who is exhibiting symptoms of Alzheimer's disease, and her 80-year-old brother, who serves as my grandmother's primary caregiver. Plus, she is still chief cook and bottle washer for her beloved 15-year-old twin grandsons, who split their time between their own mother's home and the house my mother lives in.

My mother does not just preach about faith and healing, she lives it. Her example serves to give all of us a goal. Four out of her five children are college graduates. This woman, who once dropped out of high school, earned her associate's degree at forty-four and her bachelor's degree at the age of forty-eight, and just prior to her sixtieth birthday completed her master's in social work.

Mom has faced and overcome many things in her life. But she sees them more as challenges to be overcome rather than paralyzing obstacles. She has come through as a result of her faith. We are thankful for her love, her resilience, and her example.

DEALING WITH DEMENTIA

Kathy Davis

As I walk into my mother's house, her eyes, which used to be so full of life, stare at me blankly. I begin to say, "Hi, Mama," but change my greeting to "Hello, Mozelle." My mother does not readily respond to "Mama," but she still recognizes her first name. Alzheimer's disease has torturously, inch by inch and step by step, taken my mother away from me. She really does not know me anymore. Her frail body is on death row, and only God knows when her sentence will be up. In the meantime, we make sure she eats and gets her fluids and makes it to the rest room in time.

I give big kudos to my youngest brother and older sisters, who are full-time caregivers for my mother. Mozelle is seventy-nine years old and behaves like a three- or four-year-old. Most families would have put their loved one in a nursing home by now (it has been over ten years), but my sisters are insistent that, as a family, we shoulder this responsibility.

I was the one who wanted to put Mozelle away and hide this shame from the world. I was newly remarried, and my children were still very young. I did not have time to "baby-sit" an adult, as I put it. Taking care of Mother was a constant battle. But my sister Gussie stated, "The only way Mother would go to a nursing home was over her dead body." At this point, I gave up. Gussie moved in with my mother and began a journey that none of us would ever forget.

My younger brother, who was unable to work at the time, had been living with Mother. He first noticed the changes in her and became alarmed. Mother, he said, would bounce back and forth between reality and fantasy. She began to see things that were not there; her paranoia was downright frightening. When we tried to convince her that it was all a part of her imagination, it made her angry. She was convinced she was being watched, and tried to cover every window in the house. The biggest problem we had with her were her wanderings.

It was a nightmare. That is the only way to describe the behavioral changes my mother has gone through. As the side of her brain she used most started disappearing, personalities we never knew existed came to light. There was the workaholic domestic, always sweeping and wiping and trying to cook. Then there was the runaway. This was the most dangerous personality of all, because in her mind she was never at home; she was always threatening to leave, and if you turned your back, she would. Mother had wandered off many times. We never knew what happened on many of her outings, but in each instance, she came back unharmed; a few times the police or someone in our extended church family would bring her home. But not knowing where she was, and the panic of searching, was one of the worst experiences we had to face.

Mozelle had been a quiet and reserved woman and a dedicated wife and mother. She loved to cook and clean; worrying about her children was her favorite pastime. She would gladly baby-sit her grandchildren and would call us every day, listen to our problems, and give us advice that we rarely heeded. I really loved my mother, but I also resented her for getting this disease. In my own limited understanding, I felt Mother was selfish to cause her children anxiety and stress by running away.

I brought up the possibility of nursing facilities again years later. Mother needed round-the-clock care and had to be watched to prevent her from running away. And my brother, who was her live-in caregiver most of the time, was getting burned out. But my sister didn't want to hear it. She knew that if we put Mother in a nursing home, her care could be compromised. We had heard about the abuse and neglect that went on in those places. My sister got that look on her face, and I reluctantly gave in.

If we had not found the Adult Day Care Center my mother attends, I believe our family might eventually have reconsidered that decision. Getting help with the daily supervision of our mother allowed my brother to regroup and get some much-needed time away from her. Occasionally all the siblings lend a hand as well. It has been a long ten years, but we have hung in there.

Mozelle is winding down now. She no longer tries to clean everything in sight and does not have enough energy to run away. Although these traits have lessened, we still have other obstacles to face. Dehydration, loss of appetite, and loss of control of some bodily functions are just a few of them.

We always knew that Mother was forgetful; it was a family joke. The words we said to her most often were "Now remember, don't forget!" We also learned that Alzheimer's disease can be hereditary. Now, the reality of being forgetful is no joke for any of Mozelle's children. The fear of becoming like my mother in my old age has made me look at life much differently. Each day scientists make great strides in the race to find a cure for this devastating disease, and I pray that they are successful in time for my family. I have already started hearing my children say, "Write this down, Mom," or the dreaded phrase "Now remember, don't forget!"

No one knows the length of time we have on this earth. Most people agree we want to live our lives with dignity and respect and to be as comfortable as possible. Our family has given these things to our mother. But in return she has given us much more. She has shown us how to be strong when it would have been much easier to give up. She has shown us that love can conquer all if you let it. I have grown in acceptance of the burden our family shares. Although my shoulders bear only a small portion, I have been made a better person for the experience.

The blank stare that I receive from Mozelle used to hold love and joy when I came to visit. That wonderful voice, so like my own, would call me "baby girl" and "Miss Kat" and ask me if I wanted something to eat or drink. Her biggest joy was always her large family, because she was an only child. I cannot say that I have always been there for Mozelle. But I want to let the world know that she has always been there for me, and she will always be with me in mind and spirit.

A MOTHER'S STORY

Paula Penn-Bradley

Over the past three and a half years, I have experienced a lot of personal pain. My husband and I separated after many years of marriage, and my son, my only child, was diagnosed with inoperable brain cancer. Everything happened so fast, and I was unprepared to deal with all of the loss. I knew that my marriage wasn't perfect, yet I was willing to work through whatever our issues were. I had supported my husband through his military career and I thought, naively, that we could make it through the hard times if we just worked together. When he walked out of our lives in August 1998 my whole world started to crumble apart. My son, who was seventeen years old, took me by the shoulders and told me no matter what happened to hold my head up, everything would be all right.

Paul was born March 29, 1981, and died June 22, 2001, at the age of twenty, after battling cancer for two years. It is truly his journey and wisdom that I share. The sadness that I feel is overwhelming, yet it is also where I find comfort in the early-morning hours or the dark of the night. Paul and I loved each other. Paul used to tell me that life with me was an adventure. You never knew on any given day what would happen or how we would adjust our lives to meet the needs of those around us. When he was diagnosed with cancer in May 1999, my heart broke. I was a substitute teacher and had just gone back to work after the summer break, so we didn't have much money. My husband was unable to assist us, and I worked as much as I could to make ends meet. The symptoms that Paul exhibited in the beginning were not significant; I thought his skin discoloration was due to a fungal infection. Months went by before we found out what was wrong. In March 1999, Paul was admitted to the local hospital the week before his eighteenth birthday. We were told there was no evidence of a brain tumor. They thought he had a neuromuscular disease. He was scheduled for an appointment at the University of North Carolina (UNC) medical center at Chapel Hill. Due to conflicts in

schedules, Paul was unable to be seen until May of 1999. The ophthal-
mologist who saw him, Dr. Cooper, told us that the original hospital had
missed the diagnosis and that there was in fact a tumor on Paul's brain.
Paul, a skater and basketball and football player, soon experienced physical changes that quickly became more pronounced. By the time Paul was
admitted to UNC in May, he had lost his sense of balance, had palsy in
his eyes, and was suffering other symptoms. During the summer of 1999,
Paul received thirty-one treatments of radiation. During his treatment,
without adequate finances and no other immediate family, my son and I
struggled along the best we could. I would bring him home from the hospital, make him comfortable, and leave to go to work. Meals were difficult because he could no longer hold plates or glasses without spilling the
contents. Yet Paul never complained. He focused on going back to school.
He told me that it was stupid to get this far and not finish. I arranged with
the school system for him to return and finish in the fall of 1999.

Throughout his last year of school, Paul received therapy to increase
his fine and gross motor skills and improve his speech, which had been
affected by the tumor and the radiation treatments. Paul was diligent in
working to complete the requirements necessary for graduation; he
attended school as much as he was physically able. He had an aide who
assisted him during the day. Some students would make it a point to have
lunch with him, and when it was time for his high school prom in May
2000, he had two dates instead of one. As the students got used to Paul's
condition, some who knew him before he became ill and some who did
not rallied around him in his fight against cancer. They helped us hold a
number of fund-raisers at different locations around the city we live in.
We held one on Mother's Day 2000 at Blockbuster Video on Ramsey
Street. Paul sat in his wheelchair holding a sign announcing the car wash,
and a couple of us began to wash cars. I would check on him in between
cars, and he listened to music. At the end of the day Paul said to me,
"Mom, only you would do this for me." He gave me a small bag with an
orchid that sits on my living room table to this day.

I would have done anything to give Paul the life he deserved and anything to take away the cancer that was robbing his life. Prayer was constant. Though I shed many tears, my talks with God helped to sustain us
throughout Paul's journey, to renew our faith for better tomorrows. Paul

kept saying that God must have something special in mind for us, and he did. There were no boundaries, no limits, nothing that could have stopped me from helping him meet his dreams and achieving his goals. His goal was to graduate; my goal was to save my son's life.

On June 1, 2000, Paul accomplished his goal, walking across the stage using a walker with the assistance of an aide to receive his high school diploma. He received a standing ovation from his peers and their families in a coliseum of people. The courage that it took Paul to complete that journey is not one that I take for granted; God helped Paul discover his faith and his purpose in life. By his desire to complete what he started, he set examples for all of us to follow and honor in our lives. He never gave up; he just kept forging ahead. He never cried out for the loss of friends who deserted him because of his declining physical abilities; he found compassion in others where there had been little for him.

On January 5, 2001, Paul was diagnosed with a secondary tumor located in the frontal lobe of his brain. It was a glioblastoma, the fastest-growing kind of tumor. It was the worst diagnosis Paul could have received. He had surgery on February 7, 2001. I remember walking into his room in the intensive care unit after they had told us they could not wake him from the anesthesia and that they had tried all they could. They had not tried the love of a mother for her son; as soon as I spoke his name and touched him, he raised his finger in response. He had been unable to speak since October, and so we had created a different form of communication between the two of us. He worked so hard to live a while longer, so that I would have time to accept his death. He spent the next two months in the hospital and came home on my birthday, March 28. He turned twenty the following day.

As a result of complications from the surgery, Paul needed nursing staff sixteen hours a day. The other eight hours I was with him. My day was not complete until he was settled in and all the machines around him were monitoring him correctly. Dr. Moore from Pitt County Memorial Hospital in Greenville, North Carolina, assisted us in getting the necessary services in my home so that we could be together. I would be forever grateful to his kindness and understanding. Paul's dad was able to come out to visit him twice before he passed. Our last journey together was a trip to my younger sister's house in Virginia the week before he passed. It was the best of times for all of us. He was peaceful and knew he was loved. Darlene, his day nurse, accompanied us and drove the van through the Blue Ridge Mountains. We took time to smell the flowers. I will forever remember the feel of his skin beneath mine as I kissed his cheek or wiped the sweat from his brow. I was always hugging him and telling him how much I loved him.

Yet I can never say that I was prepared for the day that he died or express how I have felt since then. There is so much emptiness in my life; there are times when the sadness is so deep that each breath is filled with loss. Yet, in my heart, I know that Paul lives on through all of this.

GAINING FROM OUR LOSS

Ray Thomason

Many times people associate the effects of love with some sort of telltale sign or earth-shattering event. The world somehow slows down while music swirls or some smooth-voiced singer croons the soundtrack of your moment just as every detail of that instant falls in line with perfect precision. Ideally, that's how things are supposed to flow. In reality, life throws an equation at you that can be neither solved nor studied for. A man will do his best to fix this minor imperfection in life. After all, that's what men do—fix things, solve problems, and move on, right? Not quite. A man may have thought an emotional situation was under control only to find it still current and, in turn, controlling him. It's in these situations where the power of devotion is truly discovered and felt. It was how I discovered just how infinite and far-reaching that power is.

I'll never forget the total shock I felt in November 2000 when I heard my wife's panicked screams. At the end of her first trimester, she had just miscarried. I did what I could for her and got her ready for the paramedics' arrival. That's when the finality of what just happened hit me. We weren't going to be parents any longer. All the joy I had felt at the discovery of her pregnancy was taken away in an instant, and the vacuum left from its departure was the cruelest and worst feeling the mind could ever endure. But I couldn't dwell on that fact. My wife needed me to be strong for her. As much as I was suffering, she surely must have been close to total devastation, and my coming apart at the seams wouldn't do the both of us any good. The following days would give me a glimpse of just how mighty devotion is.

The days spent in the Women's Health Center would be some of the longest and most wrenching days either one of us had ever experienced up to that point in our lives. I sat by my wife's side, holding her hand, as the nurses and technicians drew blood and stuck several IV needles into her. I watched through my tears as the remains of the fetus were removed from her, wishing I could take her place in the receipt of pain. All I could do was *watch*, to be nothing more than a spectator wanting to fix what was harming my wife. To my amazement, though, she was thinking of me. She would ask if I was all right; can you believe that? Within a period of forty-eight hours she had lost a child and undergone minor surgery, and she still was more concerned about my well-being. How much love can a person have for another in order to fight through those circumstances and have enough energy to try to provide comfort to someone else? I had no choice but to be strong for her no matter how tired or heartbroken I was. She provided living proof of the strength love gives to those during their most desperate moments.

The day finally came for her to be discharged from the hospital, and I was happy to have her home even though home would be an alien place. We spent the next few days, weeks, and months dealing with the aftermath of the loss coupled with learning how to deal with one another during that period of adjustment. We stumbled through it, without a doubt. She, being such a strong woman, never had to rely totally on someone as far as her emotional needs went, but for the first few days she had to lean on me. At that time, we'd been together eleven years and married for six. During this eleven-year period she had never had to use me to prop herself up the way she did then. Without a doubt, it was scary. I was shown another facet of love coupled with trust that I hadn't experienced up to that point in time.

Once she found her balance again, she returned to work in an effort to gain some "normalcy" in life once more. I did the same, hoping to stay busy so I wouldn't go insane thinking about the cruelty of our experience. I returned to work with individuals who had children but didn't appreciate the glory of their situation, so eventually work wound up reminding me more of the irony of life. We were trying so hard to have our first child, while many of my coworkers minimized the blessings they possessed. At least my wife had the support of colleagues who had gone through similar experiences. They could tell when she was hurting and would console her at that time. I just muddled through my suffering and prayed constantly.

With time we moved on. That's all that we could do, considering the circumstances. People don't ever get over this sort of thing; they either move on or suffer for the rest of their lives. I never knew just how much love could be generated for someone that I'd never met.

Time doesn't heal all wounds; rather, it gives a person the skill to live with the damage inflicted by whatever caused the harm in the first place. Such was the case with us. We definitely grew closer to one another instead of letting our loss pull us apart. Ironically, nine months passed before we decided to try again to start a family. Careerwise, I'd been promoted and my income could handle the addition to the family, so my wife didn't have to work. We were blessed once again late in the summer of 2001, and we were so happy to be given another chance to help bring life into the world. Things fell into place for me professionally and personally like a new beginning. Naturally, we were cautiously optimistic, given what we'd gone through, but the joy of possibly being parents once more helped balance out whatever concerns would creep into our heads. I stayed in prayer instead of worrying about circumstances beyond our span of control. Once the first trimester passed successfully, we just knew everything would turn out to be fine.

We'd decided to wait and see what gender our baby would be. But my wife told me one day she had dreamed that our child would be a boy. I was kind of annoyed that she'd brought the subject up, and I snapped back, "Why don't we just go ahead and find out what the baby will be?" She looked at me as though I'd gone crazy and had lost some common sense. Maybe I had, but I just didn't want to get into discussing whether the baby was a boy or girl. All I wanted was a healthy child. I didn't want to allow myself to fall into a comfort zone only to be let down by some unforeseen event. I jumped into the shower feeling bad about how I had just snapped at my wife. Minutes later she pounded on the door and alarmingly yelled, "We gotta go!" I distinctly remember saying, "Oh, no!"

Her water had broken! She was in the middle of her fourth month of pregnancy and her water had broken. She stayed calm while I raced around to get dressed and grab everything that might be needed at the hospital. I was in a state of disbelief because we had just been to the doctor that Wednesday, and it was only Friday. We got to the hospital and shortly thereafter found ourselves in the maternity ward. My wife held it together until we were left alone in the exam room, and once again I became a spectator to events found in my nightmares. The doctor who had seen my wife a few days before stopped by, and I could tell he felt more than terrible. The previous Wednesday a mix-up in scheduling had meant that my wife saw this doctor, who didn't specialize in high-risk pregnancy. Usually in such pregnancies an ultrasound is performed to monitor the baby for any indications of trouble. Had this been done, perhaps we would have seen signs of trouble. Only God knows why events occurred as they did.

More doctors stopped by and eventually gave us their diagnosis of the situation. Our baby didn't deliver, but was still inside the womb without the amniotic fluid. It was explained that my wife could either go home and wait for the inevitable or be admitted to the hospital in order to attempt to carry closer to term. To us, there was still hope. We prepared to make the hospital our second home for the next few months. This was no small feat, being that my wife despises hospitals, but for the sake of the child, she would stay for years if it would make the difference.

My wife told me that in spite of all that passed during those terrifying hours on January 4, 2002, she had an overwhelming feeling that all would be fine. That, in itself, calmed me some, because this hadn't been the case during her first pregnancy. I was so proud of the strength she displayed and the determination shown in a moment where she had every right to fear for the worst. She was my hero. I prayed that the Lord would be merciful enough to grant her courage and strength to endure whatever lay ahead. I prayed for strength for our child to hold on until he could be treated.

I was still on holiday break from work, so I was able to stay at my wife's side for the first few nights. Each time the nurse would come to check the baby's heartbeat in the early-morning hours I'd wake from my troubled sleep to listen. The heartbeat was good and strong and offered hope in a situation that otherwise was nonstop despair. Once I returned to work after the Christmas break, I settled into a routine of spending the evening at her side in the hospital and leaving late at night to get ready for work the next day. I was willing to hold this routine until her ninth month, just so I could be there with her every step of the way. We both accepted the situation as a part of our life that had to be dealt with. After all, our child hadn't given up on us; he was fighting for life, and we would be there for him no matter what it would take. I felt horrible inside, but I leaned on my faith to get us through that period.

The evening of January 9, 2002, I returned to the hospital from an errand to find my wife's hospital room empty. Faith was all I had in this world to deal with what I knew had happened while I was away for those hours.

I asked someone at the nursing station where my wife had been moved to. I was guided into some sort of room that looked like a midway point for women about to deliver. I found my wife there, alone, with tracks of tears on her face. While I was away, the routine check of the baby's heartbeat revealed that his heart had stopped. We were to endure the loss of another child within a year. I felt weak, angry, confused, and hurt, and there were other emotions too numerous to put into words. Worst of all, I hadn't been there at the exact moment she'd found out our child was no longer living.

We were moved to a birthing room (an ironic place given our situation) in order to prepare for the stillbirth of our baby. Hours passed as we waited for the labor to complete what is normally a joyous celebration of life. During that time I witnessed a mother's agony of losing a child. I saw my wife, full of pain, throw a tantrum, asking, "Why? Why?" It was so heartbreaking to see her go through such hell, and I was powerless. Throughout the evening I made the phone calls no human being wants to make, to family and work to let them know of the situation. Early on the morning of January 10, 2002, I simultaneously witnessed the birth and loss of our baby boy, Malcolm David.

Our first experience of losing a child did nothing to prepare us for the shock of the circumstances following the loss of our second. Our first child was so early in development, we didn't have much of a choice but to allow the hospital to destroy the remains after the autopsy. With our second experience we were able to say good-bye to our son. The nurse asked if we wanted to visit with the baby one last time, and I immediately answered yes. I at least wanted to hold our son, touch his fragile skin, and look for the physical features telling us he was ours. My wife at first didn't want to deal with the power of that situation, so she declined. She eventually changed her mind later that morning.

When the time came for us to see our baby, I experienced the most amazing feeling ever felt in my life—I felt love *from* our baby boy. I know his spirit wasn't in his body, but I felt love from his soul touching mine! His broken body was so tiny but still perfect in my eyes. I saw the motherly love my wife had for this child, and I knew that the bond they had shared for the brief period of time he was with us was as real as any connection two human beings, even ones who'd known each other for years, could ever make. We were indeed parents this time—the feelings inside our hearts told us such.

I never thought I'd have to bury a child at the age of thirty; nevertheless, there we were, making burial arrangements. It was a surreal experience. The days preparing for the interment were hellish for my wife. Again she was left empty, feeling as though the rug had been yanked from underneath her. A man will never understand the bond a mother and child make from the womb—or in life, for that matter—and I witnessed how true this is. She told me how much she missed him, how she had been getting used to being pregnant without any worries. She described how alone she felt when she showered and how she didn't want to leave him alone at the funeral home, as if she were failing him again. She wanted her baby, our baby, back!

We traveled to South Carolina to have Malcolm buried near family. My work has me constantly relocating, and we wanted someone to be able to watch over his grave site. We didn't have a traditional service with a long procession and such; we just wanted to lay our boy to rest. He'd been through enough, and we wanted a simple, respectful gathering for our child.

My parents, brother, and grandmother attended and helped us shed tears. My father quoted scripture, and I said some words to express how much Malcolm would be missed even though we had known him for an instant. As I was speaking, something happened that I didn't quite know how to interpret. The wind picked up and swept throughout the cemetery, indicating a storm was moving in, yet storm clouds never came. It continued after I finished speaking and as long as my wife and I stood over Malcolm's grave, shedding tears. When we finally brought ourselves to leave our baby, the wind calmed and finally stopped. My grandmother feels it was Malcolm's spirit letting us know he was cared for, loved, and in a glorious place now. Maybe he was trying to comfort us and wipe away all the tears with the wind. I don't know. I didn't feel better, so to speak, but I did feel some comfort.

Recently, my wife asked if I ever think of Malcolm. I told her I thought of him all the time. I wake up thinking of him and go to sleep thinking of him. I see parents with their children and think about what could have been. It hurts, but I wouldn't change anything that's happened. That little boy showed me what true love is and how infectious it can be. He brought out my wife's maternal devotion, so that I could at least comprehend what a mother truly goes through. I'm a blessed man to have witnessed such events. The residue of his love still lingers on with us, and always will. He has gained from our loss, and so have we—much more than anyone will ever know!

GETTING OVER GRANDDADDY

Tamela Handie-Tilford

I experienced the power of Black love at a young age from my paternal grandfather, the late Reverend Edgar Douglas Handie Sr. Granddaddy, as I called him, lived in Eudora, Arkansas, where he resided all of his life. As is customary in the South, he pastored several churches simultaneously; at the time of his death, he still presided over two churches. I was crazy about my granddaddy, and most everyone else was too. He was respected and admired in the community, and volunteered a lot of his spare time to fight for the rights of African Americans and help ensure that Eudora's children received a quality education. Charismatic, he had the ability to inspire people through his words. Though he had only a grade-school education, you'd never know it by listening to him. He was a dynamic speaker who, through God's grace, had been able to master the English language at the level of a college graduate. He was indeed called to preach.

Granddaddy had smooth, chocolate brown skin and a bald head. He was about 5´10˝ and the most physically fit older man I've ever seen. His waist was a perfect thirty-two inches. He wore suits every day of his life, whether he was going to church or not. I don't ever remember seeing Granddaddy wearing casual clothes, other than the pajamas he wore to bed every night.

Granddaddy showered me with love and affection. Although my family lived in Kansas City, we would make frequent trips to Eudora during the summers and holidays. I looked forward to those visits because Granddaddy was my hero. He would stand in the pulpit and deliver the most powerful, high-spirited sermons that I'd ever heard. He'd have the congregation falling out like flies. As if his good preaching weren't enough, he'd top it off by singing a gospel song toward the end of every service. Those who knew him would say, "If his preaching don't get you, his singing will." I admired the way he encouraged and inspired people to keep God first in their lives just by saying a few simple yet meaningful words. Granddaddy's deep affection for the Lord was contagious, and I caught it at an early age.

It all started when Granddaddy was invited to Kansas City to do a revival at a local church. He often received invitations to visit churches across the United States. This particular church service was one that I will never forget. It was Friday night, the last night of the revival, and members of the church had enjoyed four full nights of Granddaddy's preaching. They were anxious to receive one last dose of his gospel medicine. Needless to say, he literally turned the church out. Though I was only seven, I found myself feeling the spirit of the Holy Ghost. When Granddaddy opened the doors of the church, I got up and walked to the front of the sanctuary and stood in front of him. I still remember the smile on his face when I made the decision to bring God into my life. Not once did he question whether I understood what I was doing or not. The truth is, though I was only seven, I had felt His presence within me years before that. I had been born again, and Granddaddy knew it. He placed his hands on my shoulders and continued to invite others to give their lives to the Lord. Since my parents and I didn't have a church home, they decided to let Granddaddy baptize me when we returned two weeks later to his church in Mer Rouge, Louisiana.

As I got older, my visits to Eudora became less frequent. I was suffering from those terrible teenage years when your body is changing and you're thinking about the opposite sex. With all that going on, visiting Arkansas wasn't as important as it was before. I assumed that Granddaddy would be around forever to love me, guide me, and keep me grounded spiritually. Unfortunately, that wasn't the case.

Granddaddy developed cancer in 1996. I hadn't seen him in about eleven years. At that time, I was dating a man whom I was seriously thinking of marrying. Granddaddy had married my parents, and I told them that if I ever got married, I wanted him to perform the ceremony. My mother warned me that he probably wouldn't be around long enough to marry me. She and my father had been to visit him over Thanksgiving that year, and his appearance had changed dramatically. He'd lost quite a bit of weight. But I knew how tough and resilient he was. After all, he could walk on water, couldn't he?

On his birthday in December 1996, I talked to Granddaddy briefly over the phone. He sounded weak, but his speech was clear and his enunciation as strong as ever. I wished him a happy birthday and told him I loved him and that I was coming to see him in February.

On February 13, I mailed Granddaddy a Valentine's card. I reminded him in the card that I would be there in two weeks to visit him. The day after Valentine's Day, while visiting with my boyfriend at his apartment, I received a call from my mother. She told me my father wanted to talk to me. I sensed that something was wrong. I asked her if something had happened to Granddaddy. She said no and handed the telephone to my dad. When my dad got on the phone, I received the worst news imaginable. I can still hear his words ringing in my ears, five years later: "Daddy passed away." I bent over, still holding the phone to my ear, crying like a baby. My mom then got back on the phone, and I managed to ask her when it happened. "Yesterday," she replied. "Yesterday? Why didn't you tell me?" I asked. "I didn't want to spoil your Valentine's Day," she said. I was furious. Here I was out celebrating Valentine's Day when my grand-daddy was dead. I felt horrible for dishonoring him like that. I cried the rest of that evening and throughout the night. The next few days were hell. I wanted to die. I felt so guilty for not spending more time with him. I would've done anything to bring him back.

Five days later, we left for Eudora to attend Granddaddy's funeral. I saw him in the funeral home. The despair I felt when I initially found out that Granddaddy passed away was nothing compared to what I felt over the next three days. I didn't want to move, eat, or think. Dad was taking Granddaddy's death hard as well, and my mom had to comfort him. I've never cried so long and so hard in my life.

When I got back home to Kansas City, my grief continued. Dad was starting to heal slowly, but I was getting worse and worse as each day passed. I was the kind of person who liked to laugh and have fun, but that person was gone. I wouldn't wear makeup or pay attention to my groom-ing or what I was wearing. Music was something that I always enjoyed, particularly gospel music, but I couldn't even listen to certain songs because they would make me start crying. All I wanted was to wallow in my grief.

Not only did my grief affect my outer appearance, it affected my atti-tude. I became cynical about everything in my life and stayed that way for almost four years. It drove my mother nuts. No matter what encouraging words she or anyone else tried to offer, I would shoot them down.

One day, finally, a ray of light peeked through. I liked to watch Dr. Phil McGraw on *Oprah*. This particular day, Dr. McGraw was talking to a woman named Joanne who had been stuck in grief since the murder of her daughter almost ten years before. She was living every day as if it was the day her daughter died. I could identify with her story, because although Granddaddy had passed almost two years before, it was like yesterday to me. I relived his death every day. But several things that Dr. Phil said to Joanne that day caused a lightbulb to go off in my head. He asked, "Do you think your daughter would want you to feel pain each and every day for the rest of your life?" Joanne's eyes lit up and she responded, "No." I knew that Granddaddy wouldn't want me to allow my grief to keep me from living the life God intended for me, either. Next Dr. Phil said, "Your daughter lived for eighteen vibrant years, yet you focus on that one day, the day that she died." That statement was a turning point for me. Granddaddy had been eighty-two years old when he died, and he'd preached for over sixty years. I began to think about the many lives he touched through his ministry and how he'd lived life with passion, zest, and vigor. I had been doing exactly what Joanne was doing, focusing on the day that Granddaddy died instead of cherishing the wonderful life that he'd lived. Dr. Phil said that moving on with your life is not dishonoring your loved one's memory. He told Joanne to repeat out loud, "Lori, I love you, but I have to let you go." Joanne began to weep. I was crying right along with her, saying, "Granddaddy, I love you, but I have to let you go." I was able to let go of the grief that I had been carrying on my shoulders day after day. Unfortunately, though, my negative attitude still remained.

My mother continued to pray for me. It took another three years, but her prayers were finally answered. I was on the Internet one day and spotted an offer to attend a five-day seminar hosted by the person who had helped me to move forward with my life three years earlier, Dr. Phil McGraw. The notice said that you had to be willing to participate in intensive exercises conducted by Dr. McGraw for five days and have your story televised. In order to be considered, you had to answer a few questions about your life and submit them via e-mail. I immediately answered the questions and clicked the send button with my mouse. I loved Dr. Phil and would welcome an opportunity to let him help me. Instead of thinking, as I normally did, that I wouldn't be considered, I turned it over to the Lord. Two weeks later, I got a call from a producer of the show saying that I was one of forty-two people chosen to attend the five-day class. It was a once-in-a-lifetime opportunity, and I wasn't about to pass it up. My mom was excited, because she too was a fan of Dr. Phil's. I told my parents and friends before I left for Chicago that I was going to come back a better person. Little did I know I would come back born again!

On the first day of class, I realized how fortunate the forty-two of us were to be there. Dr. Phil had actually handpicked each of us out of fifteen thousand applicants. As Dr. Phil said, "It's no accident that you're here.

This is your chance to get it right. Not many people get a second chance, but you do." I knew it was no accident; God wanted me to be there.

During those five days of grueling mental, verbal, and written exercises, I finally was able to rid my life of the negativity that was killing my spirit and reconnect with my spiritual side once again—the spirituality that my granddaddy had introduced me to as a young child. On the last day, as we each shared our progress, I stood up and thanked God and Dr. Phil for changing my life. Tears came to my eyes as I mentioned to my classmates that I knew my granddaddy was proud of me. I could feel his spirit smiling down on me. I left Chicago feeling spiritually grounded and ready to begin living again.

Not Just a Statistic

Beverly Joan Hughley

During the summer of 1986, a letter was mailed to each and every address in the United States from the office of the then surgeon general, C. Everett Koop. The letter spoke of a new disease that had been identified in America, a terrifying new virus that was responsible for the deaths of thousands of individuals: AIDS. It appeared that those most affected were gays and hemophiliacs. As I sat at my kitchen table reading this alarming information, I remember breathing a sigh of relief. My close friends and family members were all married or in committed monogamous relationships, as was I. My baby sister, Karen, the one with a light smattering of freckles on her face and a head of thick, wavy hair, had gotten married earlier that year and was now pregnant with her first child. This new disease that was ravaging America was apparently no threat to us, based on the statistics and demographics described in the letter.

As it turns out, I was wrong. Within ten years, this new plague would visit my inner circle. In fact, April 28, 2002, will be the fifth anniversary of my sister's death from AIDS. Her name was Karen Elise Perkins, and she was a thirty-eight-year-old college-educated professional woman. She was married and the mother of a young daughter.

Karen was a dedicated and proud member of Zeta Phi Beta of south Florida. She was a gentle soul who loved working with arts and crafts and tending to the small garden in the front yard of her home. She was not promiscuous, nor a drug user. In fact, she married the first and only man she ever dated. He turned out to be the last one as well, for he, in fact, was the source of her infection. He died in 1995 of what we all thought was diabetes, since he had been diagnosed as diabetic several years earlier.

Considering the circumstances of my sister's death, it would be easy to hate my brother-in-law. There is ample evidence that he knew he was infected. However, he didn't disclose this information to his wife, my sister. We discovered a year after his death, when my sister had already been diagnosed with AIDS, that several people knew of his HIV status but chose not to disclose this information to the one who needed it most. My anger and pain at his betrayal were immense, although they have diminished over the years. I still feel hurt and bewildered by his actions.

My sister's husband had been our next-door neighbor; we all grew up together. As kids, my sister and I helped him fold newspapers for his paper route. His parents and ours were very close friends. Our mother, in fact, was his first-grade teacher. People occasionally ask me if I've forgiven him, and I doubt that I ever will. His deception ripped the hearts out of our collective chests, leaving my then ten-year-old niece with a gaping wound that would never completely heal. My niece used to roam the aisles at arts-and-craft stores with her mother and then come home and design matching T-shirts to wear the following day to school. She had her own garden tools next to her mother's. The evening after her mother's funeral, she screamed that she wanted to die too so that she could be with her mother.

All of us have suffered tremendously, but none more than she. At ten, she knew that her mother was very sick, but she felt in her heart that her mom would get better and things would get back to normal. My sister didn't have the heart to tell her daughter the truth, and she would not let me do it for her either.

My niece is now fifteen years old, and her bedroom walls are plastered with posters of SpongeBob SquarePants, Tupac, and that finely chiseled Shemar Moore. She looks just like her mom and is blessed with many of the same endearing qualities. My sister continues to live through her.

My father and I share custody of my niece, and we listen with pride when she talks about getting her first car (which she's hoping for next year) and going to college. She is still terribly wounded. Nonetheless, she is a survivor. She often talks about her mother; of how much fun they had and how much she misses her. Each time she does, my heart breaks. Sometimes the two of us will look at pictures of her mother. Although it is hard to do this, it helps us to heal.

As this next anniversary of my sister's death approaches, I am reminded of the grace and dignity she exhibited. I am reminded of the many indignities that Karen suffered because of her illness: the numerous hospitalizations and doctor's visits; the calls to my mother from so-called professional people; the innuendo and gossip that ran like an out-of-control brush fire throughout our community. And finally, the ignorance and insensitivity displayed by "concerned" individuals who probably should have checked the status of their own health before commenting on my sister's.

In spite of everything, Karen rarely complained. Expressions of anger and bitterness were rare indeed, although she was certainly entitled to express these things. She never complained, even when her long, thick, wavy hair began to fall out, or when she had to endure painful injections directly into her eyes in an attempt to save her eyesight. She so desperately wanted to live! I felt as if our small family was besieged from all sides. But we closed ranks and hunkered down for the battle for her life.

When I think about Karen, I remember the courageous way she played the hand that life had dealt her. Her graciousness, quiet strength, and optimism epitomized true class in the face of a battle that she ultimately couldn't win.

Karen Elise Perkins was not just a statistic but a daughter, mother, sister, wife, and friend who was much loved, respected, and adored. Even five years later, it has been very difficult for me to write all of this down. But I made a promise to myself at my sister's grave site that I would one day tell her story.

Grief is a road that sometimes has no ending. I'm still not over her death and, honestly, I don't know if I will ever be. But with the passage of time, I find that I laugh more and cry less, thanks to her memory.

THE REBIRTH OF WILLIAM

Celeste Bateman

For several years, conversations with my brother, William, had been few and far between. For one thing, I didn't live at home, as he and my sister, Felicia, did. But also, if William had been drinking, which he did a lot during that time, I didn't have the tolerance to engage in lengthy discussions of any sort with him. William got on my nerves. At some point in our lives, I allowed a gap in our friendship (and siblingship, for that matter) to grow almost beyond repair. But the last two weeks of Billy's life and those two weeks in mine were a pivotal point in time for both of us.

I was rushing like a fool that Saturday to get to New Brunswick, where I had been working part time at a theater. Billy followed me around like a puppy dog as I frantically threw together some lunch to take with me. I knew he wanted to talk. I noticed he had made a lot of progress in cutting down on his drinking and was making an effort to get his program together. His skin was clear and his eyes were bright. This time when he spoke, I listened. Something told me I had to.

He talked about a job he was in line for in North Carolina. He said if he got the job, the company would relocate him and his girlfriend. He told me how anxious he was about finding a boarder for his apartment so he wouldn't leave the responsibility on my aunt Bennie, his landlady.

She'd been very tolerant of his falling behind with the rent, and I could see in his eyes that he didn't want to put any more hardship on her, not after she'd put up with him for so long.

I always knew William would die young. Felicia and I often discussed it, even tried to prepare ourselves for it. From the time he reached puberty up until age twenty or so, Billy was almost always in trouble.

Billy and I were extremely close as children. When Billy reached adolescence, we began to drift apart. Suddenly, having two young sisters straggling behind him wasn't the answer for him.

An adolescent male growing up on the streets of Newark, New Jersey, in the seventies, with no father around, was an invitation for trouble. The street became his school, peers and pushers his teachers, and a police record his diploma. Once Billy got to high school, the proverbial shit hit the fan. He teamed up with his best friend, Alvie (who died in 1980), to get kicked out of two of the best boys' Catholic schools in Newark. Mom put Billy in Weequahic High School, where he dropped out a few months before graduation. Despite his Catholic school background (he had been an altar boy as a child) and good upbringing, Billy hit the streets. He was into everything from petty larceny to grand theft auto.

William had a passion for cars but couldn't drive a lick! He once stole my father's 1977 classic Mark V and ran smack into an East Orange police station.

Trouble came to Billy; he didn't have to go looking for it. If it wasn't the wrong time or the wrong place, it was the wrong crowd. Most of his friends, like himself, were brought up in good Catholic homes, and they were the craziest bunch of hellions ever to graduate from Blessed Sacrament Grammar School. They weren't *bad* per se, just boys gone wayward. They did things like jump out of the second-floor kitchen window at our house on Hedden Terrace for recreation and sniff glue for intoxication. They were all handsome and popular in the neighborhood. They were not out bustin' heads, carjacking, or robbing banks—just having what they thought was good, wholesome fun. Aaron and Lionel are the only living members of that gang now.

At age twenty-one, Billy went to jail on an armed robbery charge. He had a beef with the manager of a local movie theater where he had been employed and decided to rip off the box office. He was allegedly armed with a knife, although Billy never would have used it; he never hurt any-one unless it was in self-defense.

Eight police cars came to the house in the middle of the night and dragged Billy down the back stairs and into a patrol car. Of course, they beat him. Billy knew his luck had run out. The judge said that he had to put Billy away before he hurt somebody or hurt himself.

The eighteen months William spent in a correctional facility in south Jersey did him a world of good. I think deep down inside William *wanted* to be put away. In fact, one time he went to a police station and asked to be put away, to be taken out of society before he did irreparable damage to himself or someone else. The judge who sentenced him to Bordentown had the foresight to know that this kid could be saved but that he needed the jolt of incarceration to bring him around.

That Saturday, May 20, 1983, I received a call at work from my mother, who was inviting me to Billy's apartment for a celebratory dinner. He had just been accepted for the training program with IBM and would be relocating to North Carolina. Feeling a bit down, I begged off.

When the phone rang again, it was Mom calling, this time to tell me that the third-floor apartment—Billy's apartment—was on fire, and as far as she knew, he was up there. Billy had been in and out of many scrapes during his young life. He had been hit by a car at sixteen, slashed with a machete at twenty, beaten by the cops, jailed, and injured in car acci-dents. But in my gut, I knew he would not survive this one.

I arrived at the house about 5 P.M. The block was backed up to the corner with fire trucks. Felicia, my mother, and Aunt Bennie arrived as well. His girlfriend was standing outside looking crazy and wild. They had just taken William away in the ambulance. Someone from the Red Cross stuck a business card in my hand, and a man from the Newark Fire Department stood in front of me moving his lips while my eyes frantically scanned the scene for some sign that my brother was all right.

A hundred people stood around watching us as we returned to our cars to make that trek to University Hospital. I arrived at the emergency room first. My brother was nowhere in sight, and the nurse behind the desk asked me what seemed like a thousand stupid questions about who I was and my relationship to the patient. She told me to go to a private waiting room, where a doctor would meet with me and my family. My mother and sister arrived moments later.

The doctor marched in with a nurse trailing behind him. They settled against a piece of furniture. Three beats . . . and the news was delivered. My brother had died of smoke inhalation. Two beats later, I was screaming. My mother must have missed a beat in there somewhere, because she didn't seem to know what was happening. She didn't know why her older daughter was screaming hysterically nor why her younger one stared at her blankly.

There had to be a mistake. My brother could not be dead. He could not have died the day he had gotten that long-awaited job. Tired from working on a neighbor's house, he'd put a pan on the stove to prepare a celebratory meal for his family, collapsed on his bed, and, from all the evidence, fell fast asleep.

Pausing at the door, the doctor asked if we wanted to see William. My mother bravely followed him to the room where he lay. Felicia and I were not up to it. When Mom returned, she said William looked peaceful, his face slightly seared by the fire. Her face was strangely luminous, her manner serene and resigned.

Those next few days before the funeral were trying. Felicia and I lived off vodka and orange juice, and I lost a considerable amount of weight. I'll never forget the scene at the cemetery and the sound of the vault when it clicked shut, sealing my brother's casket from the moisture and earth. A volume in our life as a family had come to a close.

Through it all, we remained faithful and positive. We tried to view William's death not as an ending but as a rebirth. We *celebrated* his journey home to the Father. The world is too cruel for some people. Some cannot bounce back from the blows life deals. At times I considered William weak. But he wasn't weak; he was sensitive and vulnerable. The world is too wild for people like him.

It has now been nineteen years since William's death. He communicates with me and I with him on a spiritual level. He watches over me and my sons. I know he's there, and that gives me comfort. It has helped me to heal in more ways than I can describe.

THE ACCIDENT

Elnora Massey

I was lying in bed one night in June of 1994, somewhere between consciousness and sleep, for it had been a tedious day at work. My youngest
daughter, Crystal, was already asleep; Joanna, our middle child, was talking on the telephone with her friends. Wendell, my son, was on his way
to pick up his father from his night job, or so I thought. This was a difficult time for us in the transportation arena. We were all using the same
car. My van had been stolen, my husband's car was in the shop for repairs,
and Wendell's car was servicing everyone's needs. This is how the routine
went: Wendell would take me downtown to work at eight o'clock in the
morning. Jim would drive the car back downtown at four o'clock in the
afternoon and leave it in the parking lot near the building in which I
worked. At that point, he walked over a few blocks to his night job, and
I drove the car home at four-thirty. When I got home that particular day,
Wendell was on his way out the door to pick up his friends, Jason Duval
and Terrence Williams, for work. They had been working for only a few
weeks. Wendell had just completed his first year at the University of
Florida in Gainesville, and he and Jason and Terrence had a summer job
doing customer service for a weed-control company.

My daughter Joanna came running into my bedroom that night shout-
ing, "Mom, Wendell has been in a bad car accident. University Hospital
trauma is on the line." My mind barely comprehended what she was trying to tell me. My heart started to race. The trauma nurse told me he was
critical and I should come right away. As I hung up the telephone, I felt
dizzy and the bed began to twirl. This could not be happening. I called my
husband and told him what happened. I wondered then where Wendell
had been when this happened. He must have been on Interstate 10 on his
way to get his father from work. As I was going out the door to my neighbor's house, I realized that the girls should not be left alone, so I called a

friend, explained what happened, and asked if she would come and stay with the girls.

When my dear friend Barbara and I arrived at the hospital, she took that long slow walk with me inside. She realized just how frightened I was. We found the information center and were directed to the family waiting room for the trauma center. Wendell was in one of the best places he could be—the trauma center at what is now Shands Hospital in Jacksonville is one of the best in the country. My husband and his friend arrived at the hospital soon after. We all just sat and waited for the doctor to come and talk to us. As I sat there waiting, my stomach was sick with pure fear. I had so many questions running through my mind. Were Jason and Terrence with him? If so, were they alive? Was my son going to die?

The doctor finally came into the waiting room. She explained that Wendell had sustained a serious brain injury and that they were working to keep the swelling to a minimum. He also had a badly burned leg, a broken jaw, a cracked spine, and several other minor injuries. The brain injury was the most severe. He was listed in critical condition. The doctor told us that the next twenty-four hours would be crucial. When I asked the doctor if anyone else had been involved in the accident, she said that there were two fatalities, but she had no other information. Wendell had been the only one brought to this particular trauma center; he had been life-flighted from the scene of the accident by helicopter. She said that the highway patrol would be coming to talk to us and we could find out more information then. Panic gripped me—where were the other boys? Barbara called Jason's mother to see if they had heard anything about Jason or Terrence. She said Jason was not home from work yet and was late. Barbara told her about Wendell and advised her to call the police and the other hospitals in the city. I did not know Terrence, who was sixteen. Jason was Wendell's best friend. They had been friends ever since elementary school. Terrence was the younger brother of one of their mutual friends.

Waiting is always hard. The fear of the unknown can be devastating.

The waiting room at the trauma center was beginning to fill with familiar faces. Jim consoled me, putting aside his pain for the moment. All I wanted was to be alone and talk to God about this. I wanted to beg

Him for my son's life. I went out into the hallway by myself. I began to call God's name, and I was as plain and straightforward as I could be. "God, you know that my son is hurt. You also know that he is a good son. Please, God, save him. Heal his body and mind! Lord, he is worth saving! I don't know if Jason and Terrence are alive, but I am asking for mercy for them and their families, too, Lord! Please hear my prayer."

As I finished, I noticed that the highway patrol officer had arrived. He told us Jason and Terrence were dead. The boys had been on their way back from work when the car broke down on the north side of the Buckman Bridge. They had been sitting in the car, probably waiting for a patrol car to come along to help them—a sign on the bridge instructs everyone to stay in their car if it is disabled. A large sweeper truck had come over the top of the bridge traveling at high speed and rear-ended Wendell's car. Jason had been in the backseat and was killed instantly. Terrence had been in the front seat on the passenger's side. A passerby and the driver of the sweeper pulled Wendell out immediately but hadn't been able to get the other boys out because the car exploded into flames. The car had already been on fire when they pulled Wendell out. I prayed that Terrence had been unconscious when the car exploded.

I wept so many times for the boys and their families. Later, I visited them and offered my sympathies. My prayers were a mixture of praise, thanksgiving, and pleas for mercy, comfort, and strength for the boys' families. The pain on their faces was almost unbearable to see.

As I looked around in the waiting room, I saw that our friends were there by our side, and they stayed with us all night, praying for us, giving us words of comfort and hugs. I did not even remember when most of them came in. Our friend Inez let us keep her car because we still did not have any transportation. Kim went home with me to see about the girls, fix food, and do whatever she could do. That night my faith in God grew in leaps and bounds. It became clear that Wendell would live. I knew that there would be more frustrating and hard times to come during Wendell's recovery period. I knew that we would spend long, tiring hours at the hospital. I knew that more tears would be shed and that there would be more fearful moments, but I felt a renewed conviction that God would see us through it.

In the days that followed, these same friends visited the hospital often, helped us with our daily tasks, and were always by our side. They were my confirmation of God's tremendous love for us. Our families too came from near and far during the next few weeks. We received mounds of telephone calls, cards, and visits from our coworkers and church members. Several ministers came by the hospital to pray for Wendell. I met two other mothers in the intensive care unit who had injured sons. I met a wife with a dying husband. We got to know each other and prayed for each other daily. One mother lost her son while in intensive care. Yet, during her grief, she continued to pray for Wendell. The young man who had helped pull Wendell out of the car called to see how he was doing. We do not know how he got our number.

My girls went to Jason's funeral. After the funeral, Mrs. Duval took time out from her unthinkable grief to send food to our house because she knew that we were at the hospital most of the time. Terrence's mother was from Alabama, so she took him back home to bury him. She, too, called to find out how Wendell was doing and wish him well. I saw so much unselfishness and people giving of themselves.

Wendell's recuperation period took about a year. I had to be the one to tell him that Jason and Terrence were killed in the accident, several months later. He cried all night and the next day. I cried with him, and so did his father and the girls. The girls were such a saving grace in our lives during that time. They were our lifeline. I clung to them for comfort, as they clung to me.

Wendell went back to the University of Florida in Gainesville after about a year. He graduated in December of 1998 with a bachelor of arts degree. Praise God! As I stood there watching him march down the aisle, I wept once again, but this time they were tears of joy.

I learned so many things during that time in my life. Some of them I knew already, but they were reinforced by the events that took place. I learned to pray not just for my children but for others' children as well, for our prayers should not be selfish. I learned how important it is to take time out in the midst of our trials and tribulations and bless someone else who is going through hard times. I learned that intercessory prayer fortified with our own individual prayers changes things. God answered the prayers of my friends, family, and loved ones during Wendell's healing period. His blessings were immeasurable. I learned to praise His name and give Him honor in all things. I learned that all of our trials and tribulations only make us strong and increase our faith when we put our trust in God.

One night after returning home from the hospital, I was so tired I fell across my bed and cried myself to sleep. I thought that I could not go on. My mother, Margaret Edwards, who had died a year earlier, came to me that night and sang in her lovely voice, "Be not dismayed, whate'er betide, God will take care of you. Beneath His wings of love abide, God will take care of you." I could hear her voice as clearly as if she were standing right before me. I woke up the next morning refreshed, ready to start the new day and face whatever challenges it held.

Wendell will be twenty-eight years old in July of this year. He has recently moved to Chicago. He had his first seizure just before he graduated from college. The doctors had told us that there was a strong possibility that this would happen because of his brain injury. He still encounters a few problems from time to time and takes medication every day. But thank God he is alive and well. He has a strong will and a determination to achieve all the things that he sets his mind to. I know that God is not through with him yet.

The Gift of Life

Susie M. Paige

A group of students stopped me as I crossed their campus and asked me to sign up with a national bone marrow registry. They explained that there is always a shortage of African American donors, the best match for a critically ill Black person. They hoped to change that by spreading the word about the program. I didn't have to think too deeply to understand the need. Some help can come from anyone. Other help we can only give each other. But I knew even then I would be called. And five years later, I was.

From the time the phone rang and a pleasant voice on the other end of the line said I was a preliminary match for a fifty-three-year-old man with acute leukemia, my donation experience had a divine feel to it. The coordinator at the hospital recognized my name. Her mother had been my Girl Scout leader. I hadn't seen the coordinator in at least twenty years. I walked into the lab for one of my many physical and psychological tests and realized the technician on duty was a member of my church. My veins are thin, but I was genetically compatible with my recipient.

Every day for a week at lunchtime I walked eight blocks from work to the hospital for additional tests and doses of drugs needed to get me ready to donate marrow. I was built up with medicine and iron supplements while all the marrow in my recipient's body was being destroyed. If we went through this giving and receiving procedure, there was a good chance he'd live. I could change my mind at any point in the process, because everything was voluntary. But if I backed out after all the marrow was destroyed in my recipient's bones, he'd die.

Due to the size of my veins, doctors arranged for a slightly nontraditional way to collect my cells, which took about six hours. The nurse assigned to me said I was the slowest patient she ever had. She rarely left my side, and we knew each other's life story by the end of the day.

I was swollen and leaning to the side when I was taken by wheelchair to a recovery area after the collection was finished. There was a man sitting nonchalantly in a chair with a small suitcase on wheels beside him. I saw the hospital coordinator hurry in with my cells all wrapped up, placed in a small cooler.

"Where are you headed?" I asked the man, who was dressed in black, though I knew he wasn't allowed to tell me where he was flying to deliver my donation. "Down south," he said, and smiled. My recipient and his doctors were waiting somewhere in another city.

The next morning I was so sore and bruised, my upper body looked like I'd been in a fight. Except for one small scar I'd have to point out for you to see, I healed over time.

I sent a letter and gift (an angel figurine) to my recipient along with my donation. After six months I received a thank-you card and gift from him (an earring tree with mirror). These things went through the registry, so neither of us knew the other's name. He told me about his family and that he was doing well.

When the one-year anniversary of my donation arrived, the registry asked if I wanted to meet my recipient. My first reaction was yes. Then I thought about it. What if we didn't like each other? What if he felt he owed me something? Would I feel obligated to be part of his family's life? I'd always wished to be an anonymous philanthropist. While that hasn't happened yet, I'm grateful I was able to give something far greater than money, and with no strings attached. And so I declined.

On the card my recipient sent me, he asked, "How can I ever thank you?" But I have received thanks. What I knew I received was the chance to literally give a part of myself for another. God chose me as a vessel of healing; somewhere a middle-aged man is enjoying life with his wife and five grandchildren. What could be better than that?

THE LAST DOWN

Torian Colon

The weather in Detroit was beautiful for mid-October. The sun beamed through our bedroom window, and I woke up with a smile on my face. I could feel that something special was going to take place in our lives. I had just given birth to my second daughter a week prior, but my anticipation came from something else entirely.

Harry, my husband, played for the Detroit Lions. This particular

Sunday, they were playing the New York Jets. I had a good feeling about the game. He'd sat out a year before, and I had been praying for him and his career. We spoke on the phone before the game, as we always did.

"Baby," I said to him, "I think you're going to have a good game today. I'm feeling a couple of interceptions and a lot of highlights on ESPN. I think this is going to be the game! You're going to prove to them that you're the best safety on the team, and that you deserve the starting position."

"I hope so" was all I got from him in return. I knew then that he'd lost faith in himself. We said "I love you" to each other and hung up the phone.

The game was my first outing since having the baby; my mother thought I was crazy for going out so soon after giving birth. But with the weather as beautiful as it was, and me feeling as good as I did, nothing was going to stop me. I put on my new custom-made suit, and my husband's parents and I headed for the Silverdome.

In our seats, my mother-in-law too mentioned that she had a feeling that something special was going to take place in today's game. I felt Harry was going to make national news!

The big lion mascot entered the stadium as the game music began to play. The crowd was pumped up and rowdy, some with their faces painted blue and silver, and others dressed from head to toe in Detroit Lions paraphernalia. We sat in the section reserved for wives and family. My husband gave us a thumbs-up and smiled once he located us in the stands. I felt relieved; he had a calm look on his face. It had been a rough season for him. He was a five-year veteran; we hoped this comeback season with the Lions would be his ticket to bigger contracts and more years in the NFL.

Throughout the first quarter, he came in and out of the game. I wasn't really bothered—I was just relieved that he wasn't riding the bench. When Harry had a game where he didn't get what he felt was his deserved playing time, he would mope about for the remainder of the evening.

Then I saw number twenty-nine go down as one of the Jets went down. I heard the hit. But it hadn't registered in me that player number twenty-nine for the Lions was my husband. I saw the player for the Jets get up, but number twenty-nine, my husband, didn't move. I remember feeling frozen in time when I saw the stretcher come out on the field. I finally got my legs to allow me to stand up as I cried, "Come on, Harry, get up!" I had seen him get hit much harder in the past and he had always gotten up. I just knew that he would get up this time too. This was supposed to be his comeback game, his "big play" game!

Tears cascaded down my face, and panic began to set in when I saw them tape his head down to the stretcher. I knew then that the hit Harry had taken was a serious one.

My in-laws ran with me down to the locker room area. I became hysterical, and because of all the walking and excitement, I began to hemorrhage. I could feel the warm blood flow down my leg. But I had to get to Harry to see if he was all right.

Once we approached the locker room, we realized we couldn't get into the area. Reporters and photographers crowded the area outside. Finally, they let us into the locker room. My husband, the man I loved and the father of my children, was lying there with his head taped down to a stretcher. I closed my eyes and said a prayer: "Oh God, please don't let him be paralyzed."

Harry said in a shaky voice, "Baby, I can still move my feet! I think I'm going to be okay."

I responded, "It's over, Harry—it's over for you!"

"Baby, what are you talking about? I'm moving my feet!" I stood there crying and shaking my head as if to say no to him, as the team doctors prepared him to be carried away in the ambulance. Once they placed him in the ambulance, we tried to get in the ambulance with him. But he refused to allow us. He didn't want me, his mother, or his father with him. He wanted to be alone.

My mind raced a hundred miles an hour as I drove down the highway toward the hospital. I thought about how much courage and strength Harry had displayed throughout his life. Coming from a family of eleven children, he always had to be a little stronger.

I began to pray to God for strength myself. I wanted to be calm when I received the news about his injury. Part of me was worried I was going to hear terrible news about something being permanently wrong with Harry's legs. Another part of me imagined seeing Harry standing up, waiting to greet me.

When I saw Harry lying in the hospital bed, he had an expression on his face that I'd never seen before. Right then I knew everything was not going to be okay. As the doctor entered the room with his clipboard, Harry said, "Just give me the news, Doc!" The doctor responded by saying, "You have seven herniated discs in your neck, and three are bulging." As he showed us the X rays, we could see exactly the condition the doctor spoke of. Harry's spine looked horrible, and at that moment I realized that it was only by the grace of God that Harry's life had been spared.

The doctor continued, "Every time you get hit in this area of your back, these particular discs are pinching down on your spine, causing the paralysis you are experiencing."

"So can I still play?" Harry asked, as if he didn't understand what the doctor had just told us.

The doctor replied, "My advice to you, young man, would be to retire from the NFL."

Harry shook his head and closed his eyes. Although he didn't shed any tears, I could feel the pain he was going through. He had played football since he was a child. And now his playing days were over. All his years of hard work to accomplish his dream of being a starting safety in the NFL had come to an end.

That night, as Harry and I lay awake together in silence, my mind went back over the news we had received earlier in the evening. I didn't know what to say to my husband. I didn't have any pep speech to give him, nor any words of encouragement. I was at a complete loss for words.

"Well, babe," Harry said, "you said this was going to be a special day and that I was going to make sports headlines."

"Yeah, I guess," I responded, feeling guilty about my enthusiasm earlier.

"So what now?" he asked.

"Well," I replied, "God has led us this far, and I have one hundred percent faith that He's going to continue to lead us on. Just as you always knew you could make it in the NFL, you have to have the same faith that you can make it after the NFL. What happened today was not your last down!"

Several years later, Harry asked me one evening, "Hey, dear—are you bringing the girls to the game this evening?" At the time I was trying to get the girls dressed and ready for school. I responded, "I don't know, Harry. You know they have dance class today."

"You've got to come to this one! We're playing one of the best teams in the district! I mean, these boys can really play."

Harry is now a high school football coach in Houston, Texas. After much prayer, much patience, and much healing, he found his calling.

MATTHEW

Gilda Mack Benton

My husband, Tony, and I had been married four months when we found out we were expecting our first child. We had both dreamed of having children. We couldn't wait to start our family together!

I had an easy pregnancy, and my husband went to all of my doctor's appointments in order to share every moment of the experience with me. All of the ultrasounds and other tests came back showing no problems.

We began to shop together for things to fill the new nursery: a rocking chair, a crib, a dresser. We were given three baby showers by friends and family, and from these loving efforts we received everything else we needed.

In my fourth month of pregnancy, we found out that we were having a son. We decided to give our son the middle names of Tony's maternal and paternal grandfathers: Matthew Nathaniel Benton.

Matthew was born on October 8, 2000, at 4:10 on a beautiful Sunday afternoon. He weighed in at 8 pounds, 11 ounces and he was 21½ inches long. Our hospital room was filled with family and friends after Matthew was born; we could not have been happier! I decided to keep the baby in the room with me because I didn't want him out of my sight.

At about 4 A.M., when the nurse came to check him, she said he seemed a little chilly and she wanted to take him to the nursery to put him under the warmer. That seemed normal enough to me, so I didn't ask any questions. I ended up dozing off. When I woke up at 6 A.M., I was startled to realize the nurse hadn't brought the baby back yet. I immediately called the nursery and was informed that the pediatrician was doing the baby's morning checkup. As soon as it was done, they would be bringing Matthew back to my room.

About an hour later, the pediatrician came to my room and told me that she had ordered a chest X ray for Matthew, as his breathing appeared to be a little fast. She went on to explain that sometimes infants have minor breathing problems when learning how to breathe on their own outside of the womb. Although this news made both Tony and me a bit nervous, we felt that everything happening was pretty much standard procedure. Thirty minutes later, however, we received another call that an additional chest X ray was necessary. This time, we became extremely nervous.

Shortly afterward another doctor came to our room to give us the results of the X rays. In his hand was a drawing he had prepared to help us understand Matthew's condition. On one side of the drawing was a picture of a perfect heart with all its chambers and valves. The other side of the drawing was Matthew's heart; it had only one chamber! My son had a rare heart condition called hypoplastic left heart syndrome; he was born with only the right chamber of his heart.

Tony and I were devastated. We discovered there wasn't any type of surgery available to fix Matthew's heart. The only thing the doctors could do was to perform a series of minor surgeries to try to redirect the arteries so that more blood could be pumped to Matthew's organs. In essence, this is what the left chamber of the heart was supposed to do. Matthew would not live long enough to be a patient on the heart transplant registry, so that never became an option. If his condition had been discovered during the pregnancy, the only thing the doctors could have done was recommend a medical termination of the pregnancy. In God's infinite wisdom, I believe He knew that we would never have considered termination as an option.

During Matthew's sixteen-day life, he endured more than any child should ever have to. He was a good baby through it all. He didn't cry a lot, and he always seemed to find comfort in the arms of his mommy and daddy. He had more visitors than I have ever seen a child have in my life. On his thirteenth day with us, however, his kidneys began to fail. The kidney failure caused him to go into cardiac arrest, and he suffered brain damage as a result. At this point, my husband and I prayed that our son be taken back to his Heavenly Father.

The outpouring of love and support from our family and friends was indescribable. We even received letters and cards from people we had never met. They had heard our story from others and wanted to offer their support and their prayers.

We are living witnesses that the power of love makes a huge difference in one's life. Not only did Black love help us to make it through, but the love from people of all races helped us to triumph over this tragedy. Although Tony and I suffered a great loss, we feel privileged that God allowed us to share the experience of a son whose very life, although short, served to bring people closer together.

On December 26, 2001, I gave birth to another son. We call him C.J., and he was born perfectly healthy. He is truly a blessing to us. We look forward to telling C.J. about the many lives that his brother, Matthew, touched.

Miracles Do Happen

Diane Triggs

At 5:30 P.M. on Friday, February 9, 2001, a guard came to my desk at work and asked if I was Diane Triggs. He said that my daughter had been in a car accident. I rushed home; Edna, my sister-in-law, told me my daughter Jonnesse was in critical condition in Paducah, Kentucky.

In a state of shock, I waited for my husband and our other daughter to arrive back home. In disbelief, my husband listened as the hospital's recorded message repeated, "Get here as soon as you can!" My sister-in-law and two brothers-in-law drove us to Paducah.

Jonnesse was a nineteen-year-old sophomore accounting major at Fisk University in Nashville, Tennessee. When we arrived at Western Baptist Hospital's emergency room, we met a gentleman about to finish his shift. We anxiously informed him that we were there to see Jonnesse Triggs. His reply was "Good luck" as he left the waiting room area. My heart was already on the ground.

Once we were able to gather a few minor details at the hospital, we discovered there had been four female students from Fisk University in the car involved in the accident, and all four were in the emergency room. Jonnesse and another student were both on life support.

As they wheeled the girls from emergency to intensive care, we were asked to remain in the waiting room. The doctors did not know if Jonnesse would survive the night. Upon hearing this, I asked for the chaplain.

The police report of the accident stated that the wind had been extremely high that evening. As the Geo Metro Jonnesse was driving on Highway 24 passed an eighteen-wheeler, the wind got under it and threw the small car into the median. The car flipped six times, throwing all four of the students out. From pictures, it looked like someone had taken a giant can opener and opened the roof of the car. Jonnesse had sustained a broken neck and brain injuries. She and another student were in a coma; Jonnesse's injuries, however, were the most severe. The other two girls sustained fractured necks.

All of the students survived the night. The next morning, our daughter's doctor stated that Jonnesse was only a hair away from being paralyzed. She was kept on morphine until she could undergo surgery; if she so much as moved at all, she could end up paralyzed for life.

We did not know a soul in Paducah, Kentucky. I began to pray to God for help. As I sat there in the waiting room, a lady approached me and introduced herself as Ayrie. Ayrie and her fiancé, George, were in the waiting room because her brother was a patient in ICU. Ayrie called a chaplain friend, Mary, from another floor, Mary came in shortly thereafter, like an angel. They began to talk to me and counsel me. As we talked, I began to relax and finally I drifted off to sleep in the chair. When

I awoke, Mary and Ayrie invited my husband and me to attend their church the next morning.

Relatives of Jonnesse's classmates arrived from St. Louis at six that evening, as did our friends and family. The parents of another of the students arrived on Sunday.

We did attend Ninth Street Tabernacle on Sunday morning. At the close of the service, we were invited to the altar for prayer. We cried like lost three-year-olds. I have never seen my husband cry that hard, and I hope I never have to see him cry that way again. The next thing I recall, the female minister, Reverend Burage, began to pray and lay hands on me while Pastor Turner prayed for my husband.

When the service was over, Pastor Turner suggested to one of his members that the church secure a hotel room for us; he immediately assigned a deacon and wife to each of our four families. Each deacon-and-wife team arrived at the hospital that afternoon with keys to rooms at the Drury Inn.

Soon the news of the accident with the four girls from Fisk University spread throughout the town. Our church in St. Louis and the Ninth Street Tabernacle joined to pay our hotel bill. My aunt had a close friend in Hendersonville, North Carolina, and although she knew the friend very well, she had never met the friend's children. It turns out the children lived in Paducah, and when they were told of our circumstances, they visited us at the hospital and brought us money as well.

Jonnesse had surgery on Wednesday, the day after the accident. She had a plate placed in her neck and a halo attached to it. On the Thursday following the accident, two of the students were released. Only one of the other students required a halo for her neck. Jonnesse remained in the hospital in Paducah from February 9, 2001, until March 1, and in the hospital in St. Louis from March 1 until April 27, 2001. One year later, on March 21, 2002, she finished her last day of rehabilitation.

When she left the hospital in Paducah, two weeks after the accident, she was on a stretcher. She could not stand or walk and did not know she was being transferred. She was conscious but extremely incoherent. She had to relearn all of the God-given movements we take for granted.

Jonnesse's other classmates in the accident returned to Fisk in the fall of 2001. Jonnesse lost her scholarships because of the accident, but she is now taking one course at a community college here in St. Louis. She is determined to make it.

We would not have made it without the help of God and the entire community of Paducah. Strangers, family, extended family, and adopted family, both Black and white, came to our rescue in our time of need. God, faith, and the love of those who crossed our path during the experience helped to pull us through!

MY MIRACLE

Marc Little

As I lay unconscious in the hospital, my family and friends gathered in the waiting room, anticipating my death. Shot by a Los Angeles gang member, I had lost all but a pint of the blood in my body. The physicians held out little hope for me. But as a new college grad with big dreams, I wasn't about to toss in the towel.

The date was July 31, 1987. I had just earned my degree in broadcast journalism from USC, and was living in a campus apartment, prepping for the GMAT exams required to get into graduate school. Around 9 o'clock that night, my college sweetheart, Tegra, met up with me as I was walking home from the 32nd Street Market near the university. Living on a "peanut butter and jelly" budget, I had taken a break from studying to pick up a loaf of bread from the store.

As Tegra and I were walking back to my apartment we saw a young man on the sidewalk leaning over the windshield of his car. He appeared to be repairing something on the passenger side.

As we passed by, the youth asked if I could help him. As a West Haven, Connecticut native, I didn't have it in me to ignore his request. "Sure, what's up?" I said as I approached his vehicle.

The young thug arose from the car pointing a twelve-gauge shotgun at my forehead. "Fix this," he said. I was stunned to silence as I stared down the barrel of the gun.

Everything seemed to play out in slow motion, like a scene in a movie. I raised my hands in the air as the loaf of bread tumbled to the ground, and I watched with detachment as the robber's mouth moved, demanding money. "You better have at least a hundred dollars," he said.

I had sixty-eight cents in my pocket. Tegra, I thought, took off running to knock on doors for help; in fact, she had only gotten a few feet before stopping.

The gunman again insisted I cough up a hundred bucks. But I had no hundred dollars to give him.

He slapped me across the head with the blunt end of the gun, and I fell to the ground. As I lay on the pavement, he cocked the shotgun and shot me in my right leg, close to my private parts, hitting, I would discover later, the main artery. I believe he was actually aiming for my head, but the force of a twelve-gauge shotgun can throw off a weak shooter's aim. I don't remember feeling any pain, but I sure hollered as I reached to feel my leg.

The gunman jumped into the passenger side of the car, next to the driver, and the two sped down the road. (I later learned the car had been stolen the night before.) Residents and others in the neighborhood responded to the commotion, and gathered around me as I shivered on the ground. My entire body was going cold. A blanket was spread over me; Tegra had knelt by my side.

When the ambulance arrived to transport me to the hospital, I recall the paramedics denying Tegra permission to accompany me. I didn't have the strength to fight on her behalf, though I wanted her with me.

On the journey to the hospital, I felt a spirit beside me in the ambulance. An otherworldly voice inquired, "Do you want to live?" And I realized that I was being given the option to fight for my life or cower down and quit. It was up to me.

At that moment, I declared within my heart that I was going to make it, no matter what. My mother didn't raise a failure, and she (as a single parent) didn't fail at raising me. Nearing the hospital, I drifted off into a state of unconsciousness while humming familiar church hymns.

Upon arrival at the emergency room, I was on the brink of death. I had lost all but a unit of blood from the gunshot wound, and physicians gave me little chance for survival.

The rapid blood loss caused my kidneys to fail as well, and I began to retain water. Ultimately my body went into renal failure. I desperately needed a miracle.

Tegra stayed at the hospital praying fervently for me, her Bible clutched to her chest.

Hospital staff called my mother in the middle of the night and alerted her that I was near death. "If you want to see your son alive, you'll have to come out right away," they advised. She took the next flight from Connecticut and came straight to the hospital.

My father, Floyd Little, a former running back for the Denver Broncos, lived in Santa Barbara, California. A friend of his, who is the president of US Air, chartered a private plane and immediately flew him to Los Angeles. The two had been golfing together earlier that day.

The doctors warned that if I lived to see the next day, I would likely be brain-dead and blind. Essentially, there wasn't much more they could do. They didn't want to put me on life support because I was asthmatic, and blockages in my body would not respond properly to the sophisticated medical equipment.

The following morning, my 145-pound body had inflated to almost 212 pounds from retaining so much water. In addition, I suffered from hydrocephalus (swelling of the brain), which caused my ears to sink into my head. My eyes were swollen shut. It was only by God's grace that I lived through the night at all.

The doctors made another attempt at putting me on life support that next morning. As if by divine intervention the blockages in my body had vanished, and the life support equipment worked. It was the first of many miracles.

Later that day I was scheduled to begin dialysis treatments to restore my kidneys' function. But, miraculously, my kidneys began to work again on their own.

The shooting had gained considerable media attention, capturing newspaper headlines and making local television news. My attacker had been an eighteen-year-old boy engaged in what was suspected to be a Crips gang initiation. The driver of the stolen vehicle was caught the next day; the shooter turned himself in shortly thereafter. The night before shooting me, he had attempted to shoot someone else, but the gun had misfired.

I was hospitalized for the next four months. My muscles became atrophied and my weight dropped to eighty-eight pounds. I felt like a skeleton, all skin and bones. But I was determined to make it.

Eventually the wounded leg became gangrenous. My toes turned black and shriveled up like raisins. The doctors worked hard at trying to save my leg to no avail. A month later, I reluctantly consented to have my leg amputated.

My leg was amputated at the upper hip area—a hip disarticulation. I went through seven surgical procedures in all before being fitted for a prosthesis.

I had received prayers and support from all over. The walls in my hospital room were covered with cards from floor to ceiling. Local newscaster Jim Hill came and did a story on me, and people I didn't even know stopped in to see the "miracle kid," as I'd been dubbed.

My mother camped out many nights at the hospital to help me in my fight for survival. I love my mom so much—she's always gone way out of her way for me. When I was growing up in West Haven, she put off completing her education to work extra jobs to make sure I had the best she could provide, including sending me to a private boys' school, Notre Dame.

My final two months in the hospital were spent in rehabilitation. One might think the most painful part of my experience was the amputation of my leg. In fact, it was the skin graft surgery I had to endure. Once the leg was amputated, skin was shaved from my detached leg and used to close up the stump. When the anesthesia wore off, it burned like a french fry dipped in hot grease.

In rehab, I had to learn how to walk again. With the muscles in my remaining leg atrophied to the thickness of a large stick, I faced one of the most difficult challenges in my life. On one occasion during my rehab process, I fell down, and I had to relearn how to get up again, and how to walk with a cane.

I finally checked out of the hospital on November 16, continuing outpatient occupational therapy after moving into a friend's apartment with my mom.

My father, who at the time owned a Lincoln-Mercury dealership in the L.A. area, was also a pillar of strength. I had first gotten to know my father, as well as my two sisters Krya and Christy, better when I came to L.A. to attend USC. Though he didn't raise me, through my healing process, we became best friends.

The love, support, and encouragement of my family and the community—and Tegra—made the ordeal so much easier to bear. I learned how blessed I was to have Tegra as my girlfriend. She remained with me every step of the way, and played an important role in my healing. I don't know how many relationships could weather the kind of emotional and physical roller coaster we went through. I'm honored to say that she is still with me now, as my wife.

Once I was physically capable, I launched an organization called "Fight the Good Fight." This was my attempt to motivate and encourage urban youth. I traveled the country addressing school-aged audiences about my experience, to inspire them to make positive choices and avoid gang life. I spent two years on the road in all, which contributed to the process of my own healing, while giving me a chance to do something important for urban youth.

At a certain point, I felt like the time was right to get on with my education. Out of the blue, I received a phone call from Jeff Keith, an amputee who had run across the country on a prosthesis. He told me about a scholarship opportunity for physically challenged athletes known as "Swim with Mike."

Through Jeff, USC offered me the opportunity to attend graduate school on the same scholarship. Seeking acceptance to their law school, I took the LSAT and GMAT exams but my scores weren't high enough. I'm a solid B student, and that wasn't enough. But I felt I had what it takes to get the job done. Still, USC kept telling me over and over again, "Your scores aren't high enough to be admitted to our law school."

After four attempts, USC recommended I apply to another law school, do well there, and try to transfer back at a later time. That was heartbreaking in a way, because I could use the Swim with Mike scholarship only at USC.

Nevertheless, I followed their advice and attended Whittier Law School for two semesters. My grades were exceptional, and in August of 1992 I transferred to the USC School of Law. Finally, I was able to access the scholarship I'd been awarded.

I earned my Juris Doctorate degree in 1994 and took the bar exam in July of that year. Tegra and I got married in September, and I learned in November that I passed the bar on the first try. One month later I began my own practice, specializing in entertainment law and civil litigation.

Today I have a thriving law firm in Los Angeles with a roster of clients that include professional athletes, record companies, and producers in the entertainment industry. In addition, I have a promising venture in South Africa that, I hope, will create jobs and other opportunities to empower the people of South Africa.

Not only has God granted me success with my entrepreneurial endeavors, but He's given me a great season of ministry at my church, Faithful Central Bible Church, where I serve as chairman of the Board of Elders.

It would have been just as easy for me to give up during that ambulance ride to the emergency room. But God had a plan that the enemy could not derail. Even with only a pint of blood in my body, and doctors and friends assuming I would soon die, the voice of His spirit proclaimed life.

I am convinced the attempt on my life happened for a reason. It was the Lord's design that I serve as an example of His miraculous power and prove that His word is alive today. My life is evidence of that. More important, no one is exempt from that same awesome power.

HOPE AND
OVERCOMING

Hope

Tavis Smiley

During my senior year at Indiana University, I came to Los Angeles to do an internship with Tom Bradley. It actually took me nine months, from January until September 1985, of writing, calling, and faxing his office, as well as using my student aid money to fly twice to Los Angeles to try (unsuccessfully) to meet with him, before he finally granted me an internship.

The unpaid internship lasted for one semester, from September through December of 1985. Through the course of my internship, I got to know the mayor fairly well, and when my internship was over, he told me he would hire me as a member of his staff once my studies were completed if I was interested. I returned to Bloomington, Indiana, to complete my degree, and one year later I packed up everything I owned into my Datsun 280Z and drove out west to Los Angeles to work for Mayor Bradley. When I arrived in Los Angeles, I discovered that the city's economy had taken a downturn, making it necessary to impose a mandatory hiring freeze on all employment opportunities. As a result, he didn't have a job to give me. The best advice he could give me at that point was to stick around until the hiring freeze lifted and he would bring me on staff right away.

The hiring freeze ended up lasting over a year. I found myself stuck in Los Angeles, without money, without family, and without a job. I was ashamed to admit to my college buddies back home that my situation had taken a turn for the worse. Especially since I had bragged to them about my success in landing a job right out of college.

I had received an eviction notice to move out of my apartment. I looked for work wherever I could. The truth of the matter was that I couldn't find any job, not even a menial one. I was denied employment at McDonald's because I was "overqualified." No one would hire me even for a manual-labor, minimum-wage job.

When I thought I could not go any further, I reluctantly called my mother. I broke down in tears, crying and sobbing like a baby. I explained to her that I was coming home because I could not make it in Los Angeles. I could hear Gladys Knight and the Pips warming up: "LA proved too much for the man. He couldn't take it. So he's leaving the life he's come to know." I had given it everything I had, but things weren't working out and I was at my wits' end.

My mother said to me, "Honey, you can always come home. You'll always have a bedroom here at the house, and all I want is for you to be happy. Come home, stay as long as you like, regroup, and do whatever you need to do. We are your family—we're here for you, and we'll always be here for you." I thanked my mother for her words of comfort, although I was very disappointed in myself. I did not want to go back to Indiana with my tail between my legs.

When I finished talking to my mother, I made it into the shower. In the midst of my tears, I reconciled myself to the fact that it was time for me to go home. "Things cannot get any worse for me," I thought. At that very moment, a massive earthquake hit the city of Los Angeles. I started slipping and sliding in the shower with soap and water flying everywhere. All of a sudden, the voice of the Lord spoke to me and said, "Things can always get worse; they can get *much* worse."

Hearing the voice of God made me realize that as long as I was alive and had breath in my body, there would always be hope. There are times when hope is the *only* thing we have to cling to. I didn't have a job, I didn't have any food, and I didn't have any money, but I always had hope.

I managed to make it out of the shower in one piece, and right away my phone rang. It was my friend Harold Patrick, calling to see if I was all right. When I answered the phone, I was still upset and trying to process all that had taken place. Harold became concerned about me and rushed over to my apartment. We ended up having a long conversation about my circumstances and my feelings about leaving Los Angeles and returning to Indiana.

Harold listened to what I had to say. Then he replied, "I will support you in whatever decision you make. But I want you to know that I am not going to give up on you until forty-eight hours after you have given up on yourself. I want to give you enough time to change your mind. I have great expectations for your future. I believe in you; you are the hope of my dreams. I'm going to be here for you." I was extremely moved by his words.

As I thought about God's message in the shower and Harold's unshakable belief in me, I saw in that moment my own sense of hopelessness through the lens of the blood, sweat, and tears of my ancestors and the sacrifices they had endured to pave the way for those coming behind them. We became the hope of *their* dreams, and the purpose for which many of them gave their lives. I thought, "I have a whole lot of nerve giving up on anything." Here I was talking about giving up hope and going back home to Indiana because I didn't have a job, because I was being evicted from my apartment. How could I compare my situation with the experiences of my ancestors who had survived the journey to America on slave ships, survived the institution of slavery, and lived through segregation?

Those two back-to-back moments that morning in 1987 set me straight about what it meant to be hopeful. Since that day, I have never taken hope for granted. There is always hope, and hope springs eternal. Whether we have money or not, whether we have good health or not, and whether our mates walk out on us or not, we need to latch on to hope and never let it go.

OVERCOMING ADVERSITY

Iyanla Vanzant

There are two kinds of adversity that we experience in our lives: the kind that is thrust upon you, and the kind that you put yourself in. For the first sixteen years of my life, I lived through adversity that was thrust upon me. The reality of growing up in poverty without real parenting caused me to develop certain ways of dealing with life, certain outlooks, and certain perceptions of life and of myself. This is a natural part of growing up where our development of how we think and feel about ourselves can be influenced by the adversity thrust upon us by the environment we grow up in.

My self-perception was definitely influenced by the poverty in my environment, as well as by the images of the women I grew up around and who were important in my life. Most of the female figures I grew up around struggled on a daily basis. Their struggles were built on hard work, but it wasn't the kind of hard work that advanced you or got you ahead in life or got you acclaim and notoriety. It was just basic day-to-day struggle.

At the age of sixteen, I started making choices and decisions on my own. Unconsciously, I brought adversity into my life by putting myself in situations and creating experiences for myself where I had to struggle. For example, I had my first child when I was sixteen. This made me discover that it was hard being sixteen, not having an education, not having any money, and trying to raise a child on my own. These were clearly experiences of adversity that I created for myself. In trying to overcome this self-created adversity, I married somebody who was not capable, who was not ready, and who, quite frankly, was not even willing to engage in a marriage and in raising a family at the time. So instead of correcting the situation, I ended up thrusting even more adversity upon myself. I moved from the place of unconsciously creating adversity for myself to the next stage of my life.

Fast-forward. . . . At the age of thirty, I had three kids and I began the process of consciously examining and evaluating my life in order to make different choices and decisions, but this time consciously. This process of self-reflection was hard for me, because the major question that kept popping up in my head and my heart was How do I keep any sort of faith in my life when all I've known is adversity? What is it that gives one the strength and the courage to know that there is something better for you? For me, it was a feeling of deep belief; not even a practicing faith, but a deep belief that God, somehow and in some way, had something for me to do and that He would present the opportunity for me to do it.

My first opportunity happened while I was riding on a bus, coming from a welfare center. I passed a sign that read, "If you're ready to change your life, come to Medgar Evers college." For me, that demonstrated an opportunity. When one lives in adversity, there comes a time when you literally have to move in blind faith; you cannot waste time asking questions—you just have to move! Because the minute you start thinking, the deceptive intelligence will remind you of how many other things didn't work and you will stop yourself.

So, I went to college; me and the three kids. I took things day by day and moment by moment. I think faith is a second-by-second thing. When you have a deep sense of knowing a certain thing, it's the same as having faith. My faith and my deep sense of knowing allowed me to feel that, with every fiber of my being, God had something for me to do, although I had no idea what it was. However, faith kept telling me that God had a definite purpose for my life. In this respect, I had to hold fast to my faith and let it guide my direction and my journey. In times when I feel I am in the most trouble, unable to see any direction or purpose for my life, my faith leaves me and I often revert to my human thinking, which was, for me, loaded with adversity. So, because of my faith, coupled with my deep sense of "knowing," I went to college and to law school.

Fast-forward. . . . I started practicing law in Philadelphia, and I was just miserable! I did not want to do what I was engaged in doing because it conflicted with my belief that God had something better for me to do. I had come from a situation of being on welfare with three kids and in an abusive marriage, to practicing law as a criminal defense attorney in one of the largest and most prestigious defense offices in the world—the Philadelphia Public Defenders Association. The PPDA was the second-largest public defenders association in the nation, yet I was miserable working there. What it took for me to walk away from my job was, again, that deep knowing that God had something better for me to do with my life. Here again, I had no clue what it was, but that's when the principle kicks in—you have to let go of what you don't want in order to get what you do want. Looking back, I guess if I had thought about it more, I would have stayed in the PPDA office, gainfully employed, and kept actively searching for my purpose while constantly asking God for clarification of purpose. But I was impulsive and so I left. Sometimes you have to be willing to walk in the darkness and not be able to see until this thing that you "deeply know" develops. It's almost like a photograph that starts off as a negative and transforms into a clear image. A friend of mine described it this way: "When you're in the darkness, God is developing you. There is a new image that is going to be impressed upon you." So I ended up walking in the darkness of being unemployed, getting evicted from my house, living in a friend's basement, and having my youngest daughter come home pregnant, but yet, there was still this feeling of "deep knowing" for a higher purpose working inside of me.

Fast-forward. . . . I took a job teaching life skills on how to reenter the workforce to women who were on welfare. I put together a little workbook for them which basically said, every day I want you to do this and do that. I called the workbook *Tapping the Power Within*. When I sat down to review the workbook, I realized it had thirty-two pages. So I took it to Kinko's to have it photocopied, added a cover page to it, and ended up with a pamphlet for the women in my life skills program. Throughout the course I kept working on the pamphlet, and it kept growing until it finally developed into seventy-two pages, at which point I thought, *This is a book!* I wrote Alice Walker, who had her own publishing company at the time, about the possibility of publishing my pamphlet. Her response was "Nice idea, but I can't publish it right now." I could have taken her rejection of my work as an act of adversity, but I simply said, "Okay." Then another opportunity presented itself when I was encouraged to call an agent by the name of Marie Brown. She also responded that it was a lovely idea but she was not ready to publish it. Finally, two years later, Marie Brown called me to say that she knew of someone who was interested in my book. During times of adversity in your life, when you have a deep sense of knowing that you have divine purpose, you've got to exercise patience and hold the vision.

Fast-forward. . . . *Tapping the Power Within* was published and the news of it began to create a buzz in circles here and there. Another friend encouraged me to write Susan Taylor of *Essence* magazine as a way of generating more support for my work. Mind you, there were many others who said I would be wasting my time in writing to Susan Taylor because so many others had written to her and never received a response. Two weeks after I wrote to her, she responded to my letter and *Essence* magazine ended up publishing my story in April 1988. After my story was published, I started getting offers for speaking engagements. In order for me to come and speak somewhere, I asked that I be sent an airline ticket and be paid $500. As a result, I traveled all over this country speaking at different locations, without a dime in my pocket, hoping that when I got to where I was going, they would feed me and knowing that I would come back home with $500. Sometimes you just have to move your butt!

One day out of the blue, the same agent I mentioned previously, Marie Brown, called me about an offer from Simon & Schuster to write a book they had a concept for. At the time, I was still living in my friend's basement, my youngest daughter was pregnant, and I still didn't have a dime to my name. Another friend gave me a computer (without a printer, mind you), and I started writing the book *Acts of Faith*. I was basically writing about things that I needed to know about. In adversity sometimes you have to be your own teacher and your own support. *Acts of Faith* was published and I continued to travel around doing speaking engagements. Things started to move slowly and then they just took off.

Fast-forward. . . . It was now 1998, and I was seven books into my career and I get the phone call that Oprah wants me to come on her show. After I picked myself up from the floor, I started doing *The Oprah Winfrey Show*. But it was a really weird experience for me because, like most offers, I thought, *If I could just get on Oprah and people know I'm out here, I'll be okay*. By the time I got to *The Oprah Winfrey Show*, however, I had already been out there and people already knew I was okay, so I didn't have this particular motivation in mind. Instead, my motivation became to be able to reach the greatest number of people in the shortest amount of time. And, in doing her show, that is what she provided me with the opportunity to do. So I did my first show on *Oprah* in February 1998. I came back to do the show in May 1998, September, October, November, and

December of 1998. I ended up becoming a fixture on live television through her show.

While there at the studio getting ready to do the *Oprah* show, I received a telephone call to attend a meeting with Barbara Walters on the possibility of doing my own show. After I picked myself up from the floor, once again, I met with Barbara Walters. At end of the meeting, she asked me to consider the possibility of doing a show with her. I explained to her that I was already happy doing *The Oprah Winfrey Show* every week. Barbara told me that if I ever changed my mind, to let her know. "Okay, but I don't think I'll be changing my mind," I told her.

I went home the same evening, sat down, and did what most human beings do that ultimately gets them into trouble: I started thinking. Thinking can be hazardous to your health. I thought to myself, *This is very bizarre!* "Okay, God—what are you trying to tell me?" I immediately went into seven days of prayer and fasting, praying for clarity of purpose. On the sixth day I felt I received the message "The time is now!" For me this meant the time is now for me to stand on my own; the time is now for me to get my message out to reach the greatest number of people in the shortest amount of time; the time is now and this is the opportunity. But, in the back of my mind, I couldn't imagine myself leaving *The Oprah Winfrey Show*.

I ended up going to Oprah and sharing the news with her of the opportunity I had to do my own television show. I asked Oprah if I stayed with her show, would she be willing to eventually produce my own show for me. Her response was "Absolutely." But here again, it was about timing. At the time Oprah was getting ready to launch her magazine, she was teaching a course with Stedman, her show was at its peak, and the movie *Beloved* had just come out. Things were incredibly busy for her as well.

In the end it was my impatience, my naïveté, my ego, and my everything that took me out of *Oprah* to Buena Vista Pictures. We shot one pilot, and the pilot didn't sell. One year later, the producers came up with a new concept and I went forward and did the show in the new format. It was the biggest mistake of my life! Oftentimes when we have to walk through adversity, we are unaware of what we're actually going through. Ultimately, I got stuck on doing the show and forgot about my vision, reaching the greatest number of people in the shortest amount of time. I focused on doing the show and not on the vision of what I wanted the show to really be about. The producers were focused on doing the show as well. Once I got into the notion of doing the show, I realized that the producers were not aligned with my vision. Vision is part of the "deep knowing" that I mentioned earlier. It is vision that will bring you through adversity. Vision represents what you stand for. It represents what you are doing and why are you doing it.

Fast-forward. . . . After twenty-six weeks on the air, the tragedy of September 11 happened and television audiences were down. My show was in the sixth major market at night and so my viewer numbers didn't count and I didn't know dip from diddly about doing television. I ended up surrendering my inner authority and inner guidance to those who throught that they knew more about the industry than I did. Then I received a call from the producers, who told me, "We changed our minds about the show and we're done with you." So I packed up my things and I went home. Afterward, I heard from gossip out in the street, "What did you think you were doing, anyway?" My doing the show ultimately confused some people, angered others, and even attracted others. It was at this point it hit me that I had aligned myself with folks who weren't in alignment with my vision. I realized that I had made a big mistake.

Looking back, I know within my own self that I am a good student. In making the mistake of doing my own television show, I had to sit back, reevaluate things, and look for the lesson in what I had done. This is what I learned: that in all my adversity from my younger years, from my growing up in poverty and struggle, in the confusion I experienced and in the lack of identity I had—all these things I had experienced collectively came to a head. If I had stayed on *Oprah*, it would have been absolutely grand for me. But I had to make it hard for myself. I had to go to New York and struggle and fight to try and prove myself and move through adversity, because adversity was my condition. As we examine and evaluate our lives, we have to be real and conscious about how our conditioning as children manifests itself in the way we make choices in our adult lives. Once you realize what you've done, you have to take the appropriate steps to correct yourself as soon as possible.

Right now, I am in the process of reclarifying my vision, reclarifying what it is I stand for, and aligning myself only with people and activities that are in accord with who I am, what I stand for, and what it is that I believe. To quote a line from one of the old Negro spirituals, "I don't feel no ways tired." How many people get an opportunity to have their own television show? For me, it was a blessing and it was part of my divine purpose, because there may have been no other way for me to learn the lesson that I'm addicted to having it hard, that I'm addicted to struggle; the lesson that if things are too easy, I'll make them hard. What *Oprah* gave me was a gift, but it was too easy.

How do you keep the faith? Have a vision. How do you keep the faith? Walk through the darkness knowing there is something better and something more grand for you to do. How do you keep the faith? Keep yourself in check and when you find that you're out of order, self-correct. How do you keep the vision? Stay away from thinking—don't think! God speaks to us in our hearts and in our spirits, and if your head, your heart, and your gut are not in total alignment and in total agreement, recognize this as a situation that is not God, but a situation of you and your conditioning. Self-correct as soon as possible. My head and my heart and my gut were not in alignment with me going to Buena Vista Pictures because I didn't know enough about television and I didn't feel comfortable with the people who were producing my show. I saw who these people were and I ignored what I saw. If there is a piece of advice I can give from all of this, it is to *never* surrender your own authority. Sometimes you will have to say no to someone or to something and it won't make sense. But do it anyway. Just say no! Have a very strong no and a very strong yes, because if you don't have a very strong no, it disempowers your yes. Say yes only when you mean yes and no when you mean no, and don't compromise. I realize that I did not have a strong yes and I did not have a strong no. If I had had a strong yes to *Oprah*, I would have had a strong no to Buena Vista.

Finally, I'll be back! I don't know in what form, but I know that I'll be back, because I'm real clear about what I stand for and I'm clear about aligning myself with people who support my vision. My vision is about healing the planet and the universe. In terms of keeping the faith, if your house is not in order, you can be coerced into doing things that you wouldn't normally do. I went to television because I wanted to, not because I had to. Television seemed a natural extension of the work I was already doing. In that sense, my house was in order. If I had done it for the money or to satisfy some need that I wasn't aware of, I could have been coerced into doing some things that would have compromised me as a person. My mistake was the result of my naïveté and my lack of clarity. The one thing that saved me and that I believe will ultimately save others is to never let your integrity be compromised. This is so critical for us.

I am grateful to have had the opportunity to do my own show. Even when you are sitting in the midst of adversity, look for the blessing. As I count my own blessings, among them are the fact that I am healthy, I'm surrounded by people who love and support me, I have a wonderful family, and I'm absolutely gorgeous. I could have been ugly and broken down, but thank goodness, I'm not. And always, always, find something to laugh at when you're in the midst of adversity. Looking back, I can remember the days of being in New York and shooting three and four shows on the same day, arguing with the producers and trying to figure out what the heck I was doing; just all kinds of mess! But I found joy in eating chicken wings! The message is to find something to make you feel good or to laugh at. You have to keep this in mind no matter what is going on in your life. Sometimes we take life too seriously. One thing I've discovered is that you can't mess up your inheritance, your destiny, your greatness, your divinity, or your ability. You can create messy situations, but as long as you don't get stuck in the mistakes you make, the poor choices and the bad decisions you make, and beat yourself up, terrorize yourself, and brutalize yourself, you can recover from anything. I think we lose sight of that sometimes because we come from a history of adversity. But if you can manage to always find something to laugh at while in the midst of adversity, you will always be able to make it!

OVERCOMING DYSLEXIA

Danny Glover

When I was a child, I was diagnosed with dyslexia. Although you never fully get over it, it had a much more profound impact on my life during my childhood. It is in childhood that we first learn to believe in ourselves. Having dyslexia as a child can impact the child's self-esteem, and the way they see themselves in the world. It can cause them to feel they are dumb, or unworthy, or that they are a disappointment to their family. I felt all these things.

I am almost fifty-five years old now. When I grew up in the fifties, there weren't any programs about how to overcome dyslexia and learn to adjust to it. I was already tall, lanky, and awkward; having the dyslexia seemed to add the label of "dumb" to this list. I didn't, however, experience the kind of peer pressure that can help destroy a child's self-esteem. I guess this mainly had to do with the fact that, in the end, I went to all the dances and I still ended up walking home with the girls.

One of the things that saved me early on was that my second-grade teacher recognized I had an affinity for numbers. The mark of a good teacher is his or her ability to encourage you by supporting the things you do well. This particular teacher was instrumental in recognizing the fact that I was good in mathematics, and encouraging me. When I would stand in front of the class to read, I would be miserable and scared, and outside of math, I did very poorly in school. But knowing that I was good in mathematics helped me to overcome my fear and maintain my self-esteem; it gave me something I could take ownership of. The fact that I was good in math became a saving grace.

The other thing that gave me a sense of balance against low self-esteem was the fact that I had a tremendous capacity and willingness to work hard. Many of the jobs I worked were manual labor jobs. I had a paper route for five years when I was a kid that included a hundred customers. I worked this paper route with pride. I treated my customers as if they were special, and it gave me a great sense of pride and belief in myself. When I was nineteen,

I was afraid to apply for a job as a bank attendant, but I washed dishes at a hospital and at a women's college. Even though these were manual labor jobs, they still bolstered my sense of self-worth. I grew up in a family with four other siblings and my parents worked very hard to do the best they could for all of us. The fact that I could work a job here and there and help my parents out in the household meant a lot to me. All these things helped me to affirm and validate myself, and take attention away from my dyslexia.

As a teenager, I discovered that I had some sort of chemical imbalance in the brain resulting in epileptic seizures. I started having seizures at fifteen and continued having them until I reached the age of thirty-five. But looking back, there were some good things that came out of this condition, as well. Because I had epilepsy, I had to take a medication that required I not drink alcohol. As a result, I never acquired a taste for alcoholic beverages, and to this day, I still do not drink them.

I grew up during the time of the civil rights movement, and I actively participated in programs that helped to advance our civil rights. I also worked with kids in a tutorial program. Later, I attended San Francisco State University and became inspired by all the artists who read poetry aloud on the campus. When it came time for me to read Frantz Fanon's *Wretched of the Earth* as a class assignment, however, my dyslexia cropped up again. I think I read it and struggled through the book at least twenty times before I was able to understand it. But I was encouraged to struggle through my reading assignments because of all the positive feedback from the civil rights activism I was involved in. Being able to understand this piece of literature, even if I did have to read it through many times, provided another source of validation for me. Though it took me longer than anyone else to read the literature and class assignments, I was able to overcome my learning disability and adjust to it. I was finally able to succeed in understanding written literature; going on to become a successful actor was just an extension of this process.

When speaking to children today about overcoming dyslexia, I tell them that it is hard to do. But it gets a little bit easier the more you feel you have value and worth, and that you matter to others.

COURAGE

Linda Spruill

To hear my brother James tell it, we were so poor, he had to walk to school with cardboard in his shoes. Being poor was the furthest thing from my mind when I was growing up. Always at the back of my mind was one question: What kind of mood is Daddy going to be in when he comes home? Is he going to come home with a beautiful white smile on his dark brown face, or is he going to come in resentful and full of anger?

We lived in Williamston, North Carolina, right across the street from his mother, Grandma Ethel. I don't have very good things to say about her because I learned very early that if he stopped by her house first, it would determine the kind of mood he was going to be in. When he came home angry and began a fight with my mother, she would *always* finish it. Martha, my mother, was the eldest of six children and the only girl, and she would fight with her brothers to the finish. I guess she carried that fighting spirit over into adulthood.

One Sunday evening in late August 1968 after visiting Jean, a friend of Ma's, for the afternoon, we had settled in for the night. A few minutes after Ma went to bed, Daddy pounced on her and started choking her. He was angry because she had taken us to visit her friend. He didn't know that she had placed a wrench on the windowsill near the bed; as he choked her, she reached over and grabbed that wrench. That night would forever change my life and that of my nine siblings.

This wasn't the first time he'd hit Ma. It didn't matter what Ma used to defend herself—you knew it wouldn't just end with her getting a punch to the face or a fist in her chest, and she had the broken bones to prove it. I don't need to go into the painful details of the fight, but for Ma it was the last straw. She had been saving paychecks and decided it was time for her to leave. I was twelve years old at the time and don't remember the events of the rest of the night. I thought she had left us to stay in that house with Daddy. I cried most of the night and the next day. We had not heard from her and had no way of knowing where she was.

About four days later, she called on the phone to say that she would not be coming back. She told my sister Valerie and me to dress the younger children and walk over to her brother's house. Since Daddy could not bear to see us leave, he left the house before we did. He cried before he left but did not try to stop us. We walked the two or three miles to Uncle Garland's house, passing familiar homes, the E. J. Hayes School, and so many other landmarks that we had seen at least a hundred times. Imagine ten children walking down a wooded path with just the clothes on their backs. This walk was very different from all the other times we had walked over to Uncle Garland's house. We didn't stop at the graveyard to tell ghost stories. We didn't stop at the creek by the railroad track to pick up tadpoles. We didn't run through the pile of peanut shells on the grounds of the peanut factory. We just kept walking, wondering what would happen next. When we arrived at Uncle Garland's house, he gave us a bag of food, put us all in a station wagon, and drove us to the town of Windsor, where we caught the Carolina Trailways bus to New York's Port Authority bus terminal. Garland told us that we would meet Ma in New York and that we would not be coming back to live with Daddy.

Our lives began to look up again when we saw Ma waiting for us in the most massive, cavernous bus station I had ever seen. Growing up in Williamston, life was either Black or white, but this place held so many different kinds of people. I don't think any of us had ever heard a foreign language or even seen an escalator.

Since I was an avid reader, I thought the streets would be paved with gold and that it would look like Emerald City in *The Wizard of Oz*. Instead, we ended up at my aunt Hattie's apartment in a stinky, funky building in the Flushing Avenue projects in Brooklyn. We thought we were going to die from the stench as the elevator took us to the fifth floor.

Well, to make a long story short, my mother, Martha Spruill, is sixty-seven years old now. She has taken care of her ten children, their children, and their children's children. She was also a foster mother to three other children for about two years. Ma got a job at the New York City Board of Education School Lunch Services, earned her GED, got a driver's license, and worked until retirement. She is a strong, proud, courageous woman who has survived in spite of all the odds stacked against her through the years. And she is the person who brought hope back into my life.

DRAGGED THROUGH THE MUD

Sandra R. Bell

We owned a business, a construction company called BellincCo. We'd been in business since 1984, mixing concrete and doing other subcontract work. However, in 1991, with a federal freeze on new construction and a little cash in the bank, we decided to fish a little closer to home. We bid on and won two projects: a community building for the local Housing Authority and Fire Station #5 for the city.

It was the beginning of a nightmare. The city council and the Housing Authority Board told us that we weren't qualified to do the projects, although we had the performance and payment bonds for the projects. Most people think of construction bonding as insurance; it's not. Bonding is like getting a loan from a loan shark; you sign your name and a company puts up a paper guarantee in the amount of the contract that you will perform. Then they put up another 50 percent that you will pay everybody. If the owner claims you aren't doing either of those things, he can cash those bonds in.

The powers that be did everything in their power to stop us, from forgetting to inform us that one of the sites was an old dump to telling our employees not to come to work and suppliers not to deliver materials and equipment. With costs mounting, we decided to stop working on the city's fire station project until we could get compensation for the additional work.

That night, a steeple wall above the bay doors for the fire station fell. It was blamed on us when in fact the design of the project didn't have any bracing or ties to anchor the wall to the building.

The next thing we knew, the local ABC affiliate was putting the story on the news. The mayor was out of town when the first, seemingly sympathetic story aired. Later, negative articles appeared in the paper. It was claimed that we weren't working on the other job, even though the community center was well on its way to being completed. The Housing Authority director decided that the community center was not to be built by our company. In fact, he was quoted in the newspaper as saying that my husband had never had any intention of finishing the job and wasn't a decent person.

Not to be outdone, the mayor staged an ambush for my husband at the project site. The mayor showed up with his driver, the city attorney, and a full entourage of Black city councilmen. That night on the six o'clock and eleven o'clock news, there was our white mayor, at 6´6˝ towering over my 5´8˝ husband, demanding that he do the job the city was paying us to perform.

The stories continued. Our motives were assessed and our character was examined and attacked. We were informed by friends that "they're going to get you and they're going to get whoever tries to help you."

Another business owner told us some of them were going to get contracts as a result. He added, "Sorry it had to be at your expense." All I could think of was how unfair it was for us to be treated this way. I had never felt so down.

Then I remembered falling in the hog pen when I was a child. My grandparents had had about fifteen hogs in a fenced-in area. After a rain, a small tree had fallen from outside the fenced area into the pen, acting like a bridge. My cousins and I had double-dared each other to climb the bridge. When it got to be my turn, somebody shook the limb. Not too hard—just enough for me to land in the hogs' mushy dirt.

I got it in my eight-year-old head that I wasn't moving. After I'd been out there sitting in the mud for an hour, Grandmomma came down the lane with her cane. Some time before, my uncle had sent Grandmomma a fancy cane from Liberia, and she always used it to walk to the mailbox, which was about a half mile from the house and only a couple of hundred feet from the hog pen.

When I heard her coming, I told my cousins, "Now y'all going to get it." To my surprise, instead of getting the plum switch, tearing off the bark, and giving them a beating, Grandmomma opened the gate and lit into me. She started beating me right there on the ground, until I came up out of the mud like a jack-in-the-box. Then she switched me all the way back to the house.

Stripped, crying, and soaking in the big tub on the back porch, I couldn't figure out why she had done this to me. "They pushed me," I cried.

She finally said, "Sandra, it doesn't matter if you ended up in the mud because you were pushed, you accidentally fell, or you just got it in your head to jump in. It only matters that you get up." "But that's not fair," I cried. She responded, "Fair ain't got nothing to do with it. When you down, you got to get up. You got to pull yourself up, and just like getting out of that hog pen, it might be slippery, you might stumble and fall again, but you got to keep getting up."

Suddenly, I realized that all the bad articles, media coverage, half-truths, and misrepresentations of the facts had put me back in the hog pen. Right then I knew I had to get up!

It took a few months to salvage something of our lives. My husband and I cut our losses and eventually moved to another city, where we reestablished ourselves. But our persistence and hope had carried us through.

HAMS AND TURKEYS

Billy Mitchell

I'm often asked where I got my passion for advocacy. It came in part because of my grandmother, Addie Mitchell—Nannie, as her grandchildren called her. Her physical being left us three days shy of her ninety-fifth birthday, but her spirit remains to this day.

One time Addie Mitchell was marching with the civil rights leader Reverend Joseph Lowery and others in Dickens County, Alabama, trying to help two women who were accused of voter fraud. All the two women had been doing was teaching sick folks how to cast absentee ballots and helping others to register to vote. But in the sixties in the South, civil rights were at best a novelty that African Americans did not enjoy.

Their plans were to march from Pickens County to Montgomery, Alabama, tie up the traffic on the highways, bring attention to this injustice and Alabama's intimidation tactics in general, and get the women out of jail. Word had gotten out that the sheriff of Pickens County was going out to all the Black folks' homes, giving out hams and turkeys. He was telling them not to get involved with the march. "We've got good relations here in Pickens County," he would say. My grandmother told me that at the time she thought it was nothing to worry about. Black folks would not sell their souls for a few hams and turkeys.

They were expecting some three hundred people. But when they gathered at the place where the march was to start, there were only about fifty people there. My grandmother asked herself, "Could Black folks actually be selling their souls for hams and turkeys?" Recognizing that God was on their side, they decided to go on.

It was February, and it started to sleet. When they finally got to their first stop, Aliceville, Alabama, people thought my grandmother's face was wet from the sleet, but it was wet from tears of sadness, thinking that Black folks had sold their souls for food. She prayed for some kind of sign as to whether she should keep going, for it was a long, cold walk to Montgomery. When they turned the corner in Aliceville, there waiting for them were over four hundred others with their marching shoes on, ready to join them. And they had baskets full of ham sandwiches and turkey sandwiches to feed the hungry marchers!

They went on to march to Montgomery and eventually got the women out of jail.

Love and Self-Love

Edith Ross Gray

In the Name of Love,
  I sacrificed;

In the Name of Love,
  I paid the price.

In the Name of Love,
  I compromised;

In the Name of Love,
  I accepted lies.

In the Name of Love,
  I accepted infidelity;

In the Name of Love,
  I believed what he was telling me.

In the Name of Love,
  I accepted his excuse;

In the Name of Love,
  This was only mental abuse.

In the Name of Love,
  He treated me so unfair;

In the Name of Love,
  It was more than I could bear.

In the Name of Love,
　　He didn't tell me this tip;
　　That he had two daughters during our relationship!

In the Name of Love,
　　I allowed his mother to move in;

In the Name of Love,
　　I wouldn't do that s—— again!

In the Name of Love,
　　I swallowed my pride to raise his child;

In the Name of Love,
　　Where's my sanity?—and that's just to put it mild!

In the Name of Self-Love,
　　I got a divorce;

In the Name of Self-Love,
　　I made a better choice!

In the Name of Self-Love,
　　I rise;

In the Name of Self-Love,
　　No more compromise!

In the Name of Self-Love,
　　I went to counseling and began to take back, for myself, what he took;

In the Name of Self-Love,
　　I can now smile while I write this poem for this book!!!!

YOU DON'T KNOW LIKE I KNOW

Sonia Clark

On January 17, 1995, my twenty-sixth birthday, my two children and I became homeless. My mother-in-law, without remorse or feeling, threw us out of her home.

At that time, my daughter, Brittany, was three years of age, and my son, Ronald junior, was a year and a half. Besides my in-laws, I knew only a few people in Wilmington, North Carolina, and I was miles away from my parents, who lived in New York City.

"What am I going to do?" I asked myself. I could not go back to my husband, because he had proven time and again that his attraction to women was more important than his wife and kids. I couldn't go back home to my parents; I had been down that road before and was too embarrassed. Nonetheless, I called home. I wasn't sure what my father was going to say, since we had had words during the recent Christmas holidays. Through my tears, I explained to him what had happened. To this day, every time I think of his advice, I smile from ear to ear. Without hesitation, he said, "Get your things and get out of there. Go to your sister's place in Greensboro. I'll be down in a few days to help you get situated."

The next day we arrived at my younger sister's one-bedroom apartment. Sherri took us in and helped me put my life back together. I started working for UPS at night and my sister kept the kids for me. During the day, I looked for another job and a place to stay. Sherri will always be my hero for giving me a hand when I had less than nothing.

My ex-mother-in-law's eviction occurred just after I had finally decided to get a college education. After high school, I had gone into the military, where I met my husband. When I left the military, I had children and wound up going from one dead-end job to another. While I was in Wilmington, a sister working at the unemployment office stressed to me the importance of going back to school while my kids were young. Naive in the ways of the world and those of academia, I told the woman that it was impossible because I did not have any money. Nonetheless, her words haunted me until I decided I would try it.

After the kids and I got settled in Greensboro, I asked Sherri how difficult it would be to get admitted to North Carolina A&T, where she was a student. She felt that I could still get in for the spring semester, but I wanted to take it slow, and so I applied for the fall semester. The paperwork was not very difficult. My sister walked me through everything, showing me a few shortcuts, advising me about whom to see when I had to go to the financial aid office or the registrar's office, and encouraging me to "just relax and have fun."

The only thing my sister and I disagreed on was my decision to move into the worst housing project in Greensboro. Morningside Homes had a bad reputation from one end of the Triad to the other. However, we had been staying with my sister for four months, and I felt we needed our own place. Moreover, I wanted a cheap place so that I could concentrate on my studies and not have to worry about rent all the time. On my son's second birthday, I signed the lease. I prayed and asked God to watch over us; He did. He blessed us with a few neighbors who looked out for us and treated us like family.

However, almost on a daily basis, I had to deal with women whose lives consisted of baby-daddy drama, trips to the welfare office, and spending all their food stamps in one day. I could hear the whispers as I came to and fro: "There goes that stuck-up girl from New York with the car. Yeah, she think she hot shit because she go to A&T. She a nigger just like us." When I went to school in the morning, there would be a group of "player haters" standing around outside. When I came back home, they were still there.

My mother called to encourage and sometimes threaten when I wanted to drop out of school. My father, too, supported me at every turn and kept me rolling in whatever car he could get from the auction.

Sophomore year, my estranged husband stopped paying the court-ordered child support. Nonetheless, I made the dean's list both semesters, got over my fear of water and learned to swim, and decided to start putting my journalism skills to the test via the student newspaper.

Senior year I became managing editor at the *A&T Register*. For four years, I struggled to be a parent, a student, and a Black woman trying to simply be herself. I would not have made it if God had not blessed me with a family whose love is never-ending. In addition, He strategically placed some special people in my pathway who understand that love and Aggie (A&T) pride go hand in hand.

There was Andrea Cummings. "Dre" was one of only a handful of my classmates who wasn't too scared to come to the Grove. Matter of fact, folks thought she lived at my house 'cause she was always there washing clothes or having her usual plate of mac and cheese with a glass of ghetto Kool-Aid. Not only did Dre encourage me, she was there when family could not be. My sister moved out of state in 1996, which left the kids and me without any real relatives in the area. Dre stepped up to the plate and helped as much as she could. When the kids got the chicken pox, we took turns watching them and going to class. The next semester, I got the flu, Ronald junior had an earache, and Britt had a touch of pneumonia all in the same week. Dre would stop by in between classes to help cook, get our medicine from the store, and help keep the apartment clean. She was also there for the heartbreaks and the bad-hair days. To this day, I don't think she knows how much her friendship means to me.

Dre; Lisa, my next-door neighbor, who served as my alarm clock and inspiration for three years; Mrs. Wiggins, my academic advisor and friend; Dr. Styles and Mrs. Tonkins, two of my teachers; Mrs. Bea, who befriended me during my freshman year when I worked part time at Sears; Mrs. Cook, A&T's financial aid advisor; the Durhams, who managed to keep my car running and gave the kids gifts at the holidays; my journalism teacher, Mr. Johnson; and my family all showed love at a crucial time in my life. On May 15, 1999, North Carolina A&T State University awarded me a bachelor of arts degree in English.

The past seven years have been an example of what a determined person can do in the face of adversity. However, I know that I did not get here by myself. My success was made possible by the love and sacrifice, individually and collectively, of people who understand that no man or woman is an island, and we must all work together.

Dream a Little Dream

Germaine Sibley Gordon

About five years ago one of my close friends organized a group of ladies she called an empowerment circle. In this circle of sister friends each woman took the time to reflect on her life's events. "Guard your thoughts," my empowerment sisters would always say. "Guard your thoughts" became such a powerful statement to all of us because it meant that if the mind can think it, you can achieve it.

At one point in my life I found myself in a deep emotional rut. I was spiritually unfulfilled with my job, my boyfriend, and myself. Less than six months before, I had received my graduate degree and felt ready to take the world by storm. But in the months since, I realized having just any job and any man was not fulfilling at all.

By January of the following year, I'd had enough. I knew I needed and deserved better. I quit my job and focused on a positive outcome for my life and a career I truly enjoyed. Bills, rent, and others' opinions didn't matter. On some days I questioned my decision (especially when the bill collectors called). Fortunately, I had my sister friends to talk me through the fear.

A few weeks after quitting my job, I quit my relationship. My heart knew I needed someone who was going to add to the happiness I chose for myself. My current relationship was draining, and if I was going to change, I needed to let go of things that kept me down.

I was living in Chicago with no immediate family; most of my friends lived out of state. Talk about scared! Deep inside I knew that if my life was going to change, I was going to have to change as well. My lack of respect for myself and my need for companionship was evidenced by my tolerance for verbal and spiritual disrespect.

For the first time in my life I was alone and open to the world and what it had to offer. I had no job, man, family, or school (I had been in school almost continually since kindergarten) to hide behind. It was scary yet invigorating. In the following weeks, my life began to change for the better as my personal faith began to deepen and my understanding of God's love began to increase.

While visiting the house of one of the few sister friends I had in the city, I met a nice guy who had come to visit her husband, and he and I started up a conversation. We had seen each other before but never had much to say to each other. This day, though, something was different. For the first time in months, I felt energized about my life. Like two old friends, we spoke as if reunited after many years apart. There was an immediate comfort with him, and at that moment I knew we were going to be closer than mere friends. A few days later, we went out on our first date, and a week after that we were inseparable. The relationship was refreshing, as we both worked to learn more about each other and about ourselves. He knew I wasn't interested in anything less than 100 percent commitment, and he respected my spiritual development.

Three weeks after we met, I received a phone call from a local university. The director of the youth program knew my new beau and had spoken with him a few days before. He had given her my name as a possible dance teacher for a spring-break arts camp. As God would have it, I was hired for a one-week workshop. With the money, I was able to pay off some bills and catch up on my rent.

As a result of "cleaning house," my emotional rut had turned into emotional riches. I felt better about myself, which in turn resulted in better outcomes in my life. My understanding of "that little voice inside," the God spirit that is within all of us, had grown.

I am now married to the guy I met, and we work constantly to grow together spiritually. I work every day to direct my thoughts in a positive way in my relationship, my career, and my life. Like everyone else, I have my days of uncertainty, but the spirit of God that lives within always pulls me through. "Guard your thoughts" is a powerful reminder of how we can live our lives.

I continually strive to be of service to others who are working to develop a deeper spirituality, as I believe that whatever we do, our thoughts have the power to dictate how far we go and how successful we come to be!

ADDICTION

Sharon Ewell Foster

There were two hundred women in white in front of me. Women of all colors and all faiths, from all social and economic groups—women bound by a common goal: change. What was so moving about them was the sense that transformation was in the air. It sizzled and crackled during the time we shared. It was a spirit; it was alive.

I was not speaking in a church or in a theater. My audience was a group of inmates dressed in prison uniforms at Dawson State Prison in Dallas, Texas—each one of them in a program designed to help them recover from addiction. Some of them were drug addicts and dealers, others prostitutes, some gamblers, and still others thieves. Their addictions were characterized by their reliance on some outside force that would make them feel better—something that would take away the pain.

What could I possibly tell them that would make any difference in their lives? I wasn't even sure how I'd come to be among them. A single mother of two, a former Defense Department employee, I had taken a detour from my book tour to talk with the women. I hoped to say something to them that would encourage them.

As I spoke to them, I looked for opportunities to walk among them and to hug them. It occurred to me, as I talked, that there were few differences between them and me.

For years, while I worked for the Department of Defense, I applied for job after job. I sought promotion after promotion. I looked and prayed for raise after raise.

"This job will be the perfect one," I would tell myself. "Everything will be all right if I can just make some more money, if I can just get a better job or a better supervisor."

It was called having a career, and most people applauded me for it. Lots of people have careers, and you shouldn't confuse them with me; my need for promotion consumed me. While I enjoyed the last two years that

I worked as a civil servant, most of the time I was dissatisfied or miserable. I hid how I felt behind suits, lipstick, pumps, and stacks of paper piled on my desk.

For the sake of more money and a better title, I moved to places I never wanted to live. I neglected or abandoned important relationships and ruined my health. I dressed and behaved in ways, and tolerated treat-ment, that violated my sense of who I was and what I believed. I needed those promotions, the recognition, the money—those fixes—to help me feel better, to make me complete. That sounds pretty much like addiction to me.

As I stood among the two hundred women in white, jailed because their addictions were illegal, I realized that we had so much in common. There was a woman from my hometown, East St. Louis, Illinois. There were single women, married women, women with children, women who had had careers. There were women who could pray and quote scripture as well as corner girls. I shared their joy, and like them, I was free. They no longer needed their "fix"; I no longer needed to spend hours scouring employment lists. (There are many trees in the rain forest breathing eas-ier because I am no longer sending out hundreds of résumés each year.)

Like them, I was forced by circumstances to face my behavior and to commit to making a change. But it was not until I stood before them that I realized that I had shared a similar transformation. It was then that I was able to tell them how I became a new creature, how I wrestled to find my true purpose and promise. It was then that I was able to offer the women hope and to share with them the joy that I have found—the joy that we shared—on the other side. It was standing in front of a group of women, sharing our scars, that I realized that I was free indeed! Gathered in the arms of the women, I prayed the same prayer for all of us: "Lord, help us to face ourselves, to change, and to become all that you have destined for us to be."

GETTING OFF WELFARE

Sharon Blessman

I am a registered nurse in the inner city of Detroit, Michigan. My job involves connecting needy people with the resources they need. Many times the people that I help are so destitute that they lose hope. Many are pregnant teenagers, single parents, or poor families whose major concern is a choice between food and other necessities in life. My major hurdle in working with this group is to bolster their spirit.

I share with these people a personal story of hope and courage that I've had the privilege to watch unfold. A good friend, whom I will call Beth D., had moved to the Detroit area when she was in her early twenties. She did all the things young people generally do—party, party, party. She went to work at a local Taco Bell. She moved in with her boyfriend, and things went smoothly for a while. Then the inevitable happened: Beth got pregnant! Shortly thereafter, he began to physically abuse her.

Beth had only a sister in the area. Her mother was deceased, and her brothers and father lived in another state. She did not enjoy the benefit of a strong support group in the area. Like many women caught up in the cycle of abuse, Beth agreed to take her boyfriend back and entered into marriage with him, hoping this would improve the situation. But the abuse continued. Finally, after two years, she decided enough was enough.

Now Beth had a baby and a minimum-wage job, lived in a dangerous neighborhood, and had limited resources. But she said to herself, "To hell with this! I deserve better and so does my child!"

So she picked herself up by her bootstraps. She used the welfare system to get her jump start. She attended Lawrence Technological University full time and did nails to get extra cash in between study sessions; my family helped out with her young son. These were hard times for my girl, but she forged ahead.

Because of her determination, courage, and strength, Beth graduated with her master's degree in business. She now holds a top position on the

Detroit school board and has the financial security to send her son to any college or university that he wishes.

My message for those of you who may find yourselves in similar situations in life is this: Don't ever allow the welfare system to run your life. Use it only to advance your life! Never be afraid to step out on faith. Keep in mind that if you believe, you can achieve. Love both God and yourself with as much intensity as you can muster. And never say "I can't," because *you can!* Keep the faith, because it will keep *you!*

A Dream Come True

Sondra Simmons

You try to keep me from reaching the top.
You throw obstacles in my path, to try and make me stop.
As I reach for a new level you do what you can
To hinder my progress, but you don't understand.
From the crown of my head to the soles of my feet,
I am a wish fulfilled, a dream complete.

You can't stop me from being what I am destined to be
No matter how you criticize and talk about me.
You make my load heavy, but I still stand.
I refuse to break, although I may bend.
And yes, I dare to walk with my head held high.
For I am a dream that refused to die.

You laugh as I stumble along my way,
Hoping for me that tomorrow will be a darker day.

You undermine every move that I make.
You give nothing as you greedily take.

Relentlessly you seek my demise,
Desiring only to see defeat in my eyes.
You ask who in the hell I think I am,
As you look at me and wish me damned.

I am the Cream of the Crop, a Journey Complete.
A Quest Fulfilled, a War That Knows No Defeat.
I am the Top of the Line, a Long Journey's End.
Ruler of the Hill, a Drinking Man's Gin.
A Cloud's Silver Lining, a Wronged Man's Just.
A Poor Man's Desire, a Rich Man's Lust.
A Drink of Water, when a hard day is through.
A Wish Fulfilled. Yes I AM
A Dream Come True.

LEAVING THE FRONT PORCH

Lamont Jackson

My father died of cancer, and my mother died violently. All of this took place before I was two. I became a victim of child abuse, spent time in the hospital, and jumped around to several foster homes.

When my guardians left the house, they would lock me upstairs in my bedroom, and when company was over, they always made me sit outside on the front porch. If I didn't comply, they would punish me by burning my hands on the stove.

One day when we had company, as usual, I was exiled to the front porch. I sat there for about one hour before something or someone spoke to me and told me to get up and run. It seemed as if the voice was telling me that I should run as far away from that place as I could, and so I ran! I spent two weeks in the hospital for burns to my hands and for malnutrition.

The day I left the front porch of my abusive guardian's house is probably the single most important and significant day in my life. It started me on a journey to find something better. I was young at the time, but God moved me to make a change, so I ran away from home. I use the word *home* loosely because there was really nothing homey about the place where I lived or the people I lived with. It was merely a roof over my head. I was never really welcome there.

After my stay in the hospital, I became a ward of the state of Indiana. I spent eight years in one foster home and two years in another. By the time I was a young man I was carrying a great deal of emotional baggage. I was filled with feelings of rage, fear, and anger. I was about to be sent off to the Family Children's Center for orphans when I was rescued by my cousin.

My cousin, whom I affectionately called my aunt, opened up her home to me and welcomed me in. She was a single mother living in a small three-bedroom, one-bath house with five daughters. My cousin, may her soul rest in peace, gave me the mother's love that I so badly needed.

At the age of fourteen, after having finally achieved some stability in my life, I tried concentrating on school. This was easier said than done, however. Emotionally, I was so unstable and so confused that it was difficult to focus on school. Living in a small house with six people was tough. We were on public assistance and often didn't have enough money to pay the bills. We would boil water in order to take a hot bath and had to wash our clothes at the Laundromat. But we all loved one another.

During my senior year of high school, everyone was talking about going to college. I didn't have a clue about going to college and doubted that I could get admitted, much less succeed there. I was a very average student and hadn't even taken the SAT. Besides, in the course of the school year I had partied a lot. But God allowed another pivotal person to enter my life.

Charles Martin Sr. was the executive director of the South Bend YMCA and often held parties for the local middle and high school students. In addition, he had developed a number of other programs to try to keep kids out of trouble and headed in the right direction. One night at one of these parties he approached me and asked, "What are you going to do after you graduate from high school?" I told him I thought I would just get a job and work somewhere. He asked me if I had considered college, and of course my response was no.

Noting my confusion, he promptly scheduled several counseling appointments with me where he took the time to discuss college and lay out a plan of achievement for me. He signed me up to take the SAT and helped me enroll in a summer precollege program at Indiana University. A short time later, I was admitted to the school!

For my first two years of college, Mr. Martin acted as a mentor, counselor, and father figure for me. He helped me to choose classes and fill out financial aid papers, and he arranged transportation to and from my home to the school. He also inspired me to become a member of the great fraternity Kappa Alpha Psi.

These events set off a chain reaction of positive experiences for me and allowed me to rise from the ashes of my circumstances and contribute to the uplifting of my people, instead of becoming a statistic. The people God placed in my life—my late cousin Sedalia and the late Charles Martin Sr.—allowed me to believe in the possibilities of man, and in the power of love!

OVERCOMING OBSTACLES

Tracy Andrus

In 1988–89, while living in Shreveport, Louisiana, and owning a small company called Consumer Financial Services, I got into trouble with the law. I had purchased a fine home and numerous automobiles and was living the life of an unsaved man. Prior to my success, I had been a very devout Christian, working faithfully in the church. I had even confessed my calling to preach the gospel.

When huge amounts of money started to pour into my business, I turned my back on God and my family and began to live a very immoral lifestyle. I had money, women, fame, and fortune. I was on television three or four times a day doing my commercials. I had billboards on the side of the road with my picture on it. I was the man and I knew it.

One day, while vacationing in Florida, I called my secretary to ask her to wire me a few hundred dollars because I had decided to take a cruise. She informed me that my account was very low and the money I needed was not available. When I returned to Shreveport, I discovered that as a result of my lavish lifestyle, I had neglected to stay on top of my business and my deposits were getting smaller and smaller. Soon, I was struggling with the lease payment for my office, not to mention my four automobile notes and the mortgage on my new home.

In an effort to avoid being embarrassed, I deposited a phony $4,000 business check in my personal account to help me meet my financial obligations, and it worked! Somehow, I was able to raise the money to put back in my account before a fuss was made.

That transaction became the beginning of my end. This practice of opening up numerous accounts, depositing checks that you know are not good, and receiving money back is called check kiting. Having discovered how to work the process, when things got tight financially I started floating checks all over the place. Before I realized it, I had obtained $38,000 from this fraudulent process, and the banks and the police were looking for me!

I tried everything I could to get this money back to the banks, including commingling funds of my clients with my personal money. I was desperate, willing to do anything! When the authorities in Shreveport tried to arrest me, I left Louisiana and took my check kiting to the state of Texas, where I kited for approximately $18,000. Looking back, I realize that all of this money did me no good, because when the police did arrest me, my bond would be anywhere from $50,000 to $100,000. It turns out I was giving most of the money to the bail bondsman and digging myself deeper and deeper into debt and trouble.

Soon I was on TV on every station without having to pay for it. I made headline news and was on the ten-most-wanted list.

When the smoke cleared, I was facing felony charges in Shreveport and Bossier City, Louisiana. I was also facing felony charges in Texarkana and Houston, Texas. I knew I was in serious trouble. I didn't deny doing any of what I had been accused of doing. In fact, I pleaded guilty to it all. I was wrong and I knew it. If they had given me a hundred years in prison, I would have had to accept my punishment and do my time, because I was as guilty as sin.

When the time came for me to appear in court, the judge sentenced me to six years on all seven counts that I was charged with, but I was blessed because he ordered that the sentences run concurrently—which, in essence, amounted to one six-year sentence. When I went to Bossier City to be sentenced, the judge there sentenced me to six years at hard labor and ordered that the sentence also run concurrently with the Shreveport sentence. The same thing happened when I appeared for sentencing in Texarkana and in Houston—the judge in each of those cities sentenced me to three years at hard labor and ordered that the sentences run concurrently with the other sentences that I was serving.

Of course, I knew that none of this happened by coincidence. I believed it was God giving me a second chance, and I wanted to do my best to take advantage of this opportunity.

I was sent to Wade Correctional Center in Homer, Louisiana, where I served as an inmate lawyer assisting other inmates with their legal concerns. I found favor with the warden and the other inmates and was made a trusty and moved to the honor dorm. I lived there for the next two and a half years, until I was sent to a halfway house.

While in the halfway house, I met the sheriff, and he helped me tremendously. Soon I was allowed to attend church, and I met the Reverend Huey P. Lawson, who served as a role model and employer for me during my final days at the halfway house.

Once I was released from prison, Reverend Lawson, who owned a real estate company, allowed me to work for him. Despite a law in Louisiana saying that ex-felons cannot hold a real estate license, I appeared before the real estate board and explained my situation, stating that I was out of prison and felt that I had paid my debt to society. At this point in my life,

I wanted to provide an honest and decent living for my family. With the help of the Lord, they voted unanimously to allow me to sell real estate if I could pass the test—and I did! I knew God was still working in my life.

Later, I attempted to look for a more stable source of employment and became a substitute teacher in Rapides Parish. When I took the exam to become a teacher's aide, I passed it. Mr. Julius Patrick, who was the principal of Reed Avenue Elementary School and the mayor of Boyce, Louisiana, became my boss, my father, my advisor, my friend, and my tutor for the next five years. I will love and remember him the rest of my life.

Mr. Patrick encouraged me to rise! He never said it in quite these words, but when he spoke to me, everything about him said to me that even though I might have lost a battle, I had not lost the war. "Keep fighting," he would say, "and stay focused; you can do it!" He believed in me, and his encouragement made me want to achieve and become even more successful. I had the support of my wife, children, mother, and other family, and somehow I knew that I could beat the odds. I was down, but I was not out.

I was able to enroll in Louisiana College, in Pineville, in the spring of 1996 thanks to the president of the college, Dr. Robert Lynn, who arranged to have my old school loans paid off by alumni of the college. I majored in criminal justice and religious education.

In 1999, I received my associate's degree in criminal justice, and in 2000 I received my bachelor of science in criminal justice. I resigned from my teacher's aide position at Reed Avenue Elementary and enrolled at the University of Louisiana at Monroe in the master's degree program. While there, I met another positive Black role model. Mr. Roy N. Shelling hired me as a full-time third-grade teacher at Lincoln Elementary School. It was my first job as a full-time teacher. I knew that God was working mightily in my life.

In August of 2001, I graduated from the University of Louisiana at Monroe with a master's degree in criminal justice. I then sent in an application to the new juvenile justice Ph.D. program, the only one of its kind in the nation, located at Prairie View A&M University, in Prairie View, Texas. Shortly I received a call from Dr. Frank Williams, who informed me that I had been accepted into the program! I laughed out loud and thanked the Lord! I recognized that without Him none of this would have been possible. He had given me the faith to try. I kept knocking, and he kept opening up the doors.

Today, I am a Ph.D. student at Prairie View University teaching Introduction to Criminal Justice to college students. I have worked as a research assistant for two of the most brilliant people I know. I hope to receive my Ph.D. within the next two years. The God I serve has made it possible that men like me can transform their lives from prison to professorship. With the help of the Lord, I was able to overcome.

PERSISTENCE OVERRIDES RESISTANCE

Joylyn Wright

I must have read the letter at least one hundred times. I nearly fainted when I read the first line: *I am pleased to inform you that your application for admission to the Thomas M. Cooley Law School has been accepted after review by the Faculty Admissions Committee.* Yes, I understand that millions of people receive letters like this every year, so why did I nearly go comatose when I read it? Well, maybe because this moment had been in the making for two long, frustrating years, and it all started with me falling asleep at my desk.

I was working at an insurance company as an administrative assistant. The job was very uneventful, and so was the pay. Many days I found myself surfing the Internet (on the down low, of course) searching for other jobs. I felt like my youthful years were flying away, and I wasn't doing anything constructive, much less having any fun. One day, a friend of mine was applying to graduate school and asked if I would help her write her personal statement.

When I finished the statement, I found myself with no work to do and sitting in my cubicle staring at a blank computer screen. Suddenly, without warning, I just felt my head get heavier and heavier. Luckily, I jerked myself awake before anyone noticed.

It was then that I experienced an epiphany. I asked myself, was *this* the way I wanted to spend the rest of my life? Working in a mindless job, with terrible pay, no life, and no purpose? Did I want to wake up every morning to a going-nowhere job just to pay the bills and after twenty-plus years find myself being escorted out the door with a gold watch and a one-way ticket to that financially precarious state of employment called early retirement? Well, my answer was an overwhelming no, and at that moment I decided it was time to make something of my life.

I had known what I wanted to do with my life since I was sixteen years old. I wanted to be a lawyer! Years before, I'd tried to get into law school; I even took the Law School Admission Test (LSAT) twice. However, I was so disappointed with my scores that I buried them in a drawer in my old bedroom in Bonneau, South Carolina, and abandoned my dream for three years. I look back on this time as if I was mentally asleep. However, when I woke up from my little nap I realized it was time to take the risk of a lifetime and fight for my dreams.

I had no idea that I was in for one of the hardest fights of my life.

I started applying to law schools like a madwoman. Give me a form, and I would fill it out; I didn't care where the school was located! I never thought about how I was going to get there, how I was going to pay for it, or even if I had a chance of getting in. I was on a mission to apply anywhere I could. By the end, I had applied to approximately thirteen schools. I thought for sure I would be accepted by someone; after all, what were the chances of my being turned down by all thirteen schools? Well, my chances were excellent, because that is exactly what happened. All thirteen schools had denied my application!

I had never felt so rejected in my entire life. One by one the rejection letters came with their pleasantries: *We have reviewed your application for admission, and unfortunately, we cannot offer you admission into our incoming class. . . . Thank you for your interest in our school. . . .* At first, I was defiant. Every time a school rejected me, I would just apply to another one, and another one, and another one. I refused to be ignored. However, by the eighth letter, I was beaten and broke! Applying to law school was expensive. I cried night after night, pleading with God to have mercy on me and give me one acceptance letter, but it never came.

By May 2000, I was through with the idea of attending law school. I was tired of the disappointment and the rejections. I tried to comfort myself by saying that I did my best, so I could convince myself I had nothing to be ashamed of. Finally, I decided that I would just stay at the insurance company and work toward my gold watch.

But, despite my efforts to forget about law school, I simply could not. I kept hearing, "All things are possible with God." So, after a few weeks of recovery from the onslaught of rejection letters, I decided to begin the application process again. But this time, it would be different. This time I went to students, attorneys, and school administrators and asked what I needed to do to get into law school. I went to a law school forum and met with recruiters, bought a book on how to apply to law school, and called some of the schools that had turned me down and asked why they hadn't accepted me.

With motivation from a small group of friends and family who had believed in me, I took the LSAT for the third time. I studied every day. I even brought the study guide to work and studied during my lunch break and at my desk when my workload was slow. Luckily, God blessed me with an understanding boss who never gave me a hard time about it.

Now, it was time to reapply! I followed the book to the letter. I wrote the best personal statement I had ever written, or so I thought. I had several people, including an English instructor, review my statement, and I asked all the right people for letters of recommendations. My applications that year were perfect! I ended up applying to twenty-four schools, including some of the schools that had denied me the year before. I thought no one could turn down this great application. I was certain that I would get in somewhere!

However, again I was wrong. This time twenty-four schools sent twenty-four rejection letters. It was the year 2000 all over again! Coincidentally, I was also let go from my job and had a car accident. I was devastated.

Several people suggested to me that "perhaps God does not want this for you" or "you most likely won't ever get into law school with those grades." I was ready to believe them. Then one night, while in my apartment feeling sorry for myself, I found a book I had purchased at a book fair a year earlier. It was a small volume with quotes of wisdom from successful African Americans. While reading it, I came across a quote that changed my entire outlook on school. It read, "I wasn't the 'did everything right and got into medical school' type person. My motto became persistence overrides resistance."

For me, it was as if someone had turned on a light. For the first time in my life, I felt that there was someone who understood what I was going through, because I obviously wasn't the did-everything-right-and-got-into-law-school type of person. The quote reminded me about an example from the Bible, of a man who knocked on his friend's door and asked for food late at night. Jesus said that the friend gave the man food not because he was a friend but because he saw the man's need through his persistence. The lesson was that we needed to have the same persistence when approaching God or any other situation. I immediately had hope again, but most importantly, my faith was restored.

By the fall of 2001, I approached law school with a different perspective. This time I didn't rely on the "right people" or the "perfect personal statement" or anything I did, because none of these things worked. This time, I relied on one thing . . . God! My mother had always told me to put God first in whatever I did, but I'd forgotten that. I'd put so-called important people and my abilities first, which, I believe, is why nothing had happened. So I simply braced myself, turned the situation over to God, and allowed Him to do the rest.

I went to Atlanta for another law school forum and got as many brochures as I could get. Then I went home once again and began to fill out applications. This time I trusted God, not myself, and it worked!

I received my first acceptance letter in December 2001, about two years and three months after I nodded off at my desk. Having received thirty-seven rejection letters, countless negative advice, and an academic suspension in college (that's another story altogether!), this kid from a single-parent home in rural South Carolina was finally accepted to law school. I had a school that was willing to give me a chance. I now fully understood the quote I had read earlier. Persistence definitely overrides resistance.

MAKING A DIFFERENCE

Regina Little-Durham, M.S., M.P.H.

One evening in May 1985, after parking my car near my co-op apartment in Jamaica, Queens, I was approached at knifepoint and robbed. The man then took my car keys out of my purse, opened my car door, choked me with a scarf, abducted me, took me to what I later found out was his mother's home, and raped and sodomized me. I'm a twenty-six-year-old professional with a strong belief in God and a background in hospital administration and social work. I started to talk to the brother to try to save myself, because I believed I was going to die—I had seen his face. Although my throat was raw from being choked and I was in tremendous pain, I said to him, "I forgive you . . . I know you don't mean to hurt me." The brother said nothing. I said, "You must really be hurting inside to do something like this . . . how old are you, anyway?" I was shocked when he responded, "I'm twenty-eight." "Oh," I said, "and when is your birthday?" He said, "October." We continued to talk, and I was able to get additional personal information out of him. Finally he said, "Let's go." He put a blindfold on me, took me back to my car, drove me about half a mile from where I live, and jumped out of the car. Shaky and bleeding, yet thankful to be alive, I drove back to my home and called an ambulance.

When the ambulance came to take me to the hospital, one of the emergency techs said, "You must be the fourth or fifth rape in this area in the last three months." I was astounded! I had heard nothing on the news; nothing had been posted in my development. When I contacted the Rochdale Village administration, they admitted that they had "heard about alleged sexual assualts" but had elected not to say anything because they didn't want to upset the residents unnecessarily. I was furious. But in a way this was a good thing, because it gave me a focus, a way to regain control, which is critical for a rape victim. I spent the next few weeks receiving counseling for post-truamatic shock and working with the police. Because I had seen my attacker's face, they were able to draw a reasonable sketch of him. I went out with the police trying to approximate where he had taken me. Subsequently, he was caught. He turned out to be a former security guard for the complex where I lived! Several of his other victims and I testified in court, and he was sentenced to fifteen to twenty years. (I received notification recently that he was denied parole.)

I decided that I was going to take a stand. Security in Black neighborhoods, even in nice ones, is an issue. Why weren't we notified of a possible attacker on the loose? In any predominantly Caucasian community, it would be all over the six o'clock news!

I hired an attorney and forced the development to hold a community meeting to alert residents to the situation. I then found out the names of three of the other victims. One of the victims had been stabbed, another left naked on the side of the road. It took some doing, but I was able to convince them to file a class-action lawsuit against the development. As sisters, we had a duty and responsibility not to let this go. The case was subsequently settled out of court for over $1 million. Management was forced to revise their security plan and develop a written policy about notifying residents of possibly dangerous situations.

And so with God's help, something truly positive came out of an absolutely awful experience. I believe that God knew that I could handle the situation and help make a difference.

THE LITTLE ENGINE THAT CAN

Audra Washington

On Thursday, May 18, 2000, at 11:30 A.M., I was called into the human-resources department. Thinking we were going to discuss a contract with my employer, a music publisher, I was informed by my boss that I was being fired! The reasons he gave were personal use of the company's messenger service and discrepancies in my expenses. They had already planned my exit. Termination papers were neatly typed and placed in front of me, awaiting my signature. A company car was waiting downstairs to take me home with my belongings, and security was waiting to escort me back to my office so I could pack up my things. As I sat there, I still could not process what was taking place. I had heard stories of how people in the music industry were let go, and now I was joining the ranks! Fired, terminated, and downsized.

After signing a waiver that I would not sue them, I walked away with severance, unemployment insurance, and a settlement that was heavily taxed, not to mention a year's worth of medical insurance at their expense. But I kept thinking, How could this have happened? Where were the warnings? What had I done? How was I going to live? What now?

I had given birth to a beautiful baby girl the previous September. I was very much still in postpartum depression. I was the sole financial and emotional provider in my home, since my daughter's father had lost his job ten months earlier. I considered myself to be an extraordinary sistah—a Bennett College graduate, a member of Delta Sigma Theta sorority, and a music industry executive with a salary and perks in the $100,000 range. I was well-spoken and articulate in the boardroom as well as on "Sony" avenue. I had worked in the music business for ten years and knew a lot of songwriters, producers, artists, executives, and the white men who controlled the music industry. How could this have happened to me?

I left my former employer in a state of humiliation. How was I going to explain this to my family? What would happen to my reputation in the business? Would I find a job to take care of my family? What would happen to me emotionally? I was already drained physically, emotionally, and spiritually. I had always been in control of my life, but now, for the first time, my situation controlled me. I had been fired! Downsized!

With the little pride I had left, I declined to take the company car home. I walked home from Fifty-second Street and Avenue of the Americas to Ninety-sixth and Columbus Avenue, just to clear my head. I broke the news to my family and friends, and they too could not believe what had happened, or why. I did not believe the company's reasons for laying me off were justified. But what was done was done, and I had to move on. Later I discovered it was a setup to get rid of me. They had a contract under negotiation and they needed my salary to meet their numbers for the merger they were working on.

After a month, I was still in shock. The phone calls of "Hey, girl—what's up?" and "You are on the guest list of . . ." stopped completely. Things had gotten so bad between my daughter's father and me that I just wanted out, or so I thought.

I must admit that although my mother was with me physically in New York, it was actually my dad in Atlanta who held on to me emotionally. He suggested to me, "You need a change; why don't you come to Atlanta? Whatever you decide to do, I will support you and your daughter, Sierra." With that reassurance, I decided to pack up and move to Atlanta, Georgia, believing this would heal my pain internally. But it ended up only making matters worse—I hated Atlanta!

Nearly three months later, I moved back to New York City with more appreciation than before. I was happy to be back on concrete and not grass (if you can believe that), taking the train instead of driving everywhere, eating hot dogs and drinking vanilla egg creams.

My daughter's father had left our apartment. I began to realize I was not only single, but a single mom.

The Christmas holidays were quickly approaching, and I was anxious to see them come and go. What did I have to be joyous about? I didn't have a job, though I had looked everywhere—temp agencies, monster.com, and hotjobs.com. I followed up on every lead. I reached out to old contacts and asked that they keep me in mind. I looked in every conceivable area where I thought my skills could apply—all to no avail. Then my unemployment ran out and I was denied any extensions. I couldn't even get public assistance! The only person who kept me going on a daily basis was my daughter, Sierra. Through my tears, her presence in my life allowed me to continue smiling. I knew I would have to continue pressing on for her, and for us!

My savings completely exhausted, rent and every bill past due, I relied on my friends emotionally and financially to get me through 2001. My family and friends not only gave me money to pay my rent, but gave me something much more important. They gave me the encouragement to continue pressing on. They were able to convince me that I was good at what I did. By the grace of God, in March 2001 I started my own company. The Sable Group: A Music-Related Service Company is a boutique agency that handles music publishing, creative exploitation and expansion, special events, and corporate sponsorship.

My "aha" moment came when no one was willing to hire me. I felt I had no choice but to create my own opportunity—to use what I had learned in the music business and make it work for me instead of working for someone else.

Has it been easy? Absolutely not! But it has been fun and extremely challenging. And yes, it has been worth it! I am enjoying being a business owner, creating ideas and seeing them come to fruition in an industry I love and an area I am passionate about. I love Black music and feel I have been chosen to preserve and educate others about Black music in all its richness.

I must admit that I do get nervous when money is short and bills are due. But I am blessed to have a strong church family who have stood by me financially and spiritually and continue to pray with and for me. I am also blessed to have friends who refer me and my company for other projects and to other contacts they have. I have learned to live within my means and not get caught up in who is wearing what, driving what, and going where. I have learned to focus on the real me—the cliché "to thine own self be true" has taken on a new and deeper meaning in my life.

Most of all, I have learned to love my daughter more and to spend quality time with her each day. And I am learning to rely on God and His will. In my darkest hours, at those times when I cannot see the solution to a problem, and even when the smallest of blessings comes my way, God reminds me that He is the one who brought me through. I will forever be grateful to my friends and to Him for teaching me the true meaning of "keeping the faith."

EDUCATION

My Second-Grade Teacher

Tavis Smiley

Malcolm X once said, "Education is our passport to the future. For tomorrow belongs to those who prepare for it today." When I think where I've come from and the life that I've been able to build, I am reminded of the impact that teachers have had on me. Whatever I am, and ever hope to be, I owe in part to my second-grade teacher, Mrs. Vera Graft. Mrs. Graft was the person who, early on in my life, inspired me to believe that I could achieve anything that I wanted. Thanks to her unyielding support, and the abiding interest she took in me, I was convinced that the only thing that could determine my altitude was my attitude.

I grew up in north-central Indiana, where I attended Nead Elementary School, a school that was overwhelmingly white. I don't recall there being more than one or two other Black kids in my second-grade class. In the midst of this sea of whiteness, I was virtually alone, which made it difficult for me in many ways. In first grade, I did not distinguish myself as a particularly talented or gifted student, and when I reached the second grade, I wasn't doing much better. The difference was that Mrs. Graft took an interest in making sure I didn't become a lazy student or a student who slacked off from stretching toward his potential. She was able to see that I had the potential to do something special with my life.

I attended preschool in Gulfport, Mississippi, where we lived before moving to Indiana. All the students in my preschool class were Black, and my preschool teacher, Mrs. Warren, took the same interest in me that Mrs. Graft did. Mrs. Warren would not allow any of us in her preschool class to do anything less than our absolute best. A strict disciplinarian, she ran that preschool class as if it were a top-notch private academy, even though most of us came from a disadvantaged background. She always insisted that we do our work and that we apply ourselves. I quickly became accustomed to this kind of attention and level of expectation.

As a result of our move to Indiana, I was transplanted from a Black community in the South to a rural white community in the Midwest. All of a sudden, my whole world changed dramatically, and I had trouble adjusting at first. But Mrs. Graft was not going to let me sit in her classroom with my brain set on stall. At the beginning of the school year, whenever I was challenged by a problem that I wanted her to help me figure out, or one that I wanted her to give me the answer to, she would say to me, "You've got to quit quitting, Tavis. You have to develop the discipline to sit here and work through this problem. Tavis, think; think through this material. We have studied this and you know this. You cannot sit here and allow your brain to be set on stall. You've got to apply yourself and you've got to process this."

What hinders extraordinary performance in our children is ordinary expectation. Mrs. Graft did not have ordinary expectations for me. She had extraordinary expectations for me. From her I learned not only the value of applying myself, but also what it meant for someone else to expect something of me. I went on to become, according to her, one of the most outstanding students she had ever taught.

Nowadays I often get asked the question, "Of all the issues facing Black America in particular and the nation in general, what primary issue should we focus on?" I never have to ponder that question, because the answer is always the same. The primary goal of our society ought to be the educational excellence of our children, because everything else flows from this. We live in the most multicultural, multiracial, and multiethnic America ever, and yet in so many ways we are abrogating our responsibilities to educate, in a more excellent way, the least among us. We fail to recognize, sometimes, that many of those who are less privileged will be the ones who will inherit America and be expected to lead us triumphantly through this new millennium. I believe that it is child neglect on our part to not provide our children with a quality education as surely as it is child neglect for them to not have prenatal care, proper nutrition, food, clothing, and shelter.

When it comes to education, we have to do three things. First, we have to make it our number-one priority; second, we have to demand more of America's schoolchildren; and last, we have to, as Malcolm X suggested, recognize the true value of a quality education. We have to see education as an investment in our future, which is exactly what it is.

When there are educators in the classrooms who care about those for whom they are responsible, so much can be accomplished. All of us can look back on our academic lives and recall the name of some teacher whom we admired and adored. I have never met a single person who succeeded at anything and didn't acknowledge a teacher somewhere who inspired them, motivated them, empowered them, and enlightened them. Teachers can have such a long-term impact on the lives of their students. Somebody, somewhere put something into these students; demanded something of them; expected something from them; hoped something for them; and instilled something within them that to this very day has made a difference in their lives. Whether they are thirty or ninety, the fact remains that if they have been successful at anything, they can point directly back to a teacher who helped to shape their lives.

We need to appreciate the role that teachers play in our lives. I have often said that teachers are the most undervalued folks in American society. And if teachers are the most undervalued persons in our society, then parents are the most underutilized in our children's educational process. I have traveled throughout this country and have spoken at all kinds of educational institutions—inner city and suburban; Black and white; rich and poor; endowed and unendowed; public and private—and I have learned one thing of which I am certain. The schools that do best in this country are the schools where parents are involved. If we really want to empower our children and empower ourselves toward building a brighter future, then every parent of every child must involve himself or herself in their child's pursuit of educational excellence. There is a role in this country for every parent to play, and the time is now for parents to step it up, to pick up the pace.

As I mentioned earlier in the book, I am one of ten children. Nonetheless, my parents never missed a PTA meeting, never missed a parent-teacher conference, and would not hesitate to come to our school to meet with our teacher, our principal, or when necessary, the school district superintendent. My mother and father loved each of us dearly, sacrificed for us, and would have done anything on earth to see us succeed. But they made it very clear that if we ever got into any trouble at school, and they had to come down to the school and meet with the teacher, principal, or whomever, that we had better be on the side of right. They let us know that if they learned that any of us had been cutting up in class, misbehaving, not turning in homework, talking too much in class, and not concentrating on what we were supposed to be doing, we would pay the price for such behavior later at home. I cannot tell you the numbers of times my siblings and I were punished for not behaving in the proper manner in the classroom. Even in a family as large as ours, my parents stressed the need for each one of us to get a quality education. Every Black person has heard the statement (as a parent points his or her index finger at your head) "What you put in here, no one can take away from you." We have to prepare our children and give them the ammunition they will need to overcome the obstacles that life will present them. There is no better preparation for life than a quality education.

And, by the way, thirty years later my second-grade teacher and I are still in contact. We talk to each other and write to each other regularly. I will forever be indebted to her, and she claims to still be one of my biggest fans.

NEVER GIVE UP!

G. Jean Thomas

In 1974, at the age of twenty and with a junior-college secretarial certificate in hand, I moved to Atlanta, Georgia. I had just married my high school sweetheart a month earlier. Upon our arrival in Atlanta, I was ready to begin my job search. Although I possessed a secretarial certificate, the truth of the matter is that I could barely type forty-five words per minute. Practically every other job seeker was typing at least sixty-five words per minute. It didn't take me long to realize I was not prepared to compete in the job market. Reality set in.

I enrolled in the Metro Atlanta Skills Center, an educational training program that targeted minorities. Even though I had taken typing classes in high school and junior college, I had never approached typing as a skill I should master. Having been raised on a farm in southwest Georgia, I was naive enough to believe that a typing speed of forty-five words per minute would make me as competitive as I needed to be.

At Metro Atlanta Skills Center, within a few months I was able to greatly improve my typing skills. Through persistence, hard work, and a lot of practice, I became confident enough to seriously approach the job market again. This humbling experience had taught me two things: never to settle for mediocrity and to do things right the first time. I emerged from my experience as a true competitor.

In 1977, my husband and I became parents. Four months later, at the age of twenty-three, we purchased our first home. Looking back, I can say that this was the beginning of a series of tests, trials, and tribulations in my life.

The responsibility of maintaining a home and being a parent was overwhelming! I had also become a surrogate mother for my youngest brother—my mother had passed away several years earlier, when he was five.

There were many times where there was not quite enough food to go around, so I made myself the last one to eat. Together, my husband and I wrestled with the responsibility of our daughter, my younger brother, and our house note. Then our marriage broke up and my husband and I decided to go our separate ways.

At this point, I had been working long enough to realize that I would never be able to seek other opportunities without acquiring additional education and skills. So I submitted an application to Georgia State University to pursue a four-year college degree. Within a few weeks, I received a letter from the admissions office stating that my application for admission was being denied. The letter informed me that I was entitled to an appeal of the decision from the admissions office. I went through with the appeal process and was admitted to the university.

Without two incomes, I was unable to keep up with the mortgage payments for the house. In addition, I now had the responsibility of a car note and weekly day care expenses for my six-month-old daughter.

I decided to take things one day at a time. I recalled hearing my parents and grandparents when they used to talk about what the Lord had done for them. I decided to turn to a higher power for strength and asked God for faith to simply hold on. I was determined to have faith and not give up.

My first major challenge was in figuring out a way to bring my current mortgage up to date. I needed approximately $2,000. My earnings were a meager $12,500 per year, and a certain percentage of this was automatically deducted for a retirement account. Although I had five years of seniority on my job, I decided to resign from my job in order to gain access to my retirement funds. With the money in hand, I was able to bring my house note current.

The first winter after my divorce was particularly difficult. In Georgia, the weather is generally warm. However, this particular winter was unusually harsh. The furnace in our home was not working properly. Sometimes it failed to turn on at all. Even when it did work, it resulted in an electric bill in excess of $350 per month. Eventually, the furnace stopped working completely. I bought two space heaters from Kmart and an electric blanket. I kept one heater in the bedroom where my children and I slept and the other one in the bathroom, where we got dressed each morning.

During the Christmas season that year, we experienced blizzardlike conditions in Atlanta. The space heaters were totally inadequate, although at least they kept us from freezing. When we were home, we would spend most of our time in the bedroom, where there was a space heater. At times, it seemed colder inside the house than outside; ice formed on the inside of the windowpanes.

I never let on to my children or anyone else in my immediate family the extent to which we suffered that winter. My pride, determination, faith, and desire to make things work would simply not allow me to surrender. I continued to have faith that God would see us through.

I came down with a severe case of bronchitis that kept me out of work for two weeks. Because my funds were so limited, I tried to avoid going to the doctor. Although I had health insurance from my job, even the copayment was too much, not to mention the additional expense of prescriptions.

I prayed to God to help me come up with a solution to improve my life and my family's situation. When I finished praying, what came to my mind was the idea of selling our present home and purchasing a more affordable one. I decided the time had come for me to finish my education as well.

I put the house on the market; it was under contract six days later. At the time, I was living from paycheck to paycheck and borrowing money from everyone I could. After my home was sold, I was able to buy another, smaller home in a different city in the area, where my family and I spent the next ten years.

I reentered Georgia State University. But because of my limited finances, I was unable to attend classes on a consistent basis. I would attend one quarter and have to drop out the next. The stop-and-start process was terribly frustrating and seemed endless as well. Then, halfway through completion of my program, the university decided to discontinue the major that I had selected. I was forced to choose a new major and had a new set of classes to complete. I refused to give up, however.

During the last two quarters of my senior year at Georgia State, I attended school full time and worked full time as well. It took me thirteen years to complete my undergraduate degree in political science. But I finished. I had entered, dropped out, and reentered Georgia State University four times before graduating. By the time I marched down the aisle, my daughter was a sophomore in college herself at the University of Georgia! I was euphoric. Looking back, I still find it difficult to believe that I did it!

Somewhere during those thirteen years of completing my degree, I managed to find the time to attend paralegal school. I attended classes two nights a week and every other Saturday. I would leave work at 4:30 P.M., pick up my daughter from after-school care, drop her off at my sister's house, drive to the MARTA train station, and then ride the train to Lenox Square, where my classes were held. When class was over at 9:30, I made the reverse trip. We would usually arrive home at 11:00 P.M.

Currently, I am attending graduate school at Clark Atlanta University in pursuit of a master's degree. My daughter and I are making family history; we are both pursing master's degrees and working full time!

Through persistence, hard work, and determination, I have come to realize that every experience in life carries a lesson to be learned. I may never have wealth, but I am truly thankful for all that I have accomplished. All it takes is a little hard work, and faith.

JUST GET THE KNOWLEDGE

Sandra J. Easterling

The green and white three-bedroom house with the large porch was perched at the end of a dirt road in the borough of Wheatland, Pennsylvania, located some eighty miles from Pittsburgh. The house sat alone at the end of the street like some huge forlorn castle that boasted a view of country living on the one side and cows peeking curiously through the long wire fence on the other.

My mother had returned to my grandmother's house to get a jump start on life. Dad had proven he wasn't the husband or father type even after many years of practice. I learned from him that a real fun guy who can play a mean bass and outdress the next guy does not automatically qualify as husband and father material.

When she wasn't cooking or cleaning around the house, Momma worked in a big office building in Sharon, Pennsylvania, emptying wastebaskets, mopping the floors, and dusting the furniture at breakneck speed. The telephone rang frequently for "Sweetie," as my mother was affectionately called by her sisters and close friends. She wasn't one to dish out a lot of advice but was more the great listener. Being a wise woman, she knew that most people didn't heed advice even when they asked you for it.

The toughest lesson I had to learn as a young child came one day while I was in my first-grade class. Sitting in my classroom going over the assignments, I raised my brown arm frequently in an attempt to answer questions. The teacher, however, refused to call on me. After much frustration, I started passing the time by talking to my classmates. This became bothersome to the teacher, and she began to wave her finger in my direction and send me a cold stare. I ignored her and continued to talk to my friends. Finally, she beckoned me to the front of the class, and to my horror, she sat me across her knees, pulled up my skirt, and proceeded to spank my behind parts good!

When I arrived home, I sat down and confessed my story to Momma.

I hadn't cried, because I was too humiliated to do so. Momma had me sit on the hassock and talk to her while she ironed. She asked me, "Did you know the answers to the questions?" I replied, "Yes, ma'am; I knew them all." She continued, "Well, if you know the answers and you know the teacher isn't going to call on you, why bother raising your hand? Knowing the answers is enough! Just keep learning more of the answers. Don't concern yourself about impressing others with your knowledge; just get the knowledge!"

And that's what I did.

A WELL-EDUCATED BLACK

Lana Rucks

I grew up in suburban Cleveland about twenty-five years after *Brown vs. Board of Education*. In both my immediate and extended families, learning was a priority. When finances would allow, my sister and I were enrolled in a variety of enrichment activities. Often during the summer, my father would hold "basement school," in which he would reinforce lessons learned from the previous school year and prepare us for the next year. Our analytical thinking, critical in any endeavor, was developed at the kitchen table with regular discussions and debates on myriad topics. My parents had moved to this suburb because it had one of the best public-school systems in the nation at that time. The combination of my parents' efforts and the quality of the schools should have been enough to ensure a quality education. It did, but not without a fight.

The transition from elementary to junior high school introduced us to tracking—placing students in "appropriate" learning levels. Some have argued that tracking is a modern version of segregation. One day toward the end of sixth grade, my teacher distributed notices indicating where she had tracked us for the following year in English and math. I was shocked to see that I was placed in a standard English sequence. "Standard" was actually below average. I quickly folded the notice and put it in my backpack before any of my classmates could see it. I had always considered myself smart. That was the first time that I can recall thinking I was dumb.

I showed the notice to my mother, who immediately became angry. My mother, who was a native of Cleveland, recalled her own school experience. She had had a math teacher who would not teach her class math because "you do not cast pearls before swine." My mother crossed out the word *standard* on my paper and circled the next-highest level. I was eventually placed in advanced English.

This marked the beginning of a six-year battle with various teachers, guidance counselors, and administrators. The next year my parents urged the school to have me placed in gifted-and-talented courses, a move that was supported by my grades and standardized test scores. Nevertheless, their request was met with resistance. My father, who was raised in a small town in the segregated South, was extremely sensitive to the issue of educational expectations. He told us of an experiment in which average students were divided into two groups and assigned a teacher. One teacher was told that the students under her care were below average, and the other teacher was told that her students were gifted. At the end of the school year, the students assigned to the gifted classes outperformed the remedial group. Because of his involvement with the community and with the schools, he knew that upper-level classes reinforced students' abilities and confidence.

Eventually, I made the transition to gifted-and-talented courses during the second half of seventh grade. (My math teacher, in a fit of pique, required that I complete nine weeks of homework assignments in a week.) There were only seven other African Americans in the gifted-and-talented program in a class of eight hundred at a school that was 50 percent Black. Together we developed an organization that provided a network for parents and students at the high school level, and mentored junior high students to help with retention in the program.

There is a profound and lasting impact on kids who are told daily that they are smart and capable. If the schools are not doing it, then we adults must tell this to our children. We need to expect and encourage our children to do marvelous things, and eventually they will. Most importantly, parents must be involved in their children's education. My parents attended every open house, scheduled meetings with teachers, and were involved in parent organizations. They understood that the educators needed to see that they were concerned about their children's education, because if they did not care, no one else would. Our school system did not understand the intricacies of becoming a "well-educated Black," but thank God, my parents did!

EDUCATION IS A TICKET OUT

Virginia D. Banks-Bright, M.D.

I came from a family that was always politically involved. It just made sense to my mother, a civil rights activist, to have us march in Raleigh, North Carolina, for the integration of hotels, schools, and restaurants. I would come home from school in the ninth grade in 1962 and do all of my homework so that I could go with my mother and sister to the church where all the marchers collected. The father of the former mayor of Atlanta, Bill Campbell, was one of the civil rights activists at that time, and he also participated. We would sing and march in the streets nightly to such songs as "We Shall Overcome" and "We Are Soldiers in the Army." Slowly, hotels and restaurants opened their doors to "Negroes."

At the time, I was attending a Black junior high school, and my parents felt that my education would be enhanced by going to the white high school across town because they offered more courses, especially in German. My mother petitioned the school board, and I was accepted.

The school had been integrated, reluctantly, two years previously, and there were three Black students there.

In September 1963 I enrolled at Needham B. Broughton High School in Raleigh. Every day was a day from hell. Although the teachers, for the most part, were okay, the students were unforgiving. I was called the N word on a daily basis. There were times in class when the teachers had to force the students to sit next to me in class. In biology class we had to sit at desks made for two people. No one, of course, would sit with me. The teacher would hand us items to look at and then we would pass them on to the other students. When the teacher would hand something to me and I would pass it back, the students would laugh and let it drop on the floor. Then they would get up and get a paper towel so that when they picked it up, they would not have to touch it.

When we entered the auditorium or the gymnasium for special programs, whoever was behind me in line would automatically start a new row so he or she would not have to sit next to me. There would sometimes be an entirely empty row where I was sitting. My stomach was in knots most days. I wanted to give up, and told my mom and dad that I did not think I could do this. My mother instructed me to go back in there and just prove that I deserved to be there.

The first exams came along, and I made A's on most of them. Then some of the teachers pointed out to the class that I was the only one who sometimes made 100 percent on an assignment. Some of the students started coming around when they found out that I was smart. Believe it or not, some of the most racist ones asked me to help them with their homework.

That experience made me tough. My mother and father were strong parents who had a vision. Black parents, in those days in the South, knew that education was a ticket out and could lead to success in the future. I don't know if I would have continued to let my children go to a school where they were constantly berated and humiliated.

Today I am an infectious-disease specialist. I have not been back to my high school for any of the class reunions. I do realize, however, that the human spirit is capable of much, and those of us who integrated schools in those days must serve as role models to our children and to other children as well.

From Pregnant Teen to Ph.D.

Tanya Dugat Wickliff, Ph.D., M.B.A.

The phone rang and the voice of my best friend at the other end said, "Dr. T, are you ready for the big day?" I stood speechless for a moment (as hard as that is to imagine for anyone who knows me). "Dr. Dugat Wickliff, are you there?" Finally I replied, "Good morning, Shay. Quit tripping, I'm just Tanya." "No," she said. "Today is your graduation, and after all that you've been through, I'm going to call you by the name that you've earned, thank you very much!"

Realizing that there was no negotiating with my best friend, I answered her inquiry regarding the after-graduation party that my family had planned, and excused myself from the conversation. Instantly, as if on autopilot, I began to shout, "Thank you, Jesus!" The tears welled up in my eyes. Perhaps you'll understand my behavior better when I share with you my story.

Years before, while playing in a Liberty High School basketball game (serving as the vertically challenged point guard), I received the ball on a fast break after our opponents had missed a free throw. But everyone was able to pass me on the court and set up in the zone before I got down to the other end, even though I had had a head start. Though not the star player, I was not *that* slow. Coach called a time-out and benched me, yelling, "Dugat, what is wrong with you?" I didn't go back into the game. Afterward, I was forced to divulge the news that I had found out earlier that day—I was pregnant! Paralyzed by confusion, shame, and fear, I plowed through the next months of my life in a daze. I knew my life had been forever altered. I had no idea what to expect or how to handle it.

Immediately the murmuring began. The "good girl" had been found to be "bad," and the spotlight was turned on high beam! I was not met with much friendliness from family, friends, school administrators, or the community at first. "Look at her. And they thought she was going to be something. Ain't gonna be nothin'." "Might have had book sense, but didn't have a lick of common sense to go get herself in that condition!" And the worst thing of all was the silent treatment. My mother was in shock—she had already been in and out of hospitals from a permanent, debilitating work injury. My father drank an extra bottle of Crown for sure when he heard—"You were my little princess. You were going to be my little Barbara Jordan. I should have had your sisters teach you some stuff. I really thought you would do something."

The people who mattered to me most—my parents, grandmother, aunts, church family, and everyone else—were disappointed in me. And the pain I felt inside was excruciating! I had let everyone down—even God!

I understood how I had ended up in this situation, but it just didn't seem fair. I was fifteen, lived in a single-parent household as an only child (I had nine siblings by my father but none in the household), had a sickly mom who was away a lot in hospitals, and was picked on by seemingly all my peers for being a geek or a Goody Two-shoes. I was lonely in my small east Texas town with no one to talk to and no one to show me that I mattered, except for the boy who became the father of my baby.

That summer when my son, Jamar, was born, I made a life-changing decision—to provide my son with the absolute best that I could. It didn't seem like a big deal, but it became the driving force for me to do my best in whatever I pursued. I didn't have material things to give him, but I could give him the best me that I could. This decision motivated me to excel in speech, debate, sports (I tried hard anyway), band, flag corps, and academics, which resulted in membership in the National Honor Society. Two years later I was the only Black honor student among the LHS graduating class of 1982. I enrolled in the University of Houston (with no help from the guidance counselor, who had obviously written me off the way so many others had) and majored in mechanical engineering.

During this time, I learned the meaning of the phrase "character-building experiences." For example, in the second semester of my freshman year I was stranded, literally, without any transportation to school. School was fifty miles away, and we didn't have a car. I made arrangements with four different people to get to and from school and prayed for God's grace and mercy to get me through. I got a job at McDonald's making $3.85 an hour, the minimum wage in 1983, and got an apartment in the fall of my sophomore year. With only a few pots, donated groceries, my clothes, and a borrowed kindergarten exercise mat to lie on, I proudly moved into my apartment. Between then and the spring of 1989, when I completed my bachelor's degree, I commuted via Metro buses and Greyhound between Liberty and Houston to attend my son's Christmas play, school field trips, and every activity I could when he wasn't attending classes or school functions with me. I was determined to be a good mommy while making a better life for us.

We had a big fish fry hosted by my fiancé. However, the celebration was short-lived. Five days later my grandmother, who had helped to raise me and my son, was diagnosed with inoperable cancer. She died two months later. Although devastated, I didn't have much time to mourn. I married Tony later that year. We were a family of not four or five but six. My mom lived with us, I gave birth to a second son, Raymond, and ten years after the birth of my oldest son, I gave birth to my youngest son, Cortlan. In only one year, I experienced graduation, loss of life, creation of life, a new job, a new husband, relocation to a new city, and growth in my family.

My husband, Tony, and I were just getting adjusted when my mother caught pneumonia and unexpectedly died. I don't think my husband and I ever fully recovered; several years later we were divorced. We remained extremely good friends, however, so much so that we discussed a reconciliation and began to make plans.

I had completed a master's degree and had just enrolled in a Ph.D. program at Texas A&M University after working in industry for nearly ten years. One Wednesday night I talked with Tony until approximately 11:45 P.M. We were planning a big date in New Orleans for the following Saturday after the concert given by the gospel choir that I sing with was over. Since it was late, we agreed to work out the particulars the next day.

Shortly after noon the next day, my officemate on campus informed me that I had missed a call. "Someone called to tell you that your ex-husband died. I'm so sorry!"

Tony had died of a heart attack in his sleep at age forty. This could have been the straw that broke me. But I refused to let it. I took things as best I could, one day at a time. And now, miraculously, I'd arrived at this important milestone, graduation day. Today I would receive my doctorate of philosophy in engineering.

Humbly, through tearstained eyes, I paused to reflect on the amazing journey that had begun a few decades before. My life had been full of challenging and tragic lyrics. The melody, however, resonated with faith and with God's mercy, grace, and favor. I've come to truly understand that success, for me, has been and will continue to be measured by the people I touch and the positive difference I make in the lives of others.

RUBY LEE

Wylencia Monroe

This is a story of a woman who knows the meaning of persistence. Let's call this woman Ruby Lee. Ruby Lee, as the name much suggests, was born in a small town in Alabama in 1939. She was raised by two parents, attended and excelled at the public schools available to her at that time, and went on to college. After college, she began her teaching career and later married. She had children a little later in life than usual and hoped that her children would have the opportunity to get an education as good as or even better than what she had received in the segregated public school system.

Although she was born and bred Baptist and had raised her children in that faith, in the mid-seventies she started sending her children to a Catholic school. She did this for approximately three years; then the costs became more than the family could bear. Ruby Lee decided to give the local school a try for one full school year, but the school didn't quite measure up. Ruby Lee's children were often bored at school; they often found themselves serving as office assistants, delivering messages, or tutoring other students.

The next approach was to look for a public school outside their community. One school offered special programs and had won awards, but the admission process was based on a lottery, and Ruby Lee's luck had run out. The next school the children attended offered special programs and had won awards, and it appeared that Ruby Lee's hopes for her children had been realized. But when the school learned that Ruby Lee and the kids lived outside the school's area, it was necessary to find another school option.

With some experience in maneuvering within the public school system, Ruby Lee then found a magnet school. This time she used her parents' address in order to make sure everything looked right on paper. After one and a half years at the magnet school, the ruse was discovered and the children were informed that they would be released because they did not live within the school's area. By this time Ruby Lee had had about enough. She went to the city board of education with her children and tried to enlighten the board about the difficulties she had encountered. She explained that she had been teaching for a little over twenty years now, that she valued education, and that she wanted only the best education for her children. She explained that the local school had not met her standards and that she did not have any other options for her children.

In parting, she made one demand: "If my children cannot finish out the school year and remain another year at their present school, then they will not attend school at all and I will not return to work. Now, you try to find someone who can come in during the middle of a school year and teach a hundred and fifty ninth and tenth graders. Try to find someone who enjoys teaching and has more than twenty years of experience doing it, and try to find someone who has a sincere interest in their students learning as if the children were their own. I'll be waiting to hear from you."

Well, the first day Ruby Lee was at home with the kids she heard nothing. The children wondered, and Ruby Lee worried. But by the third day, the board called and said the children could return to school. Ruby Lee was relieved, and the children were thrilled! Although the children had moaned and griped about changing schools so many times, they later came to know the meaning of persistence and to value their mother's efforts.

FAMILY, FRIENDSHIP, AND HERITAGE

Sassing the White Man

Tavis Smiley

My maternal grandmother, Daisy Mae Robinson, affectionately known to me as "Big Mama," was the daughter of a sharecropper in Mississippi. I loved her so much that I often share with my radio audience some of the advice and words of wisdom that she imparted to me.

It was always fascinating to sit down and talk to Big Mama about our family, legacy, heritage, and culture. I learned so much from her during these moments. Every time I had the chance, I would say to her, "Big Mama, tell me about the story of what happened on such-and-such a day," or "Tell me about that time when so-and-so happened." Big Mama would always say, "Boy, I've told you that story a hundred times," and I would say, "I know, but tell it to me again." I used to love listening to her tell stories of what it was like to grow up as a sharecropper's child, and what it was like growing up in the South during segregation. Just to hear her stories of struggle firsthand was enormously empowering.

I was able to gain a great sense of the historical contrast between the life and experiences she had growing up and those I had. As I listened to her talk, I was able to see the progress we had made as a country and as a people. There is a lot more to be done, of course. But when Big Mama talked, it became abundantly clear to me how grateful I should be for the opportunities that had come about in my life as a result of the struggles my ancestors, and Big Mama, had gone through.

Here is one example of the contrast between our lives. My grandmother had come to live with our family, and one day she was in the family room watching TV. All of a sudden, my mother, who was in the kitchen working, heard my grandmother scream out in the most wretched, awful, wailing voice she had ever heard. Big Mama was in tears, weeping, "Oh, Jesus, Oh, Jesus." My mother dropped what she was doing and ran to the family room to see what could have happened to my grandmother. When she got there she discovered Big Mama watching a debate on television between a conservative white male commentator and me. We were both giving it everything we had, going back and forth and matching each other point for point in an ideological debate.

My grandmother, however, witnessing this, was fit to be tied. Here she sat watching me argue with, talk back to, and sass a white man. She said to my mother, "Has Tavis lost his mind? Girl, do you know what they're going to do to that boy? Where is he? We've got to go and get him right now and bring him home." Big Mama was scared to death that I would be thrown in jail or lynched for sassing a white man.

My mother burst out laughing. Once she caught her breath, she tried to calm my grandmother down. She explained to Big Mama that I was only doing my job, which entailed debating issues on television. She tried to explain to Big Mama that I had been asked to come on television by the white people who programmed the show to debate the white commentator in the way she was witnessing.

My grandmother, however, couldn't understand it. How could I get away with sassing this white man on television? Because of her life experiences, it didn't make any sense to her. "They ain't gonna put Tavis in jail for this?" she asked. "They ain't gonna beat or lynch him for this?" "No," my mother said. "That's what they want him to do on the show."

My grandmother still couldn't believe it, and her spirit could not rest. My mother ended up having to contact me and ask me to call my grandmother to assure her that I was all right. That evening I called Big Mama on the phone. It was only after assuring her that I wasn't sassing a white man and that I wasn't going to be lynched or go to jail for talking to the man in this way that she started to calm down. Then I hit her with the punch line—not only had the producers of the show wanted me to talk to the white man the way that I did, I told my grandmother, but the white man had actually *paid* me to do this. She literally laughed until she cried. "Lord," she said, "I never thought I'd live to see the day when my grandchild could sass a white man anywhere, much less on television where people all over could see it happening."

It was a fascinating example of how far my grandmother, and African Americans, had come, that the daughter of a sharecropper could witness her grandson on television sassing a white man. History had brought her, and us, a long way.

HERSTORY

Gigi Steele

When we speak of Black history we speak of adversity, strife, obstacles, helplessness, and hopelessness. We rarely acknowledge that the adversity generations of our people went through gave way to later generations of strong Black people.

My history begins with three generations of strong, educated Black women, three generations of Spelman women. The first of these women led the way in bringing the rest of us into being. My history, thus, begins with an account of HERstory.

My grandmother, a strong Black woman of eighty-three years, was able to instill hope, inspiration, and determination in her family. My grandmother loved her family and sacrificed tremendously to make her family walk the path of salvation and prosperity.

Being raised by Grandma offered me a shining example of what the future could be. Although it was hard to see while growing up, the reality of her sacrifice is so clear to me now. When I reflect on my history, all of my memories are linked to my grandmother. She devoted her life to raising her five grandchildren. When the burden of raising grandchildren was first thrust upon her, she carried that weight without ever showing us that it was a burden.

Back in the sixties, when owning a house was just a dream for most Black folks, I remember standing outside in the Georgia red clay watching our house being built. This became the house where we all grew up. My grandmother single-handedly kept a roof above our heads.

There were seven of us, and sometimes more, depending on when the older two daughters needed shelter. Although the girls had to share a room and the boys shared a room, we had food, clothing, and shoes on our feet. We even had a crystal chandelier in our dining room! I never understood why Grandma cried the day I broke one of the crystals on the chandelier. It wasn't until I became an adult that I realized what a sacrifice that chandelier had been, earned through Grandma's toil and hard work, brought into our midst to provide an example of the beauty of what could be, instead of the darkness of what surrounded us. I never understood why we had to take baths in less than a foot of water, or why we had to bathe together, until I realized that to make ends meet, we had to conserve water. Or why at night when the house was cold, rather than turning up the heat, she would always say, "Well, honey, if you're cold, get a sweater." She ran this household alone.

I still remember the day that we all dressed up and she put on a black robe with a red scarf draped around her neck; it was the day she was going to get her master's degree. At the time, I didn't know what this master's thing was. But, because of her efforts, I, too, could envision getting a college degree one day. Everything that I am today is because of her and who she was.

I was able to raise my own children with the same values and strength. I could show my children what could be instead of what was. Although my grandma is now old and sits in a well-deserved easy chair in that same house that we grew up in, each time I visit her, I try to let her know that she is the reason that I am who I am. And I can tell that she is proud of who I came to be. Even when she leaves this earth, her spirit will live on in all five of her grandchildren, who will pass that spirit to their own children and grandchildren.

As a people, we can all look at our generations and find a grandma somewhere who possessed the strength and courage to carve out a path for those coming behind her, someone wise enough and strong enough to instill in us the same strength and courage to look beyond adversity and forward into the future.

AGGIE

Bennis Blue

The other day was my sister's sixty-eighth birthday, and for the first time that I can remember, we pulled one over on her—a surprise, that is. Agnes has cared for three generations of siblings and their offspring. This she has done despite having never completed high school and without having a spouse. She is known affectionately to nieces and nephews, grandnieces, cousins, and kin as simply "Aggie."

My sister spent her days growing up in rural North Carolina working on our farm and tending us siblings. When our mother died in 1957, Agnes, at the age of twenty-three, set off for the city to seek employment. She spent most of her meager wages buying clothing and food to pass along to our maternal grandmother to help with the upkeep of two of my other sisters, my younger brother, and me. A kind cousin convinced her to find a place to rent in Raleigh, North Carolina, so that the rest of our family could stop being passed among relatives and settle down to someplace called home.

That home was a three-room house with no heat and no running hot water. The unpainted house was located on a dirt street. However, we were all thrilled. Shortly afterward, the family—four younger siblings, one sister who returned after eloping, and Daddy—settled in with my sister Agnes. The neighborhood was blessed with several mothers who sat on their porches to keep an eye on all of the neighborhood urchins, such as my brother and me. Our next-door neighbor was the mother of a librarian, a public school teacher, and a college professor; down the street were several librarians, public school teachers, and a beautician who gave me my first paying job (sweeping up the beauty shop, emptying trash cans, washing dishes, and running errands).

Agnes rose at six-thirty each day to leave for work, wearing her pink or blue uniform. She worked as a counter girl in the cafeteria at one of the best-known supply businesses in town. Before she left, she prepared breakfast for us and made sure that we each had clean clothing to wear to school. Daddy was frequently away from home working as a mason, carpenter, or landscaper, or hanging out with his friends and drinking. Despite working long hours, my sister always found some way to brighten up our day.

I remember the day she brought home our first television, a black-and-white Zenith on a rolling cart. We felt we had arrived! I grew up during a period of rising civil unrest; my sister never sat at the back of the bus and told us never to sit there either. In fact, we were told to exit the bus if we were ever asked to sit in the back. I never was.

It was my sister who made it possible for me to earn a doctorate, although she herself never received a high school diploma. She now takes care of my three nieces, ages seven, nine, and ten—her inheritance from our baby brother, who died of a massive heart attack shortly after his forty-first birthday. Her own enormous heart makes her ministering to the children all in a day's work.

My son, a college sophomore, regards her as a role model and listens intently to any advice or criticism she has to offer him (I would encounter great resistance for offering him the same advice). She retired from her minimum-wage production job to raise my nieces, yet my sister is always praying and singing the song "How I Got Over."

Because she always gives to others and never expects anything in return, surprising my sister on her sixty-eighth birthday meant a lot to me. Her eyes lit up when we sang "Happy Birthday" to her. For that one moment, we gave her a tiny measure of the joy that she has brought continually into the lives of all of us.

A Special Identity

Linda Robertson

I awoke to the whir of the ceiling fan above me. The slight breeze did little to permeate the morning heat. Still in bed, I realized I had been dreaming. I felt tears streaming down my face, but with so much to do, I could not afford to languish under the lone sheet. I began to think about the journey that had brought me to the funeral of a woman I barely knew. The funeral was only hours away.

My eyes darted around the room. I was sleeping in the room where Mother had spent her final days. Years earlier, my youngest sister had died in the bed where I slept. Medicine bottles surrounded me. I saw sedatives, painkillers, and blood thinners as well as aspirin bottles. On a chest of drawers was a Styrofoam mannequin head. Pinned carefully to the mannequin was Mother's fashionable brown wig. As I hugged my pillow, I felt chills. The room was filled with reminders of Mother and the illness that had taken her life.

I reached for the sheets of paper that were folded on the nightstand. Since our initial meeting I have carried Mother's first letter to me in my purse. We would exchange many letters over the course of our brief relationship; however, it was the first that remained with me always.

Dear Linda:

Your phone call was without a doubt the most pleasant surprise of my life. I had given up hope of ever hearing from you. I did not contact you because I would never have done anything to hurt your family.

I have never met more remarkable people in my life. They were also instrumental in you becoming the wonderful young lady you are. Your accomplishments made them very happy.

I was deeply saddened to learn of your grandmother's death. I'm sure sometimes it is very difficult for you. I will remember all of you in my prayers.

I am at work now, on a break. I retired in 1985 after teaching in five different elementary schools for thirty years. Following my first year of retirement my mother was terminally ill with cancer. Being an only child and with my father dead, it was my responsibility to care for her. My daughters did what they could to help, but they were both working. My mother died in 1986. The next year I kept Karen's baby while she worked. This is my fourth year on the job I have now. I am the community liaison at an elementary school. I don't have much contact with the students. I work mainly with the parents.

My daughter Beverly is thirty-four years old and has a fifteen-year-old son and she works for UPS. Karen is thirty-two years old and has a four-year-old daughter. Karen teaches special education. Break time is over. Answer when you can.

Love,

Mom

I don't know where I found the courage needed to make that first long-distance call to Florida. Armed with information from my maternal adoptive grandmother, I secretly sought my birth mother's identity and located her easily. I traveled to Florida to meet my mother, stepfather, and new sisters after exchanging several letters and talking endless hours on the telephone.

I met my mother for the first time just after her sixtieth birthday. She was born in Homestead, Florida, and she had lived in south Florida for most of her life.

Shortly before graduating from Florida A&M University, she discovered she was pregnant. The father of her unborn child was also a college student, but he was already married. He somehow forgot to disclose that fact during their courtship.

It was 1953 at the time, and my mother was determined to have her child and begin life anew. Her parents had other plans and forced her to relocate to California, where she would live (and hide) with an aunt and uncle. Once her child was born, she had plans to get a job as a schoolteacher. She missed her family and friends but was certain she could start life anew. There were those who had doubts about her ability to provide a good life for her new baby daughter.

One family in particular befriended my mother during her stay in

California. They were neighbors who checked regularly on the progress of her pregnancy. Mother received a visit from them following my birth. They asked that the baby be given to them to raise as their own. In return, the child would be provided with a wonderful life. My mother could return to south Florida and start a career in elementary education.

Mother, realizing that a solid family unit would offer her daughter so many more opportunities than she could provide, did just that. No legal documents were ever signed, and no money was ever exchanged. Hugs and kisses sealed their bond.

Now, some thirty-six-plus years later, Mother finally had a chance to spend time with the daughter she gave up. Our wonderful reunion, however, turned tragic when my sister became ill. Having contracted AIDS from an uncaring husband, she eventually died. I had hoped that I could bring comfort to my mother in the face of her loss. Instead, I watched helplessly as Mother succumbed to numerous physical maladies, in addition to the pain she endured over the loss of her daughter. Some felt Mother had grieved herself to death.

Today, for the second time in as many years, I will sit in the front pew of the church as the funeral service celebrates the life of a loved one. I will introduce myself to the countless family members who don't really know me but often remark on my resemblance to my mother. Well, that's not surprising. I am, after all, my mother's daughter.

MY BOSS'S WIFE

Angela Pea Stroble

My job had become my life. I would come into the office around 8:30 A.M. and some days it would be 7 o'clock the next morning before I would leave for home, only to return several hours later. I worked all the holidays as well, including the Fourth of July, Labor Day, Christmas, and New Year's. I was unaccustomed to taking time out for myself because I was happiest being in charge. I like it when people are unable to do without me. So I would have never taken the time to do something for myself, even in this situation.

In October, nearly four years ago, while viewing a commercial on breast cancer, I did a routine breast exam and found a big, suspicious lump in my left breast. Because I have a history of fibroid tumors, I passed it off as such. The next morning, I was busy trying to help to prepare my boss, an attorney, for an upcoming trial. Just then, in walked his lovely wife, Wilhelmena, who is also my best friend. I mentioned casually to Wilhelmena that I had observed a knot in my left breast, but assumed it was a fibroid tumor. Wilhelmena said I should wait a few days and if it was still there, I needed to make arrangements to have it checked. I replied, "Sure thing!"

Over the next three weeks, I watched several breast cancer commercials on TV and never really gave my own breast a second thought. But Wilhelmena certainly thought about it. During those three weeks, Wilhelmena came to the office every day to nag me about making an appointment for a mammogram. In fact, she nagged me so much it was starting to get on my nerves. Here I was trying to work and the boss's wife was following me around like a child about an appointment for a mammogram!

At the end of the third week, things were extremely busy at the office. One morning when I arrived at work, Wilhelmena was already there, sitting in my chair. As I entered the office, she said, "Well, did you make the appointment?" "What appointment?" I replied. "The mammogram appointment," she responded. I told her I hadn't had the opportunity yet to schedule one, but I would as soon as things calmed down a bit.

In the background, my boss (her husband) was screaming for a file, the phones were ringing off the hook, and clients were at the door. Wilhelmena continued to sit in my chair. Again she asked me when I was going to schedule an appointment. By now, I had *had* it with her. "I'm trying to do a job here," I thought.

Wilhelmena located the phone book and began flipping through the pages. Finally she found what she was looking for. "Call this number and schedule an appointment for yourself!" "Okay, already," I said. By this time, I was getting angry. I snatched the telephone book from her, dialed the number, and made an appointment. Later, when she asked me what day the appointment was scheduled for, I lied and told her the wrong day because she had made me so angry.

When the day came for my appointment, I arrived at the doctor's office a few minutes early. I went through the initial breast examination, took the mammogram test, and had an ultrasound test all on the same day. Then the results came back. I had breast cancer. I thought, "This can't be happening to me!" At that instant it seemed as if my life had stopped; I was in denial and shock at the same time! When I walked out of the doctor's office and back into the waiting room, there sat Wilhelmena. How she knew where to find me, I'll never know, since I had given her the wrong day for my appointment.

What I do know is that I will forever be grateful to her for her persistence and concern on my behalf. The tears began to just stream down my face. She saved my life! How can I ever thank her? Had she not pestered me during those three weeks, I would have never scheduled an appointment for an examination.

WITH A LITTLE HELP FROM MY FRIENDS

Judy Williams

The night my son, Will, graduated from high school, I sat down in a chair and cried. I felt an overwhelming sense of gratitude toward all the wonderful people who helped us reach that day. Will had been offered over

$250,000 in college scholarships. Will's big brother from Big Brothers Big Sisters, when asked about his involvement in Will's life, says, "His mother had a plan; all I had to do was follow it." My only "plan" was that Will would never have to experience in his life the emotionally debilitating things I had experienced in mine.

I was born out of wedlock, and so was he. Societal norms changed substantially for "bastard" children over the decades between our births, but the stigma continues to linger. My plan could be achieved only if Will had the self-acceptance necessary for healthy self-esteem. His understanding and consistently telling the truth about his parentage was the only way to achieve the goal.

The hazards of telling the truth about your parentage were revealed to me at age seven. My older sister and I went to sign up to become Brownies. When the woman at the desk asked us our father's name, my sister gave one last name, and I gave another. The look on this woman's face shriveled my spirit right down to my white bobby socks. We later told our mother what happened and received a whipping for divulging her shame of having had four daughters by four men. The whipping we received for telling the truth seared my soul, confirming that there was something acutely wrong with me that I could never overcome.

I didn't tell the truth again about my father's last name for almost forty years. I became such a good liar on this point that I even began to believe the different versions I told over the years. That early strike at my self-esteem took its toll inside me, despite the confidence I exuded on the outside.

We lived in Parkway Gardens, a Chicago enclave of predominantly two-parent families living in co-op apartments. The complex of three- and eight-story buildings was situated between the projects on Sixty-third Street and the middle-income working-class community of Blacks on Sixty-sixth and South Park. Every kid knew everyone else in this three-block-long, one-block-wide, densely populated sanctuary. We knew who your parents were, and who your sisters and brothers were. And if your cousins came to visit, we knew them too. Several adults had chairs and sat by the window twenty-four hours a day. Their vantage point ensured that whatever you thought you were doing in the dark soon came to light.

We lived in apartment 5A in the 6450 building. My playmates, Lucky and Delano McClendon in 2B, Pat Barrett and Reggie Clark in 3A,

Donnie Greenhill in 1D, and David Brown in the building across the parking lot, were privy to the horror in our household. I had a stepfather who was brutally abusive to the three older children who were not his. One of his favorite punishments was to beat us on the days my mother's job required her to work late for inventory. I can still hear him say, "I am going to whip you until your mother gets home." He kept his word. Kids in the Gardens made up a song about it, called "I Heard a Whipping on the Fifth Floor."

When we went outside to play, the kids laughed at us when they saw the welts on our arms and legs. We laughed with them as we played hide-and-seek and hopscotch and chose sides for softball. My mother eventually divorced my stepfather, as he had two preferred forms of reprisal for her. One was to push her into a tub filled with hot water, and the other was to push her outside with only her underwear on.

I was never called a bastard, though my cohorts had to notice that my siblings and I did not resemble each other. My older sister and I cleaned classrooms after school to pay our tuition. After school, my high school cronies Pam Walker, Mary Washington, and Priscilla Lamb shed their uniform of plaid skirt and blazer in the locker room, a tactic designed to meet boys during the trip home on the El without them knowing we were "uptight" Catholic-school girls. My tuition responsibilities prevented me from joining them. But I was a full partner in all the mischief that went on in our all-girls school, where the doors were locked when you entered and unlocked only when the bell rang at three.

I left home for the first time at seventeen because my stepfather had stabbed my mother and me. His blade found my arm when I dared to defend my mother as he leaned over the couch and repeatedly plunged the knife into her body. Everyone else, including my mother, ran from the house; I was left alone to struggle with him. Criminal charges were never pursued. The only counseling I received was from my mother. She said it would be prudent to forgive my stepfather for stabbing us. "Otherwise," she said, "he will catch you out in the street and hurt you." This was the first significant break between my mother and me. Mothers were supposed to protect their children. Telling me to forgive him was simply unconscionable.

I left again at nineteen and never looked back. Seven dollars was all

I had to my name. I didn't know where I was going to go or how I would survive. Linda Freeman and Mary Holmes saved me this time.

Mrs. Freeman didn't ask why I was out walking the street alone at two in the morning. She just said "sure" when her daughter, Linda, asked her permission for me to stay at their house for a while. Not once did they inquire why I never talked about my background or why they never met my family members.

Mary and Linda helped me find an apartment. I dropped in and out of college and partied away the next few years, until I met and fell in love with Will's father, Bill Tolbert, and uprooted myself to move to Atlanta.

Bill was my friend and lover, although he was seventeen years my senior. We held similar worldviews, although age and regional differences eventually led to the end of passion. In spite of what people may say, love does not conquer all. But Bill was gracious enough to give me his apartment, secured other accommodations for himself, and paid my apartment expenses until I found a job.

Ironically, Will was conceived at the very end of my relationship with Bill. His birth brought my life into focus. As he gestated inside me, I vowed he would never receive the reproach I had received at seven. Lack of a marriage certificate did not prevent Bill from being a friend to me and a father to his son. He did not hesitate to ensure his son had a heritage by signing the birth certificate. His only caveat before signing was this: "Don't name this child after me if every time you get mad at me, you will take it out on him." There was a better chance of the world being flat than of that happening.

Will grew up in Bent Creek Apartments, an upscale all-adult community. Like Parkway Gardens, Bent Creek was no showplace. Since Will was the first child born there, we were allowed to stay. But the rent was soon past due. I was in a panic and paralyzed with indecision about what to do. Cynthia, the apartment manager, knocked at the door to say she had located where I could go to apply for welfare if I needed to keep a roof over our heads. Cynthia also enlisted the services of another neighbor to drive me to the welfare office.

Through Cynthia's kind initiative and act of friendship, I applied, got on and off welfare in three months, secured a job, and remained in Bent Creek Apartments for eight more years. Throughout the entire time, our neighbors accepted, mentored, and favored Will and me in a multitude of ways, the way a family does for its members.

Will was five when I put our sanctuary at Bent Creek in jeopardy for something I passionately believed in then and still do today—freedom of speech. I lost my job for publishing an article in the employee newsletter. I appealed the decision in court and it took four years for the case to reach a legal conclusion. During this time, many wonderful people rescued us from starving.

Granny and Mr. Ralph Strong fed us every Sunday for nearly two years during my unemployed periods. Granny is an all-star cook. The word *chef* is too boorish to describe her culinary expertise. She tried to teach me to cook, but there is nothing about a kitchen or pots and pans that thrills me.

Theresa Stanford, Will's godmother, picked up the weekday meal slack. We had met earlier, when Will was ten months old. She learned that I was from Chicago and didn't have a support group in Atlanta. Periodically, she would send her husband over to my place with a bag of groceries. What woman do you know who would send her husband to a single woman's house in a time of crisis? But Theresa had nothing to fear from me. I would have walked through hell with a gasoline dress on before violating her trust. At Bill's funeral, Theresa and her husband, Charlie, flanked me. Although Bill and I had not been together for a number of years and I was sad to hear of his passing away, I was grateful for the settlement I received from Bill's death because it enabled me to purchase my first home.

Yvonne Page, whose friendship spans thirty-plus years, encouraged me to abandon self-pity when my car was repossessed. Her solution was for me to get up and buy another car by asking eight friends to loan me one hundred dollars each. My protest that I couldn't do it was ignored and she sent me the first check that day. All seven other friends said yes. A ninth friend, Jannie Kinnebrew, was upset that I didn't ask for her help. She literally forced me to take an additional hundred from her for insurance. Her only stipulation was that the money be not a loan but a gift. In time, I was able to repay every loan, and nine years later I remain at the job secured with the car and their help.

An account of friendships nurturing me would be incomplete without mentioning the wonderful African American men who assisted in my and Will's growth. Some were intimate friends, and others were men whose character simply prompted them to help. Imagine that! Black men who mentored a child that was not even their own, just because!

Michael Tyler and Brian Poe emphasized to Will the importance of going to college, and their actions demonstrated the benefits of earning multiple degrees. Michael Tyler is a former neighbor from Bent Creek Apartments. He and his wife, Cathy, have three boys of their own. Michael exposed Will to events and experiences far beyond what my wallet would allow. I am grateful Cathy allowed him to include Will.

Brian entered our lives from Big Brothers Big Sisters when Will was seven. He taught Will how to establish and maintain his own circle of male friends. As a reward for his all-A report card, Brian bought Will a pair of hundred-dollar Air Jordan sneakers I couldn't afford, and had enough home training to ask me if it was okay before doing so.

Brian stated in the beginning that he could only mentor Will for a year because he was going away to law school. Yet every spring break, Brian would fly Will to the campus of the University of Virginia, and he did the same for every city he clerked in during the summers. Fourteen years later, their relationship is like a blood-brother bond.

The tears of appreciation I shed the night of Will's graduation were a reaction to the incredible support he had received from our friends then, and earlier. A year after Will left for college, I returned to college; I graduated at age fifty.

None of the people in this account is a blood relative. Not a single one. Each was a stranger until we shared a history together. Each one embraced us nonetheless. Because Linda Freeman, Mary Washington, Pam Walker, and my son's father, Bill Tolbert, are no longer with us, on occasion I regret I didn't figure it all out in time to thank them for the pivotal role each played in my life. But I feel obliged to return their kindness by being kind to other strangers I meet along the way.

In a recent article in *Newsweek*, "Twelve Things You Must Know to Survive and Thrive in America," Ellis Cose speaks of the "rope of destiny" pulling us along. With a little help from my friends, the rope helped to pull me to safety!

THE GIFT

Benjamin A. Dashiell

Tuesday, December 10, 1991, began like any other workday, fighting traffic to work. As I approached my desk, one of my coworkers said, "Ben, call home immediately!" My wife advised me to come home right away, although she would not say what was wrong.

If you've ever received this type of phone call, you have some idea what I was going through. Driving home, I tried to imagine what could have happened.

When I arrived at home, my wife informed me that my father had died. My mother had phoned the news. For a moment, I stood there frozen, as memories of my life with him flashed through my mind. My entire body felt numb. I picked up the phone to call my mother. She explained that dad had passed away in his sleep that morning. I told her that I would call the rest of the family, and that I would be home as soon as I could.

Most of the rest of my siblings lived out of town. Although Ray lived in Salisbury, he was with my mother already. Kenny and our sister Medenia both lived in Delaware. Wendell, who was in the Air Force, was at Maxwell AFB, and Nate was in Virginia Beach. I lived in District Heights, Maryland. We all made plans to make the long ride home.

It was only two days before Dad's birthday, December 12. On the evening of the twelfth, one of Dad's cousins came to the house to speak to me and my brothers. Only three of us were there at the time; we went out to our cousin's car to talk. He told us that my father had another son, Russell. We were shocked. As the initial shock wore off, he explained how he had learned this information.

One day, while Russell was visiting in another town, he met my cousin's mother, who was visiting as well. Striking up a conversation, she mentioned to Russell that she had just come up from Salisbury, Maryland. Russell responded by saying that his father was from Salisbury. When asked what his father's name was, he gave her the name of our father. She looked at him in disbelief. Russell explained that my father had met his mother while he was in the military. Russell's mother worked on the base. Russell had been the product of their relationship. Although Russell had never met my father, he had the birth certificate papers with Dad's name on them, as well as a picture of Dad.

Later, my cousin's mother came to see my father to talk with him about what she had found out. My father, however, became very upset; he didn't want to discuss it. My father was very protective of us, and felt that this would only cause trouble for the family. This is how we came to be sitting in a car learning of what we came to call "the gift." Once we had heard the story, we realized his relationship with Russell's mother had occurred before my father had met my mother.

When my father passed away, Russell was contacted by my cousin and given the news of his death. Russell voiced a wish to be able to see my father and pay his last respects to him. Dad's cousin had Russell's phone number, so we gave him a call. By this time, all of my brothers had arrived, and knew the story. Russell told us that all he wanted to do was see his father, and to have some closure to this missing link in his life. He stressed that he did not want to cause us any trouble, and that he didn't want anything. He said that he would drive down to Salisbury, view the remains, and leave immediately thereafter. We assured him that it was OK, and that we wanted to meet him.

The next day, the day of Dad's funeral, we informed our sister of the news. At this point, everyone in the immediate family knew except our mother. As difficult as my father's death and making his funeral arrangements were for her, we were not sure how to break the news to her. Collectively, we decided to wait until after the funeral service to tell her. I did, however, share the news with my mother's sister, Romaine.

Aunt Romaine had decided that she would usher at the funeral service. She arrived at the church early to ensure that everything was in order. She was informed by the funeral director that there was a man and his family who had arrived at the chapel and were going back and forth to view the body. Each time they would go to view the body, they would return in a very emotional state. The young man had informed the funeral director that he was my father's son, but because we were from a relatively small town, the funeral director knew my entire family. Aunt Romaine told him that she knew who the gentleman was, and immediately went over to assist him and his family. She introduced herself and reassured them that everything was fine. We later found out that they had planned to leave before the service started, but she had convinced them to stay.

After the service, Aunt Romaine took Russell and his family to the dining hall, where they waited for us to return from the cemetery. By this time, we were all anxious to get back to the church and meet our "new" brother. Each of us went over to introduce ourselves to Russell individually; by this time, people began to realize that something unusual was going on.

We decided to break the news to our mother soon, before someone else did. So, in her hour of grief, we gathered around her and told her what we knew. Through her tears, she asked if he was there; she wanted to meet him. When he was pointed out to Mother, she went to him and hugged him! Other family members and friends had no clue as to what was going on, but it didn't take long for them to figure things out. Soon everyone began approaching him with open arms.

It's often said that God moves in mysterious ways. I know it was nothing but divine intervention that led Russell to us on my father's birthday. What should've been a day of grief became one of new beginnings. It has been just over ten years since we lost our father and found Russell. We all maintain a close relationship to this day. We were all the recipients of the gift that could only have come from our father and from above.

What If?

K. M. Ford

What if Grandma hadn't come to get me?

What if Papa hadn't cared for me as his own?

What if my family hadn't been there to support me?

What if I had let fate be my victor, instead of following my faith in God as my path to victory?

On May 25, 1968, I was born to a mentally ill woman who had been battered by her husband of three months, days before and again just hours before giving birth. When my mother was asked how she felt after giving birth to a baby girl, she laughed and only responded, "I ain't had no baby. What are you talking about? I ain't had no baby." Certainly, there was no way for me to have a normal life emerging into such a sad environment.

I was another hopeless case—poor, physically abused, born to a crazy Black woman in Newark, New Jersey, in the 1960s. The best decision the hospital could come up with was to hand me over to the local orphanage. Perhaps I would have a chance there.

"What? You'd better not give her away before I can get there! You just better not! I'll be there on the next train coming to Jersey!" yelled my petite but sassy-lipped grandmother when hospital officials called to inform her of my birth and her daughter's medical status. Almost sixty, she didn't hesitate about whether to come and get me. She just packed her bags and had my grandfather drive her the thirty miles from their little farmhouse in rural Campbell County, Virginia, to the train station in the next town over.

I often wonder what the source is of such strength and undying commitment within the Black family. What enables us to keep on going without thinking twice about the sacrifices we give . . . all in the name of love? What if Grandma hadn't come to get me?

My grandparents raised me as their own. I was always referred to as the tenth child. Although we were probably poor by annual income standards, I had practically everything I needed and could reasonably want.

My grandfather said many times that he spent more money on me than on all nine of the other children totaled.

My mother lived in my grandparents' house too for many years. We were never as close as a mother and daughter should be. Sometimes I feel she thought I really was her sister instead of her daughter. My experiences in the household would range from peace and tranquillity to total chaos and violence. The violent times occurred when my mother was off her medicine and would lose it again. The scene would get so ugly that my grandparents would have to call the police to come get her and take her to the mental institution for another treatment and recovery period. I always hated these nightmarelike scenes; it was another reminder that my family wasn't normal . . . that I wasn't normal.

At the age of five, I acquired a speech problem and began to stutter. Many times, my stuttering would become so bad that if called upon by the teacher to answer a question, I would just get caught up in a word and repeat the first syllable uncontrollably for what would feel like an eternity. Of course, this made the other children laugh and make fun of me.

And then at some point, my school decided that I must be a special-education case, because that's exactly where I went next—straight to the special-needs classes. Thank goodness my grandma lectured my teachers, stating, "This child ain't no dummy and you'd better put her back in the right class." The special testing following this episode identified me as gifted and talented, rather than a special-education student. That year, I went from special education to advanced math and reading.

My speech problem was treated with speech therapy on a regular basis for several years. Over the years I've learned techniques to smooth over those anxiety triggers so that my stuttering is more controllable in public. I moved through elementary school to high school and became very active in extracurricular activities and college-prep coursework.

Despite my shaky beginning, I graduated from high school with honors and attended the prestigious University of Virginia, where I met my wonderful husband. We have been married for eleven years now, have two beautiful and healthy children, and have established a very comfortable life, sharing careers in the financial services industry. Many times I look back and wonder how I became so blessed. What if Grandma hadn't come to get me? Just what if?

BEING BLESSED

Ky'a Jackson

In 1979, after twelve years of marriage, my father told my mother that he no longer wanted to be married to her. We were living in Okinawa, Japan, at the time and had no idea how we were going to get back to the United States. My mother sat both my brother, Michael, and me down and explained to us that Mommy and Daddy weren't going to be married anymore and that it wasn't our fault. She made sure that we felt secure in knowing that we would make it, adding, "We were a four-legged table, and now we are a three-legged table—still strong and able to stand!"

Once we arrived back in the States, we moved back into our house in Willingboro, New Jersey, which our parents had rented out while we were in Okinawa. Unfortunately, we needed at least two sources of income in order to keep the house; my mother had to start working two jobs.

My job as big sister was to try to make things easier for my mom, including staying on top of my studies. I was nine years old at the time. I would pick my brother up after school, make sure he did his homework, get his and my clothes ready for school the next day, and start dinner so that when Mom got home she could eat with us, ask about our school day and homework, and then head back out to work.

We maintained this schedule for about three years. Eventually, however, we lost the house. It was simply too expensive for us to keep. We went through some very hard times for the next year or so; we had to live with two other families until we found an apartment we would afford. But my mother never let it get her, or us, down!

On paydays, Mother would have us meet her at the diner across the street from her job after we got out of school. There she would play Ms. Pac-man with us. We would then walk to Gene's Motel. It was right across the street from the Clover Department Store, where Mom would buy us a new outfit or new pajamas. The nights we slept over in the motel, we would order pizza and soda and talk about all the things that we wanted in life and all the things we needed to do to obtain them. Atop the latter list was always offering a lot of encouragement to each other.

About a year later, we found a nice little apartment in Pennsauken, New Jersey, on Westfield Avenue, and we thought everything was going well. I was getting pretty decent grades in school, and my brother wasn't doing badly either. I was involved in just about everything in school. It was while I was in East Camden Middle School that I learned about my love for oratory and singing. I was in the choir and the drama club, and also competed in oratorical contests sponsored by Alpha Kappa Alpha sorority. I won the first oratorical contest they sponsored. But just as things began to look up for us, we were hit with hard times again.

My mother had been having problems with her legs and her eyesight. She began seeing a variety of doctors to help determine the nature of the problems she was having. No one really knew what was going on! She had always walked everywhere because we didn't have a car, but now she began to grow tired very quickly. At the same time, Grandmother also became very sick.

Mother is the youngest of seven children, and as far as I could tell, she was always my grandmother's favorite. It was hard on my mother to see *her* mother ill as well. We refer to 1984 as "our tough year" because it was the year my grandmother died and the year my mother was finally diagnosed with multiple sclerosis.

Eventually, my mother lost her eyesight completely. She went from being able to walk everywhere to having to be pushed around in a wheelchair. By this time I was in high school and Michael was in middle school. Even though my mother was burdened with so much, she still kept our needs in mind. She was worried that my brother and I would not get the education she felt was necessary from the Camden city school system, so she moved the family to Mount Holly, New Jersey.

The apartment in Mount Holly was in a great location because it was right across the street from the high school I attended. On my lunch break, I could come home and check on my mother. Mother made sure that I continued to do extracurricular activities such as singing in the choir, acting, and speaking. I even managed to compete in the Alpha Kappa Alpha oratorical contests for another three years, each time winning first place. Even though she wasn't able to "see" me, she managed to attend everything I performed in. I was able to maintain a B average in school while working part time to help out financially in the household. Once my brother reached a certain age, he worked as a waiter to help bring money home, too. Mother encouraged Michael to keep participating in his track-and-field endeavors. In fact, he competed in the Penn Relays four times and won a variety of medals. In spite of her condition, my mother never missed a home track meet.

When it came time to attend college, my mother encouraged me not to choose a school close to home on account of her. She wanted me to apply for college wherever I wanted to go. "Do something for you," she would say. But I couldn't. I ended up attending Cheyney University, a historically Black school in Pennsylvania.

We didn't really have the money for me to attend college. In fact, I'm not quite sure to this day how I made it through. I had a work-study job and a part-time job off campus while attending classes full time. I would travel back and forth from Pennsylvania to New Jersey every weekend to help with the house. My brother was still helping out as well.

I finished my college degree and today am working for a firm as a public relations specialist. I also have my own home business. My brother, Michael, is now married and has a son, Xavier. He is currently attending Laney College and plans to transfer to San Francisco State to major in political science.

As for my mother, she lives on her own in Cherry Hill, New Jersey, in an independent-living apartment complex. It is not a nursing home, but a special apartment with lower shelves, larger showers to accommodate her wheelchair, and remote door access from her telephone.

My mother never allowed us to feel that we were incapable of accomplishing anything! She always told us that we were blessed and that she loved us no matter what we chose to do. She is a shining example of a woman who knew how to fight and knew how to love. My brother and I often reminisce today on the little encouraging things she said to us growing up. We still call on her heartening words to help us keep our heads above water, especially when we are having struggles in our own adult lives.

The last time we took a family photo together was at my brother's high school graduation. To me, looking at that picture of us says love, trials, and most of all, triumph!

HONOR

Yolanda Zanders-Barr

My mother died when I was twenty-five. She had been my rock!

Never having finished middle school herself, her biggest wish was to live long enough to see her baby graduate from college. I was the baby—the youngest of nine and the first to attend college.

I graduated from Tuskegee Institute in May 1995, nine months before she passed away. This strong, independent, vital woman who was never sick turned into someone who couldn't bathe herself, who sometimes couldn't make it to the bathroom by herself, and who ultimately had to depend on other people for her well-being.

At first, I was angry. Angry at her dying and leaving me alone, angry at God for letting her die, and angry at myself for not being able to let go. I stopped going to church because I couldn't believe that the God I loved and served would take away from me the one thing that mattered most. My mother was not only my mother to me, she was my father, my healer, my doctor, and my soul.

It has been six years since Mother passed, and it has taken me this long to realize that grieving isn't enough. I must honor her. I've cried a river, but as long as I honor my mother's memory, my tears are not in vain. Every day that I get up to go to work, I honor her. Every time I go to church, I honor her. Every time I tutor someone who looks like me in algebra, calculus, or geometry, I honor her. Every time I look at her picture and smile instead of cry, I honor her. There is something no amount of money or education can buy. And that is a mother's love.

Ma Josie's Gal

Rhonda Thompson Maddox

"Ma Josie" is what they taught me to call her. "Gal" is what she decided to call me! I often begged her to call me by my name, but she never would.

Josephine Dickey, my great-grandmother, died when I was ten. I believed her to be the meanest old woman in the world! We were like oil and vinegar. Ma Josie was a master at yelling, and I hated it. She used to always yell that she was going to beat my behind, that I didn't eat enough to stay alive, and that "them young'uns" were getting on her nerves!

When visiting her, everybody always elected me to sleep with the white-haired old lady. She obviously did not like me and made me help her wash white folks' clothes in an old black wash pot. Then she would stand up and iron them in the heat of North Carolina's summer days.

She always said I would pay Mama back because I was just like my mother, hardheaded. Ma Josie lived to watch wrestling on TV, and if I breathed too loud in the process, she'd holler, "Gal, you better hush up!" Ma Josie was infamous for calling you out in a heartbeat. When she died, I missed her biscuits. But I never missed the hollering!

Thirty-one years after her death, my world fell apart. In the middle of a divorce, I became careless with everything, even my life. On a December night, two weeks before Christmas, depression took possession of me physically and emotionally. Around eight o'clock in the evening, I placed a pot on the stove and went to lie down as it heated. I had just recently moved into an old rental house and had not yet purchased a smoke alarm. Before long, I fell asleep.

Then I heard her voice softly and calmly say, "Get up, Gal." Deciding the dream I was having was about Ma Josie, I turned over and fell back into a deep sleep. However, when I heard the voice again, I knew better than to ignore her a second time. "*Gal, I said get your butt up!*" I felt like I was ten years old again. When Ma Josie yelled, I moved! I immediately sat up in the bed and realized that black smoke was everywhere!

I ran toward the kitchen to turn off the burner. I began to cry uncontrollably, thanking God for allowing Ma Josie to come and thanking Ma Josie for arriving!

At three o'clock that December morning, many life lessons became clear to me. I finally celebrated the gift I had in the white-haired old lady. Thirty-one years after her death, I could feel a great-grandmother reaching out beyond the grave to save the life of her child. That's when it hit me! It didn't matter what my real name was. What mattered was that, to Ma Josie, I was still her Gal!

On Good Ground

LaTorial Faison

I am from a small Virginia town where hardly any siblings have the same father, almost everyone is related to everyone else, and folks hold on to secrets for years.

I've always lived with my grandparents. They took me in when I was two weeks old. My mother was only eighteen at the time, and their son, my father, was not mature enough to raise a child.

My grandparents showered me with love, supported me, and supplied all of my needs. They were wonderful grandparents! I actually called them Mama and Daddy, and I still do to this day. They are the only parents I've ever known. Although my mother and I have since established a close friendship, my grandparents are still my real parents.

During childhood, it didn't take long to realize I did not resemble anyone else in the family; I looked more like the people down the street. Rumors started when I was about ten or eleven and continued for the rest of my teenage years. These kinds of small towns, where people have little else to do, thrive on rumors.

I was a teenager when I first confronted my mother about my ancestry. I told her I had heard the man she married was not my real father. She admitted that I was right. She claimed that the identity of my real father was a secret, and she promised to reveal the truth to me when I reached the age of eighteen.

Folks in town sometimes called my grandparents' house just to raise questions about me. My grandparents never said a word about any of this to me. But I eavesdropped on their conversations. After a while, I figured out I was related to the people down the street.

I later found out that my father was now a married man, living in New York somewhere with his wife, son, and three daughters. When I found out, I didn't know whether to feel mad, glad, blessed, sad, or cheated. I felt a little of all of those things; some days I still do. But my greatest joy is that, in spite of it all, I had fallen on good ground.

I was given to people who loved and cared for me and raised me as their own child. I had every opportunity to excel and to succeed at whatever I desired. And so I refused to let the rumors bother me. I became the president of my student body in high school, and I was an honors student. I decided early on I was not going to let myself down, and I was not going to let my family down.

I attended one of the best colleges in Virginia and enrolled in yet another distinguished school in Virginia in pursuit of my graduate degree. I married a man who understood me and loved me.

Today, as I work with others who are striving to succeed educationally, emotionally, and professionally, I often run into folks who are distraught and torn because of issues from their past. Like them, I could have let the question of whose blood ran through my veins destroy me. But I chose not to.

We can't help the situations we're born into, but we *can* remain positive and strong and always believe in ourselves. Family is not about blood or last names. It's about folks who are there for you when you need them most. Family is about good ground, and my grandparents are my good ground. I am fortunate I fell into their hands. Because of them, I am what I have become today: proud, independent, strong. I'm grateful to God for allowing me to fall on good ground!

THE REV . . .

Rhonda Y. C. Johnson

Our family newsletter was first produced in March 1998. At the time the newsletter was called *Umoja Times*. Our newest family members, Little Devy and RJ, from the sixth generation of traceable ancestry, were introduced on the front page. On the following page the newsletter's editor-in-chief, Envision, introduced herself. The rest of the newsletter included the achievements of other family members, a birthday list, and a classified section. There was a homemade seek-and-find puzzle and an original horoscope/funnies segment on page six. Page seven contained a crossword puzzle and a cartoon sketch. The last page announced, "Let Me Hear You Holler"—it was a request to rename the family newsletter, offering a cash reward. Although the newsletter did not look very sophisticated, it radiated an inviting warmth; those reading it felt like they belonged in the family.

By July 1998 the name of the family newsletter had changed to *Reviviscence*, from the root word *revive*. It means "restoring us all to life with vigor." *Reviviscence*, soon dubbed *The Rev*, moved up a notch in sophistication, and by the end of 1998 it was being sent to homes from Philadelphia, Pennsylvania, to Richmond, Virginia, and on down the coast to south Florida. Among the contributions were "Bad to the Bone," "See What the End Is Gonna Be," "We Are Family," "The Heirloom," "From Whence We Came," "A Proud Past and a Bright Future," "Honoring Big Ma," and "The Maat."

There were a great many stories, dedications, prayers, poems, homegoing announcements, birth announcements, and home-front news. Two family reunions were held that year: the Clarke-Coleman Reunion, in Nockamixon State Park in Quakertown, Pennsylvania, and the Patterson clan reunion, in which West Turner Street in North Philadelphia was blocked off. African violets sprang up everywhere!

The Rev kicked off 1999 with twice as many contributions and continued gaining interest. That year the family visited the Ebonics question and explored "Recipes for Living" as well as "The Fears of Memory Loss." The newsletter introduced graduates of nursery school to graduates of graduate school, announced quite a few wedding bells, recognized our armed-forces heroes, provided book reviews, and shared stories such as "Dreams Do Come True" and "Caring for the Caregiver." One of the largest contributions that year came by way of family trivia. A cornucopia of family nicknames was entered into a contest; the families were able to not only enjoy a chuckle but learn a little about each other through the origins of the nicknames.

The Rev has published hundreds of original stories, poems, letters, prayers, and photos, and plenty of laughs and jokes. In 2000, a Web page was created, and the family met a number of Oasis of Love faith ministers in the Charity International Church in Richmond, Virginia. It has included in-depth accounts of our ancestors, such as Pop Patterson, Momma Love, and Carrie Coleman, retracing their ancestral steps through various versions of their stories remembered in different ways by different family members. A detailed family tree was drafted and little-known family facts were plowed. From native German family members to the family who opened their home to adopt a child, from all the families that shared recipes and got on their knees to pray for each other to the families that sent stamps, cash, and check donations, *The Rev* sought to restore all of the African violets in our family garden by way of each and every family member or descendant of the Clarke, Coleman, and Patterson clans—with vigor. And through it all, in spite of the reunion spats and e-mail squabbles, *The Rev* never lost focus.

Five years later, having never missed a month, *The Rev* continues to document and uplift our family. *The Rev* does not focus on our flaws, but embraces all that is good in our garden, empowering us with the knowledge of our individual and unique characteristics. Combined, they make us beautiful.

Looking back, we have been grateful for the joy *The Rev* has brought into our lives. It has helped us to recognize that of all the donations one can make, the greatest endowment is the ability to reach out and focus on the glories in our own garden.

SACRIFICE

Joyce Smiley

I am Joyce Marie Roberts, daughter of Curtis and Daisy Roberts. I was born and raised in Gulfport, Mississippi. In 1947 my mother was diagnosed as diabetic and went on insulin. If you know anything about the disease, you know there can be a risk of losing your limbs to the disease. When my mother learned of the diagnosis she said, "Lord, please don't let me lose my feet or my legs or my toes." Even while I was a child, she said to me, "I don't ever want to have to go into a nursing home because of my condition; please don't ever put me in a nursing home."

My mother and I lived alone at that time; I was the baby of four children. Mother often repeated to me, "Please don't ever put me in a nursing home." Finally, one day, when I was a teenager, I promised her, "Mother, you won't ever have to go into a nursing home." I just felt obligated to say this to her. I'm sure Mother was looking for some type of commitment from us that we wouldn't put her away. I went ahead and made the commitment to her, and I was serious about it. However, we never know how our lives will play out or what our circumstances will be.

My husband and I moved to Indiana in 1969 because the Air Force transferred him there. In 1981, my mother had to have eye surgery as a result of her prolonged diabetes. She was about seventy-two years old at the time. I went back and forth to Gulfport to take care of her, and in no time an entire month had passed. My mother lived by herself, and I didn't feel I could leave her there all alone. But I knew I had to return to my home and family in Indiana. I talked to my husband and we decided that we would ask Mother to come and live with us. She did. When Mama moved in with us, I had ten children—six of my own, and four who were the offspring of my deceased sister.

Mother was still able to get around on her own when she first came to live with us. In later years, however, her health began to fail her. One day she fell in the house and broke her hip. This required surgery and an extended stay in the hospital. The hospital advised that Mother be moved to a rehabilitation hospital for physical therapy once she had recuperated. Because I felt being in the rehab hospital would feel like being in a nursing home to her, I wouldn't allow it. Instead, I brought her back home and cared for her myself. My husband and I were no longer together, so I was the only adult in the household. Mother was pretty much incapacitated and couldn't do anything for herself. I had to do everything for her: dress her, bathe her, and comb her hair. The only thing I couldn't do was give my mother her insulin shots. So I asked one of my sons to handle that task.

Mother was doing pretty good until one day she fell again in the house. I had to take her back to the hospital, and when she returned home this time, her confidence was broken. She wouldn't even try to do anything for herself anymore. That meant I had to lift her up, dress her, turn her, and so on. Sometimes I would find her sliding out of the bed, and I would have to pick her up and put her back in. I would have to lift her out of bed and put her into the bathtub to bathe her and then help her get out of the bathtub and back into the bed once I had re-dressed her. I didn't mind, because I had promised her I would never put her into a nursing home. Her condition continued to worsen, however.

I bought a motorized chair for her, which was a big help. This chair would lie almost flat like a bed, and Mother would sleep in it often. The chair would also stand Mother straight up. But because she had become so fearful of standing or walking, if the chair stood her straight up, she would just slide back down to the floor. I found myself in the position of trying to readjust the chair while holding on to my mother to keep her from sliding down to the ground. Mind you, my mother was not a little woman. She was a robust woman who weighed over two hundred pounds. As I continued to care for her, I eventually strained my back from having to lift her so much. I didn't have in-home health care assistance or anyone to help me. A health aide would come out to the house to check Mother's diabetes and her blood pressure, but I never had anybody to help me lift her or bathe her. I had to do it all myself.

The day came when I could no longer physically lift or hold up my mother. My pastor had encouraged me for a long time to put my mother in a nursing home. He could see the toll it was taking on me and the injuries I was getting as a result. I wasn't getting much rest; many nights

Mother would keep me up all night long. The days would fold into the nights and the nights back into the days. I didn't know what I was going to do. Had it not been for the Lord, there was no way I could have made it as long as I did.

My pastor continued to encourage me to take that necessary step. I talked to my children about it, and they also said that I needed to put Mother in a nursing home. Finally I reached the point where taking care of my mother was more than I was able to handle. I talked to Mother about it, and she seemed to be in agreement. My original plan was to place her somewhere only for physical therapy and rehabilitation and to have someone help her start walking again. The therapists assured me that when they got Mother back to where she could walk again, I could bring her back home.

When my mother entered the nursing home, she did receive rehabilitation. But, to my disappointment, she fell again while she was there. I don't know exactly what happened, because by that time she had started walking again. From that point on the rehabilitation was no longer successful in helping her to walk, and eventually the state discontinued funding for her rehabilitation. She wasn't making enough progress to justify keeping her in the program. This meant that if I was going to bring Mother home, it would be in the same condition in which she'd entered the nursing home in the first place—unable to walk. I couldn't take care of my mother the way I had before she went into the nursing home. So I made the decision to keep her there.

I went to visit Mother every day, and sometimes I visited her twice a day. I would comb her hair and take her to use the rest room. If her bed was in need of changing, I would change it. And I would wash her and bathe her as well, taking care of her just as if she were still in my home with me. I would take her riding around town. On holidays and birthdays, I would bring her home and keep her overnight. I don't think there was a day that went by where my mother didn't have a visit from me or someone else, except for one—the day we had a blizzard and I couldn't drive to the nursing home.

I felt bad about Mother having to be in the nursing home, because I felt I had gone back on my promise. But God helped me to recognize that even though I had made a commitment to my mother when I was a teenager, we cannot commit to certain things that are beyond our control. In my heart, I wish that nobody ever had to put family members in a nursing home, because of the treatment they sometimes receive there.

There was a nurse in my mother's nursing home who had a reputation for being mean and having an attitude. One day my mother told me that the nurse had slapped her. I talked to the nurse, and because I am a Christian, I told her that I was not going to report her but that I was going to forgive her, pray for her, and ask God to have mercy on her soul. The nurse continued to mistreat the elderly in the nursing home and was eventually fired.

I often wondered what would happen to Mother if she woke up in the middle of the night and required assistance. Would she get it? One of the things I think kept the nurses in check in my case was the fact that they knew that I was coming to visit my mother on a daily basis. Therefore they had to provide her with reasonably good care in order to not have to answer to me.

My mother did get upset with me because I had put her in the nursing home, even though at first she had given her okay to do it. I realized that she would have much preferred to have been at home. She never came out and said, "Joyce, I know you said you would not put me in a nursing home, and I feel that you've done everything you could to avoid it. I understand why you had to do it, and I appreciate all you've done for me." Nonetheless, I feel that in her heart, she didn't hold it against me. My mother had a very powerful voice; when she would see me coming down the hall, she would start screaming, "Here comes my baby, here comes my baby." She was always so glad to see me, and I would kiss her and tell her how much I loved her. And then I would go to work taking care of her. Just hearing her say those words—"Here comes my baby"— meant so much to me.

In the back of my mother's mind, I believe her real fear was that if I ever had to put her in a nursing home, she would end up like so many loved ones—abandoned. But I really loved my mother and was committed to her; I believe she appreciated the fact that even though I had to put her there, I didn't forsake her. I took care of her as if she were still living in my home. And I believe Mama appreciated me for that, too.

The day that Mama died, I was in denial. Her mind stayed sharp as a tack to the end. I asked her grandchildren to assemble at the nursing home in her room. She was lying there with her eyes closed, and I said to her, "Mother, open up your eyes. Your grandchildren are here, and each one of them wants to say something to you." She opened her eyes, and each grandchild, one by one, whispered whatever they wanted to say in her ear. When the last one was finished, Mother closed her eyes and never opened them again. A few hours later she went on to meet the Lord.

After my mother passed, the undertaker went to pick up her body from the nursing home. I didn't know the undertaker and he didn't know me. But he came to my home the next day to help me make arrangements for Mother's funeral. While we were talking, he said to me, "Your mother must have had somebody take excellent care of her and watch over her; out of all the people that I've picked up in a nursing home, no one has ever had skin as beautiful as your mother's." Other people have complimented me on the sacrifices I had made in taking care of my mother when her health was down. But the undertaker's comment was the one that stood out best in my mind. He didn't know me, and he didn't know that I had taken care of my mother. I feel that God used that undertaker to bring a sense of peace and calm to my mind.

My mother gave everything she could for her children, and worked hard to help us and take care of us. When our parents have given everything they can give to us, we ought to be willing to give back to them, to let them know this: "We love you just like you loved us, and we will sacrifice for you in this period of your life like you sacrificed for us."

BIOGRAPHIES

Born in Crowley, Louisiana, in 1962 as the twelfth child of Alice and Warren Andrus, **Tracy Andrus** earned his bachelor's degree in criminal justice from Louisiana College in Pineville in 2000. He went on to earn his master's degree in criminal justice in 2001 from the University of Louisiana at Monroe. He has been married for nineteen years to Patricia Andrus, has two sons, Desmond and Tracy Jr., and is an ordained Baptist minister.

Virginia D. Banks-Bright, M.D. grew up in Raleigh, North Carolina, where she was very active in civil rights. Since high school, she has relocated and is now an infectious-disease specialist.

Celeste Bateman is a freelance writer and public relations and events management consultant living and working in New Jersey. Ms. Bateman received her B.A. in theater arts and speech from Rutgers University and holds a master's degree in communication arts from Montclair State University. She is married to Carter Mangan Sr. and has two sons, actor Jamil Mangan and Carter Mangan Jr., and a stepdaughter, Fateisha Tullis-Mariano.

Sandra R. Bell is currently employed as a business resource specialist for the Center for Trade and Technology Transfer at Georgia State University in Atlanta. She studied journalism at Oberlin College and the Columbia School of Journalism and is a frequent contributor to the *Atlanta Tribune* and *Black Enterprise*.

Gilda Mack Benton was born January 31, 1968. She attended the University of North Carolina, Chapel Hill, and Central Piedmont Community College in Charlotte, North Carolina. She is currently an information technology specialist with Wachovia Corporation in Charlotte, is married, and has one son.

Sharon Blessman is presently working as a registered nurse case manager for a major health system. She is the divorced mother of one and is currently pursuing a master's degree in information systems.

Bennis Blue was born and reared in North Carolina. She earned her master's degree in business management and English as well as her Ph.D. in English from Ohio State University. Bennis served in the U.S. Army for sixteen years as a quartermaster officer and commanded a quartermaster unit in Germany in 1986. In 1978, she served as the first woman paratrooper assigned to the Eighty-second Airborne Division at Fort Bragg, North Carolina. She is the proud mother of a son, Marcus Townes.

Denise Bride-Frazier lives in New York City. She survived both attacks on the World Trade Center, and her story tells of the experiences as she recalled them.

Keisha Brown lives in Flourtown, Pennsylvania. She and her husband, Sherrod Brown, Jr., have three children, Sherrod III, Kaylah, and Sage. Currently Keisha is pursuing her master's degree in journalism. God blessed her and her husband by sparing the life of their six-year-old, Sherrod III, from cancer.

Ken Brown graduated from Southern Illinois University in Carbondale with a B.S. in food and nutrition. He worked his way up the ranks in the food service industry with companies such as Marriott, Wendy's, Tyson Foods, and Kraft Foods. Today he is the owner of two McDonald's restaurants in Michigan.

Juliette Catledge is a fifty-eight-year-old single mother who raised three sons, Michael and Gregory Catledge and James Bell Jr. She holds a B.S. degree in mathematics and a master of social sciences (public administration) from Florida A&M University. Presently she works as a senior programmer analyst for Computer Horizons Corp.

The author, **Michael,** left the family with a legacy of seven books that were written, but none were ever published. He was an avid reader and historian and spent many a day researching his roots while feeling a great sense of family love. He completed three years at FAMU in architecture but left to help raise his brothers. He returned to school briefly to study journalism. We miss him dearly.

Sonia Clark is a native of Brooklyn, New York. Currently she resides in west Georgia with her two children. She is scheduled to attend Georgia State University in the fall of 2002 as a film and video major.

Torian Colon is an elementary school teacher in Houston, Texas. Her hobbies include exercising, writing, and spending time with her family.

Benjamin A. Dashiell earned a B.S. degree in business administration from Delaware State University. He lives in District Heights, Maryland, and works for the Department of Defense. He and his wife, Sheila, have two children, Benjamin II and Andrea.

Kathy Davis has been writing poetry and short stories for more than twenty-five years. Currently she resides in Round Rock, Texas, with her family.

Sandra J. Easterling lives in Allentown, Pennsylvania. She is the proud mother of three sons.

LaTorial Faison is a native of Virginia and holds degrees in English from the University of Virginia and Virginia Polytechnic Institute and State University. Faison currently works as an English instructor for a college in central Texas, where she resides with her husband and their two sons. She is the founding editor of PoeticallySpeaking.net, a globally read poetry site on the World Wide Web.

Cherryl Floyd-Miller is a North Carolina native and has published poetry and fiction in numerous literary journals and magazines, including *Essence*. She is currently finishing a novel and lives in Atlanta.

K. M. Ford grew up in rural Gladys, Virginia. She is a 1990 graduate of the University of Virginia (CLAS), Charlottesville, Virginia. She is employed in risk management by a leading financial services company and is married with two children.

Sharon Ewell Foster writes gospel novels. Her first best-selling novel, *Passing by Samaria* (Multnomah Publishing), earned the Christy Award, the highest recognition for Christian fiction. Her second novel, *Ain't No River*, earned the Golden Pen Award for Christian fiction and a place on the *Essence* Best Sellers List and is a finalist for the Christy Award. Her most recent release, *Riding Through Shadows*, is a story about prayer, faith, joy, and the spiritual warfare that begins in us, in our homes, and in our everyday lives; it is already in its third printing. A single mother of two and a former Defense Department employee, Sharon makes her home in Maryland.

Nikitta A. Foston is a freelance writer who has contributed to *Honey*, *Upscale*, and BlackVoices.com. She is also a contributing editor at *N'Digo* in Chicago and is completing her second novel. She is the proud mother of one daughter, Kennedy.

Norma Gaines-Hanks, Ed.D., as born and raised in Wilmington, Delaware. She received her B.S. in sociology from the University of Delaware, her M.S. in human behavior and development from Drexel University, and her Ed.D. in educational leadership and policy from the University of Delaware. Currently she is an assistant professor and coordinator of undergraduate programs in the Department of Individual and Family Studies at the University of Delaware.

R. Lee Gamble is a full-time freelance writer with over nine years' experience writing for various newspapers in northeast Ohio, including the *Call & Post*, *Ashtabula Star Beacon*, and *News Herald*. She resides in Cleveland Heights, Ohio, with her husband and three daughters.

Cynthia Gary is health educator and program director for a nonprofit organization in North Carolina. She has a master's degree in public health and currently resides in Garner, North Carolina. In her spare time, Cynthia enjoys writing stage plays and screenplays, choreography, dancing, and community service.

Star of *The Color Purple*, the *Lethal Weapon* series and *Beloved*, **Danny Glover** received an NAACP Image Award for his performance in HBO's *Mandela*. He was executive producer of HBO's *American Dream*, and TNT's *Buffalo Soldier* and *Freedom Song*. He has been the Goodwill Ambassador for the United Nations Development Program and a supporter of the Algebra Project and TransAfrica Forum, an African American organization lobbying for Africa and the Caribbean.

Sheila J. Grant was born and raised on the south side of Chicago. She is a graduate of Northern Illinois University and is currently director of training for a social service agency in Arlington Heights, Illinois.

Edith Ross Gray was born in Chicago, Illinois, and currently resides in Stone Mountain, Georgia. She is the mother of three children, Jonathan Wallace, Julius Wallace, and Jeannie Wallace.

Germaine Sibley Gordon is an accomplished dancer, dance teacher, movement specialist, and writer. She is currently writing her first inspirational book, which includes the story presented in this volume.

Tamela Handie-Tilford is currently employed as an internal auditor for the City of Kansas City, Missouri. She enjoys writing fiction and hopes to publish her first piece in the near future.

Dawne J. Harris is an assistant in ministry at Rewarding Faith Church in Detroit, where her father is the pastor. She enjoys hosting conferences annually for Christian singles and is currently working on her first book.

Beverly Joan Hughley graduated from Florida International University with a degree in public administration. She currently resides in Hollywood, Florida, with her son, Quentin, and niece, Kristen.

Ky'a Jackson is a graduate of Cheyney University and resides in Philadelphia, Pennsylvania. While she is currently employed for a public relations firm, she is also president of Influential Images, a home-based desktop publishing business. She gives back to her community by teaching computer classes for the Center for Literacy in Philadelphia and by tutoring adults in reading.

Lamont Jackson was raised in South Bend, Indiana, and currently resides in Orlando, Florida. He received a B.S. in public finance from Indiana University and an M.B.A. from the University of Illinois. Lamont is a licensed mortgage broker and a principal in JMS Investment Partners.

Dale S. Johnson has been writing for more than thirty years. Currently he resides in Lithonia, Georgia.

Erica Johnson is a Brooklyn native. She graduated from Marymount College, Tarrytown, with a B.S. in business administration. Currently she is employed as a software training consultant for the New York City Board of Education. She is also working on her first novel and is expecting her first child in August 2002.

Rayetta Johnson is a twenty-five-year-old English teacher in the New Orleans public school system. Currently, she is pursuing a master's degree in educational administration at Xavier University.

Rhonda Y. C. Johnson was raised in the city of Philadelphia and currently resides in Ashburn, Virginia. She is humble, carefree, and nurturing and is thankful to God for her successful journey thus far.

Donna M. Johnson-Thomas is a fifty-six-year-old widowed mother of three adult children. Presently, she works as an administrative secretary in the human resources department for the court system in Detroit, Michigan.

Marsha Kelley-Sutton is currently the recruitment/program coordinator for minority programs at the University of Alabama School of Medicine in Birmingham, Alabama. She is the mother of twelve-year-old Taylor Danielle Sutton.

Carmen Lashley has a B.S. in health systems management from the University of Baltimore and is a federal employee for the Centers for Medicare and Medicaid Services. She is the CEO of Siedon Publications and has two children, Sierra and Donovan Myers, who have become successful authors writing material targeted for teenage audiences.

Ronald R. Lawson is currently the director of the Northeast Region for the Joint Agencies' Trust, a non-profit trust fund. Prior to his Dinkins' campaign experience, he worked for fourteen years in financial services for several Wall Street firms. He and his wife, Nina, have been married for eight years, and have one daughter, Bailey Wynn.

Marc Little currently resides in Los Angeles. Marc has been self-employed as an entertainment and civil prosecution lawyer for the past eight years.

Regina Little-Durham, M.S., M.P.H., resides in Ellicott City, Maryland, with her husband and two children. She is a successful health care consultant with a health care management, research, and policy firm. In addition to her client work with communities, local and state governments, and health care providers to improve health care access to the poor and minorities, she is a volunteer at a rape and crisis counseling center and donates time serving as an advocate for others who need health care advice or are having difficulties with their insurance company or other health-care-related issues. She believes that as African Americans, we must be much more proactive when it comes to our health and well-being. Only then can we truly address the disparity in health care outcomes that exists within our community.

Rhonda Thompson Maddox lives in Shelby, North Carolina. Currently, she works at a family-owned car dealership in Forest City, North Carolina. She is married and has two adult children.

Tina Marshall-Bradley lives in Columbia, South Carolina, with her husband and two children. She is currently a professor at Benedict College.

Elnora Massey is fifty-two years old and lives in Ft. Lauderdale, Florida. She has worked for a federal agency for nineteen years. It has been an honor for her to write the story published in this book. "I thought that all my tears were dried up until I started to write," she says. "Thank you."

Ebuni McFall-Roberts, M.A., L.P.C., is a licensed counselor in Atlanta, Georgia. She lives with her husband and son in the Atlanta area and will be attending law school at Georgia State University this fall.

Billy Mitchell is an elected member of the City Council of Stone Mountain, Georgia. He is also the host of *Community Forum with Billy Mitchell,* heard on WCLK-FM in Atlanta, Georgia.

Wylencia Monroe grew up in Birmingham, Alabama, the youngest daughter of Ruby M. Hood and Wiley Hood Jr. She graduated from Emory University with a bachelor's degree in English and received a J.D. from the University of Georgia. She is currently employed as an attorney in Atlanta, Georgia.

Susie M. Paige lives in Philadelphia, Pennsylvania, and is currently working on a book of Sabbath stories. She gave her stem cell donation in 2000.

Vonda Paige has been a publicist and writer for more than sixteen years. She has worked for the Associated Press, the *Richmond Times-Dispatch,* and the *Philadelphia Tribune.* She is a member of the Philadelphia Association of Black Journalists and Delta Sigma Theta sorority.

Paula Penn-Bradley lives in Fayetteville, North Carolina. Currently she works as a reservations agent for American Airlines. Paul was her only child.

Roslyn Perry is an administrator at the Cleveland-Marshall College of Law at Cleveland State University. She is thirty-seven years old and has a nineteen-month-old son, Ethan.

John Pettiford is currently a senior majoring in business administration and an honor student at Lincoln University in Pennsylvania. He is a self-taught music producer.

LaShanna R. Price is originally from New York and currently resides in Birmingham, Alabama. She is a professional stage performer continuing to pursue her career in theater, television, and writing. She is a published poet with the International Library of Poetry. Her works can be read online at www.poetry.com.

Linda Robertson was born in Berkeley, California, and graduated in 1975 from California State University in Hayward with a B.A. in speech communications. She is employed as an executive assistant for an Internet service provider in San Francisco. Currently, she resides in Oakland, California, with her son, Christopher.

Elwood L. Robinson is currently a professor of psychology at North Carolina Central University in Durham. He was raised by two loving parents who taught him the value of hard work and perseverance through their own example. He has been married to Denise for twenty years and is the proud father of two children, Devin and Chanita.

Donnella L. Rucker currently resides in Largo, Maryland, with her husband, Anthony, and two daughters, De'Ven, age sixteen, and Toni, age eleven. Donnella and her husband are very active in the Kettering-Largo-Mitchellville Boys and Girls Club, and they were honored with the organization's Man and Woman of the Year award for 2001–2002. Donnella coaches cheerleading, Anthony coaches football, and together they run the Mini Mix (five to nine years old) basketball program.

Lana Rucks is currently a graduate student in psychology at the University of Dayton in Dayton, Ohio. She provides community service work to teen mothers and women with AIDS, and currently resides in Dayton with her husband and daughter.

Sondra Simmons is a single mother of three from Clinton, North Carolina, currently residing in Laurel, Maryland. She is a full-time employee of the federal government and hopes to return to school in the near future to complete her bachelor's degree.

Joyce Smiley is the mother of radio and television personality Tavis Smiley. Currently she resides in Kokomo, Indiana.

Marilyn Smith was married to firefighter Leon Smith for over twenty years when he succumbed to the 9/11 tragedy at the World Trade Center. Leon was forty-eight years old at the time. They have three daughters: Yolanda, who at eighteen attends Johnson C. Smith College; her twin sister, Tiffany, who attends Bennett College; and Nakia, who is twenty-five years old and attends college in Brooklyn.

Linda Spruill is currently an executive assistant for the vice president and head of antiviral development (HIV compounds) at Shionogi USA, Inc. She is one of Martha Spruill's ten children.

Gigi Steele is an environmental specialist with the Georgia Environmental Protection Division. She graduated from Spelman College with a bachelor of science in 1982. She has two sons and has been married for twenty-one years. This story is dedicated to her grandmother, Magdalene T. Perry.

Angela Pea Stroble lives in Greenville, South Carolina. She works for the law firm of Fletcher N. Smith, Jr., L.L.C.

G. Jean Thomas graduated from Georgia State University with a B.A. in political science. Currently she resides in Atlanta, Georgia, where she is also attending graduate school at Clark Atlanta University.

Ray Thomason is a graduate of Fisk University and currently serves as an officer in the United States Air Force. He and his wife reside in the San Antonio, Texas, area.

Diane Triggs began working in corporate America in 1974 at the age of twenty-two. Today she takes pride in being a choir member of the True Light M.B. church in St. Louis, where she is also the coordinator of the junior church.

Iyanla Vanzant is a motivational speaker and teacher in a class all her own. For eighteen years she studied everyone and everything that spoke to personal strength, personal growth, and empowerment. She then integrated that information with her own experiences and developed a commonsense approach to addressing life's challenges. As the founder of Inner Visions Worldwide Network and the author of seven best-selling and award-winning books, Vanzant has reached millions of people with the transformational and healing power of her message.

Audra Washington's music career began in 1991 at the American Society of Composers, Authors and Publishers (ASCAP). Later she became the director of creative music and publishing at EMI-Jobete Music Publishing. Audra is a graduate of Bennett College and resides in her native city of New York.

Booker T. Washington has been the CEO of OnAire Inc. since September 2001. He is also the managing director of the holding company TomCat Entertainment, which includes OmniEvents, Inc., and OnAire Inc. He is married to Chathay Washington and has three children, Booker III, Tiffany, and Amber.

Dr. Cornel West is currently a professor in the Department of African American Studies at Princeton University. Prior to this, he taught at Yale, Union Theological Seminary, and was the Alphonse Fletcher Jr. University Professor at Harvard University, where he taught Afro-American Studies and the philosophy of religion. He is the author of numerous articles and nineteen books including *The Cornel West Reader* and *Race Matters*. In addition to his activities at Princeton, West is a guest lecturer at colleges and universities across the country.

Gay Wheeler-Smith is a nurse manager at a teaching medical center in New York City. She resides in Westchester County, New York, with her daughter and mother. She and her daughter are working on their first book, which will be published in the fall of 2002.

Judge Trudy M. White currently presides over criminal, civil, and traffic cases. She supports and encourages behavior that develops strong children, strong families, and strong communities, and is well regarded for the many civic and cultural activities that she is involved in.

Tanya Dugat Wickliff is a motivational speaker, business consultant, and community advocate promoting empowerment, enrichment, and enlightenment issues such as economic vitality, technology, self-love, and holistic health. She is president of TANCOE Resources Unlimited, national business director of the Do for Self Project, founder of the FreshStart Foundation, and consultant to many small businesses. Tanya has a B.S. in mechanical engineering from the University of Houston, an M.B.A. from the University of Texas—Dallas Executive Program, a Ph.D. from Texas A&M University, and twelve years' engineering and management experience, including international travels. She is from Liberty, Texas, and has three sons, Jamar, Raymond, and Cortlan.

Judy Williams is a parent and youth development advocate and lives in Atlanta, Georgia. She earned a B.S. in organizational leadership and is currently employed at the national headquarters of the Boys and Girls Clubs of America.

Karen Williams manages maternal and child health and minority health programs in a Detroit-area health department. A former NAACP branch president, she is a published poet, essayist, and fiction writer; immediate past president of the Detroit Writer's Guild; and a Cave Canem African-American Poetry Fellow. She lives in Inkster, Michigan.

Donna M. Woodard is the youngest of eight children. Currently she resides in Pensacola, Florida, and is working on a master's degree in communication disorders/speech language pathology at Florida State University.

Joylyn Wright graduated from the University of South Carolina in 1996 with her B.A. in English. She was born in New York City and raised in Bonneau, South Carolina, from the age of eight. Currently she works at a waste management company in Columbia, South Carolina, and dedicates this story to her mother, sister, and late father for showing her what strength really is.

Yolanda Zanders-Barr is an electrical engineer with the Department of Defense. She has been happily married to James Barr Jr. for four years.

Kaye Barrow Ziglar resides in Greensboro, North Carolina, with her five-year-old son, Garrett, and husband, Rod. She is an ordained deacon in the Presbyterian Church and also serves as hospital adjunct chaplain. Inspired by the loss of her daughter, Lauren Grace Ziglar, who passed away on March 17, 2001, she founded Motivating Grace, a motivational speaking ministry that places emphasis on topics tailored for and about women.